CHILD: DEVELOPMENT OF PERSONALITY TRAITS

CHILD DEVELOPMENT OF PERSONALITY TRAITS

Shalini Saxena Mittal

Publications

KALPAZ PUBLICATIONS

DELHI-110052

Child: Development of Personality Traits

Rs. 690

ISBN: 81-7835-071-8

Published in 2006 in India by
Kalpaz Publications
C-30, Satyawati Nagar, Delhi-110052
E-mail : kalpaz@hotmail.com

Laser Typesetting at : Master Computers, Delhi
Printed at : Salasar Imaging System, Delhi

Contents

SECTION C : MOTHER AND CHILD RELATIONSHIP

Preface

In a speech in New Delhi, in the year 1952, Jawaharlal, Nehru said, "A Human being grows and ought to grow like a flower or a plant. You can water it, you can help it grow, you can give it a good soil, you can put it in the fresh air or in the sun but it has to grow on its own, and you cannot make it grow by force". Thus Nehru wanted to ensure a congenial and harmonious environment for children in their surroundings so that they may blossom into full citizens of tomorrow.

Children are our legacy for the future. They are the building blocks of any nation. If they are provided the right kind of development, they contribute to the nation's growth in a right way. It is therefore essential that the better we understand the thinking, feeling and behaviour of children, the better we maximize their development or say personality development.

Almost all children grow up in a family. Family is the most important part of child's social network as the members of the family constitute the child's first 'Environment' and are the most significant people during the early formative years. Children interact with a mother or a father or both. Many have brothers or sisters. The personalities and lives of the people close to a child affect the child and in turn the child affects those around him or her. From contacts with family members, children lay the foundations for attitudes towards people, things and life. Therefore impact of child rearing is of paramount importance. Child rearing generally refers to all interactions between parents and their children. It is popularly assumed that children and marital happiness go together and are casually related. Studies on marital satisfaction report that marital satisfaction results in development of socially approved characteristics and traits among the children. There are various factors such as family tensions, marital discord, age of parents, socio-economic status and family background of parents which are related to child rearing practices. These factors indirectly influence the personality development of children.

The impact of child rearing done by the mother is the most important and therefore mother's role in child's personality development is very significant. There is every possibility that children with maximum behavioural problem have mothers who use unhealthy child rearing practices and have unhappy married life. Children produced by mothers with poor marital status are more assertive, expedients, emotionally less stable, reserved and poor team members. Children reared up with healthy child rearing practices and by the mother with happy marital status are possess significantly better personality traits. They are more outgoing, intelligent, emotionally stable, obedient, socially bold, self-reliant and are good team members. Thus mother-child relationship is very crucial and is of utmost importance. Mother's education, her family background, her family, status, her marital status, her culture, her family composition and her employment are important factors among many others that affects and influence the personality development of a child.

This book focuses on various factors that influence child development. The book is divided into four (4) sections. Each section is further organized into chapters.

Section A titled 'Personality 'is the first section in the book. This section elaborates scientific study of Personality Theories, provides details of Personality Development of the child and various methods of Studying Personality. ***First chapter*** in this section contains the details of ***'Scientific Study of Personality and Theories. Second chapter*** deals with ***'Personality Development'*** of the child. ***Third Chapter*** deals with ***Methods of Studying Personality***.

Section B titled 'Parents and Children' is the second section in the book. This section provides theoretical background of parenting in which various pattern studies are discussed. This section also focuses on the effect of parental personality, parental attitude and behaviour on the children. Factors in parent-child relationship are also discussed in this section. ***First chapter*** in this section present ***'Theoretical Background of Parenting-Patterns Studies'***. ***Second chapter*** is titled ***'Effect of Parental Personality, Parental Attitude and Behaviour on Children'***. ***Third Chapter*** deals with factors in parent-child relationship and is titled as ***Factors in Parent-Child Relationship'***.

Section C titled 'Mother and Child Relationship' is the Third section in the book. This section Focus on the relationship between Mother and Child. ***First chapter*** in this section discuss the mother's role in socialization and hence titled as ***'Role of Mother in Socialisation'. Second chapter*** discuss the marital happiness and its effect on the children, under the title ***'Marital Happiness and Children'. Last chapter*** contains the contents relating to the effect of mother's employment, her culture, family size and family composition. ***Third chapter*** is therefore titled as ***'Effect of Maternal Employment, Culture, Family Size and Family Composition on Children'***.

Section D titled 'Analysis and Conclusion' is the fourth and last section in the book. This section contains the review of literature referred, various plans and Procedure, results and discussion and finally provides the Recommendation and Suggestions. ***First chapter*** in this section provides the overview of the literature which was referred for the study, hence the title is ***'Overview of Literature'. Second chapter*** contains the details of plan and procedure under the title ***'Plan and Procedure'. Third chapter*** focus on Result under the title ***'Result and Discussions'. Last chapter*** which is the fourth one provides the scope of future utility under the title as ***'Recommendation and Suggestion'***.

This book would be useful for scholars, educationists, psychologists, academicians, policy-makers, NGO, Teachers, parents and any individual/organisation concerned with child development.

SECTION A
PERSONALITY

1

Scientific Study of Personality

Everybody is fascinated by the study of personality. Babies watch adults intently and seem to learn much about the personalities important in their lives. We adult focus our attention on Roosevelt, a Churchill, or an Eisenhower–we attracted by inside information about the personality of the figures that loom large over our own world.

The study of personality is indeed important to us. Marriage is an aspect of life which is of the greatest significance, and what is more decisive for happy or unhappy marriage than the personalities of the two individuals so bound together? Occupation demand different personality patterns, a study of those successfully following a given profession gives the young man a cue as to whether this would be a wise choice for him.

Meaning of Personality

Psychologist defines personality in many different ways. The word "personality" is derived from the Latin word Persona, means "mask". Among Greeks, actors used a mask to hide their identity on stage. This dramatic technique was later adopted by the Romans to whom persona devoted "as one appears to others", not as one actually is. From this was derived the notion of one's appearance as the crucial element in personality. This is, the way in which one is viewed by others has been held by many to be the central point in a definition of personality such a definition also implies that personality is essential the "mask" of behaviour a person adopts in order to present some particular view of himself to the world.

The popular, non-scientific definition of personality as the effect one was on others has two defects. First, it emphasizes only the manifest aspects of the intricate pattern of personality, the expressiveness of the individual. Second, in emphasizing only the objective aspect of personality, it does not indicate what the real personality is, the subjective or interior organization which is responsible for the expressive aspects.

"Personality" is also used colloquially to imply personal attractiveness, the ability to withstand hardships, and other specific qualities. This tendency to identify personalities in terms of a single characteristic is, of course, a common features of unscientific thinking.

Definitions of Personality

The scientific conception of personality has been worked out to some extent by trial and error. It may be helpful to the student if we summarize briefly some of the meaning attached to this term by earlier psychologists. Since these definitions show a trend in thinking, following them may quickly orient the student to the value to the final definition which will be the keynote of this book.

Most of the early psychological definitions emphasized the expressive aspects of personality and ignored or only indirectly implied the interior organization that is responsible for the observational aspects. Woodworth, for example, defined personality as the "quality of the individual's total behaviour". According to Dashiell, an individual's personality is the total picture of his organized behaviour especially as it can be characterized by his fellow men in a consistent way. Munn gave a more comprehensive analysis, pointing out that personality is the "most characteristic integration of an individual's structure and activities". It is characteristic in a dual sense because (1) It is unique, thus differentiating the individual from all other and (2) It is fairly consistent, representing the customary integration of a particular individual's structures and activities. These representative early psychological definitions stressed the manifest aspect of personality–what may be observed by others–though they implied that what a person is, how he thinks and feels, and what is included in his total psychological make-up, will be through his speech and behaviour. Munn implied this especially when he referred to the "integration of an individual's structures and activities". None however, spelled out the significance of fundamental and often unconscious drives and wishes stemming from what may be considered the real personality–the individual's evaluation of himself and to others, and how he regards his relationship with others.

Kempf (1919) has defined personality as "the habitual mode of adjustment which the organism effect between its own egocentric drives and the exigencies of the environment". As phrased, this would include practically all of human behaviour, since the vast majority of our responses do consist of just habitual way of adjusting.

According to Morton Prince (1924), "Personality is the sum total of all the biological inmate dispositions, impulses, tendencies, appetites, and instincts of the individual, and the acquired disposition and tendencies". This definition places a potentially useful emphasis on the inner aspect of personality. Like Kempfs, however, it seems to cover virtually all of psychology, rather than to delimit a particular field.

Watson (1924) has called attention to the fact that character is part of personality. He says, "Personality include not only these (character-conventional) reactions, but also the more individual personal adjustments and capacities as well as their life history. Popularly speaking, we would say that a liar and a profligate had no characters, but he may have an exceedingly interesting personality".

Symonds (1928) has defined personality as "the portrait or landscape of the organism working together in all its phases, and May (1929) speaks of "the social stimulus value of the individual".

Definitions in Terms of Stimulus and of Response. If we now examine these definitions and compare them with some examples from popular usage, we find a fairly sharp differentiation into two groups: those which consider personality in terms of its stimulus value (the effect one has on others) and those which consider it in terms of responses (what the person actually does). There is no necessary contradiction between the two. John's stimulus value for others is necessary a function of John's behaviour. There are, however, important differences between the two, and one or both may be found unsuitable for a sound scientific approach.

Personality as Stimulus. Not only the man in the street, but also many psychologists, would define personality in terms of stimulus value. This is natural consequence of everyday situations in which the concept is particularly useful, such as picking prospective employees, describing friends, or grading school children. Applicants for jobs are often chosen on the basis of their "personality" as it appears to the personnel interviewer; and this is justifiable, at least in the sense that an applicant who impresses the interviewer unpleasantly might affect customers similarly.

An attempt to use scientifically a definition of personality as stimulus leads to immediate difficulty. This is especially true if we are looking for increased logical precision and quantitative measurements of personality traits. Rigid application of this definition creates the bizarre situation in which each individual has virtually an unlimited number of personalities–one for each of his acquaintances, because he has for each a different stimulus value. He will not be evaluated in the same way by his mother, his wife, employer, his secretary, his rival for a promotion, and the man he has beaten at golf. Definition of personality as stimulus makes precision impossible, because two personalities are interacting in every instance. When Mary reports that Sally is "a malicious gossip," this may give us more information about Mary than about Sally.

Personality as Response. In an attempt to get away from the difficulties which result from defining personality in stimulus terms, many psychologists have shifted to the definition of personality as response. It is plausible, for example, that if Susan has a charming personality (and not merely a pretty face), this is a function of her behaviour. It should be possible, then, for methodical study to reveal the particular pattern of responses evoking the judgment "charming".

This is a distinct improvement over the popular approach, in that the personality is now tied down to certain objective manifestations which can be studied by the techniques of scientific psychology. Such definitions as that of Floyd Allport fall in this group. To some extent there is a danger that the definition will be too comprehensive and cover more territory than can be handled in practice; for instance, Watson's definition amounts to saying that personality is "everything you do." The problems created by an attempt to use such a definition in research are obvious.

Guthrie (1944) has defined personality as "those habits and habit systems of social importance that are stable and resistant to change." While this is more precise than the formulations of Kempf, Prince, and Watson, it still raises numerous questions. What about habits which are not of social importance? Some people like to pose before a mirror when they are alone--a habit that may not be "of social importance" although it is certainly a significant clue to personality. Does habit cover the whole of our subject matter? To many the concept of habit will seem strained if it is stretched so widely.

Personality—Mask or Substance? Numerous writers have objected to an approach limited to either stimulus value or response pattern, on the basis that each of these is likely to emphasize superficial aspects of the personality. It is suggested that we should distinguish between personality as a mask, or front, assumed in many instances merely for its effect on others, and personality as substance, the "real" or inner personality.

Clearly there is some validity in this proposal. Most of us do modify our behaviour to fit our social setting. This indicates that many of our responses are still part of the "mask" of social participation.

Personality as Intervening Variable. A synthesis of these approaches may be developed by following out the suggestion just made. It is now a truism in psychology that a stimulus does not immediately and automatically elicit a response. A stimulus affects the organism as a whole, and the ultimate response is a function of both the stimulus and the organism. (When a child is hungry, an ice-cream cone elicits one reaction; when he is satiated, the response is quite different.) There are certain intervening variables between the stimulus and the response which affect the nature of the final behaviour pattern. Such variables are the person's intelligence, his motives at the moment, his past experience with the stimulus, and his attitude toward the situation in which the stimulus appears. Thus, if the stimulus is an invitation to a dance, variables influencing the final response might be the young man's past mishaps at dances, his expectation of meeting a certain girl who attracts him, his financial status, his need to study for an examination during the evening of the dance, and so on. The decision he reaches will be a function of these forces (of which he is not necessarily conscious). Another man may reach the same conclusion, but for entirely different reasons.

Gordon Allport, after an extensive analysis of the possible definitions of personality, has found a definition in terms of intervening variable to be essential. His proposed formulation is as follows: "Personality is the dynamic organization within the individual of those psychophysical systems that determine his unique adjustments to his environment."

It will be noted that this definition covers most of the difficulties mentioned above. It recognizes the changing nature of personality (a dynamic organization); it focuses on the inner aspect rather than on superficial manifestations; but it establishes the basis for the social stimulus value of personality (unique adjustments to the environment). While it is not possible to study directly a "dynamic organization within the individual," this definition is compatible with a thoroughgoing scientific approach based upon appropriate research techniques.

It might be possible to improve in minor ways on Allport's definition, but on the whole it meets adequately all the requirements of a scientific psychology of personality. We shall therefore adopt it as a standard for the purposes of the present volume.

Allport makes no attempt to incorporate in his definition any characterization of the kind of psychophysical systems he mentions. This is perhaps good judgment, inasmuch as such a listing, once started, ought to be inclusive, and we do not now how many different systems must be included. It does seem worthwhile, however, to point out the importance of one such system: our pattern of beliefs and expectancies.

The definition of personality as an inner system of beliefs, expectancies, desires, and values has numerous advantages. From the viewpoint of research it provides a focus of investigation—less convenient than a definition in response terms, but less confusing than a definition in stimulus terms. On logical grounds it appears to unite successfully these two divergent approaches. One has no difficulty in thinking of an inner structure which determines responses, which in turn influence the judgments of others about us. Furthermore, it resolves certain problems raised by the facts of variable behaviour in different social environments and of similar responses which require dissimilar interpretations.

Personality as a Scientific Abstraction. Regardless of our choice among these three approaches to personality, personality remains an abstraction, not a directly observed phenomenon. This occurs in both popular and scientific thought; when you watch your friend in action, you feel sure that there is an underlying unity behind his acts. "I know him; what he is really working for is power; he wants to be the big boss." Thus, we confidently assert our theories about the personality of others.

The scientist, too, is concerned to develop a theory of personality. This may be a generalized theory, intended to cover all sorts of people; or it may be a special theory, a conception of Sam Wilson, what he is "really" like. In clinical work particularly, the psychologist tries to develop a picture of the "true" personality, the inner unity which coordinates and integrates all the specific actions and fantasies of the individual.

Such a conception of the scientist's efforts is disturbing to some readers. It is a widespread belief that science deals only with what is "real". But the reality may be highly abstract. No one has ever seen an electron; but the scientist has a theory, according to which, if electrons have certain properties, certain effects will follow. Experiment then is designed to observe the effects; the "real" electron is only an abstraction, not an object of experience. In the same way, the "real" personality is an abstraction from many observations and from a theory of personality. The value of a theory is based on its success in helping us to understand, or to predict, what the individual will do.

Consensual Validation. Another way to decide upon the value of a theory is to see if it leads to results which can be observed by others. The psychotic individual reports experiences which are uniquely his own; he may see pink elephants or ask for protection from the millions of little blue cockroaches following him around. In this case his inner organization—his pattern of perception and emotion—leads to a belief about reality. For him, these experiences are real. But other observers claim that they are not real. Granting that the majority is often wrong (cf. Christopher Columbus), we can still say that a personality theory which leads to results which look unreal to qualified observers is of doubtful values. Philosophers call this "the criterion of consensual validation," meaning that we can define reality by the agreement of these observers.

The foregoing examples suggest that personality is a way of looking at reality. The paranoid person may have a theory that he is being persecuted by the Masons, the Kiwanis, and the Elks. His way of looking at the world is distorted. His behaviour will be peculiar because he is responding to his world, not to our world. Within his world, his behaviour may be perfectly logical. This is another reason why it is important to find out what is behind a person's responses, not confine ourselves to a study of his behaviour. The normal personality is one whose view of the world agrees fairly well with that of people around him. A man is perceived as "queer" if he acts on the basis of a queer theory about reality.

Similarly, psychologists agree about certain fundamentals in the field of personality. This is not to deny that there are vigorous differences on theory. But certain kinds of "theories" are automatically judged to be useless. If someone tries to explain deviations in personality as due to possession by devils, he is treated as mentally unbalanced and certainly incompetent to study personality.

Thinking Scientifically about Personality

Before the specific techniques utilized in the scientific study of personality are taken up, it seems desirable to state certain general principles of thinking which are involved in this approach. These principles are not specific to the problems of personality, but are sufficiently in contrast with what might be called the common-sense approach to human behaviour that special discussion of them is needed.

Animistic versus Realistic Thinking. A substantial proportion of the average man's thinking about psychology, and especially about such complex psychological problems as personality, is animistic in character. By this we mean that descriptive generalizations are used as if they were forces explaining behaviour; that abstractions are often, erroneously, given the attributes of life.

Animistic thinking in the field of human behaviour, on the other hand, continues to be more common than is realistic thinking. Many of us still believe that personality can be changed by magical invocations (swearing at one's roommate, for example) or by human sacrifices, as in the case of mothers, whose sacrifices or their children may do more harm than good. Public opinion on crime and punishment, likewise, shows animistic tendencies. Few people think as realistically about criminals as they do about machines. If an automobile engine breaks down, we look for the cause (defective lubrication, bad fuel, improper ignition) and correct these conditions of the engine's behaviour. We should not dream of putting the engine in jail for a year and expecting that it would, upon release, decide to perform properly. Yet human beings are still handled on this animistic basis, despite the evidence of thousands of years proving its futility.

Cause and Effect Relationships. The realistic approach suggests that we must have a deterministic point of view about ourselves and others. You personally should realize the implications of this view for yourself. You can read because you have been taught; your morals are a product of training; your self-confidence, emotionality, and impulsiveness are results of your specific experiences. To a very substantial extent, what you will do tomorrow is already determined by what you are today. This is neither an argument for an attitude of reckless irresponsibility nor an assertion of the unchanging character of human nature. All organisms, but especially the human, have the capacity for seeking out certain kinds of stimulation. By deliberate choice you can expose yourself to stimulus conditions which will result in changing your personality; but it is extremely unlikely that you can produce a change merely by verbal resolution to reform.

Genetic Continuity. The preceding formulation leads logically to the principle of the continuity of the personality from conception, through birth, infancy, childhood, and maturity, to old age. Continuity does not mean unchanging rigidity. A river has continuity, but it is constantly changing. In an adult personality we can still locate infantile characteristics, but these have been overlaid by many intervening experiences. The fusion of the male and female germ cells determines certain hereditary potentialities of the individual. From that point on, environmental pressures modify, suppress, or channel these possibilities.

From infancy onward, the individual's reaction to a present stimulus is a function, in the main, of his reactions to past stimuli. Characteristics develop or change little by little over a period of time, with few exceptions. Even in the case of catastrophic changes in personality, it is usually possible to show how the person's past training prepared him to respond to his characteristic way to a crisis situation.

It is apparent that, if we accept this view, we must also accept the view of multiple causation. No stimulus ever acts in isolation. While we may successfully identify the immediate cause of a person's behaviour, background events played their part as remote causes in determining in the response which occurred. It is not, therefore, practical to search for specific one-to-one relationships, between experiences and personality traits.

Finally, it seems clear that genetic continuity means that personality is a process. In the study of the individual, we must necessarily take static cross sections and examine them; but the real, live individual is constantly changing to maintain adjustment to his environment. This will be particularly clear as we examine the extent to which the person, impelled by inner drives and expectations, modifies his environment and is in turn modified.

The Unitary Personality. The personality is a psychophysiological unit, integrated with a specific physical organism. Changes on the biological and biochemical levels affect the manifestations ordinarily called psychological, and changes of a mental character have biological repercussions. It is not correct to speak of these as body influencing mind or vice versa. These changes are simply personality events. Nothing but confusion is achieved by ascribing a glandular change to the physical realm and an emotional upheaval to a mental category.

The personality is also a psychosocial unit, being inextricably bound up with a culture and its various subgroups. No one ever escapes completely from the cultural background of his early development. Since the personality is coextensive with a single biological organism, however, it is possible to make an objective distinction between happenings within the individual and stimuli presented by the culture to which he must adapt himself. The psychosocial unity of personality is thus less apparent to the casual observer than is the psychophysiological unity.

Personality as Molder of Culture. The relation of person to society is not a one-way street. Personality is molded by social pressures, threats, rewards, and reference groups—true. But the homeostatic principle asserts that the individual will attempt to defend himself against these social variables; one such defense is to modify the culture itself.

In any event it seems appropriate to discuss the role of personality in holding culture. It is unjustifiably, pessimistic to view man as merely a creature of his glands or a helpless victim of his social milieu. The unique individual plays his role, too in shaping his social surrounding. Thus he seeks to fins tall threats which might arise, and to ensure the survival of a way of life which seems very clear to him. In today's threatening world the creativity of the unique personality may be our only defence against annihilation.

2

Theories of Personality Development

There are various theories regarding the nature, structure and development of personality. It will be useful to describe a few theories of personality in order to understand the various factors which enter into the concept of personality and affect the development of personality. Although theories abound, they can be classified fairly well into three main groups: motivational theories, trait theories and social behaviour theories.

Motivational theories, of which Freudian psychoanalysis is the most prominent, put the emphasis on the motives operating in a person where he or she shows some characteristic behaviour. Trait theories, although they acknowledge the role of motivation, try to establish a few characteristic view in which a person is disposed to act.

Social behaviour theories view personality as a set habits acquired through the basic "laws" learning. This chapter is organized around the three main groups of theories.

Motivation and Personality

(a) ***Freud.*** What is generally regarded as the most influential personality theory of the last several years was developed by a man who was not a psychologist; he was Sigmund Freud, a medically trained psychiatrist. Long before psychologist were given much attention to personality, Freud was at work in Vienna trying to construct a conception of personality based on his observations of patients. Many versions later, his theory became the most prominent of all, both in psychiatry and psychology.

Psychoanalytic theory itself is complex–probably more complex than any other personality theory. Here are some of its major ideas. Psychoanalytic theory has three parts :

(1) Theory of the structure of personality, in which the ego, id and super ego are the principle concept (2) a theory of personality dynamic, in which the conscious, the unconscious and repression of memories are important concepts and (3) a theory of psychosexual development, in which different–motives are predominants in the child at different stages of growth.

Id, Ego and Superego. The id can be thought of as sort of storehouse of biologically based motives and "instinctual" reactions for satisfying motives. The energy of these motives is termed libido. The id energy, or libido, would satisfy fundamental motives as they arose without regard to the realities of life or to moral of any kind. At birth the infant is without an ego, he is a bundle of instinctive reactions and desires. It is an undifferentiated 'it'. As the child grows and interacts with the parents and others he learns a complex system of social responses and incorporates into himself certain values which are cherished by the parents and the group to which the parents belongs.

The infant does not come into world with any interest in other; he is concerned only with himself. The infant is interested in simple pleasure like sucking, warmth, food etc.

During the first stage of development an infant does not differentiate between himself and the world and people around him. They are all one for him. It is instinctive impulses that determine his behaviour.

Later when he differentiates himself from the world, an ego is born. The ego consists of elaborate ways of behaving and thinking that are learned for dealing effectively with the world. It delays the satisfaction of motives, and it channels motives into socially acceptable outlets. It keeps a person working for a living, getting along with people, and generally adjusting to the realistics of life. Freud characterized the ego as working "in the service of the reality principle". During this stage the child becomes aware of himself as I. But even in this stage of development he has an intense interest in himself is a tyrant, he has no consideration for parents or siblings. He demands and his demands must be immediately satisfied. He cries till his demands are satisfied. He is guided entirely by, what Freud, calls, the pleasure principle, which is the avoidance of pain and the pursuit of pleasure. It is at this time that the parents try to exercise control over him. They place limit on his demand. During this period of socialization the infant loves his parents because they give him security and comfort : he wants their affection. He cries when he is left alone, he is happy when they coddle him, talk to him and play with him. It is this time that the ego emerges as the organism comes into grips with the forces and realities of the external world while seeking to satisfy the impulse of the id. The ego is a system of forces which redirects the id impulses towards gratifications appropriate to the specific environment or the situation. This is what Freud calls the reality principle, the adjustment of behaviour of the demands of the outside world.

Thus ego consists of elaborates ways of behaving and thinking that are learned for dealing effectively with the world. It delays the satisfaction of motives and it channels motives into socially acceptable outlets. It keeps a person working for a living, getting along with people, and generally adjusting to the realities of life.

The principal function of the ego is to mediate between the impulses of the organism and the limitations imposed by the environment, particularly by the parents. The attempts of the organism to satisfy the id impulses by direct action are blocked by the restraints of the society. The parent says "that is bad", "this is good" "do this", "don't do that" and so on. The child, having learnt to speak repeats these works by himself round about the age of four and restrains his impulses. This is the stage of "internalization" of the rules and values as the child sees them. They form, what Freud call the superego. The injunctions and prohibitions of the parents are internalized by the child, as a result, the superego is a moral arbiter of conduct. It function to restrain or to inhibit those basic impulses, especially sex and aggression, which society regards as dangerous. Gradually the superego becomes the 'conscience' of the child. It consists of restraints, acquired in the course of the personality development on the activity of the ego and the id. A well-developed ego and superego enables the individual to maintain adequate control over the id impulses; the ego on the basic of reality considerations and superego on the basis of moral consideration--on the basis of what is prohibited and punished in the group.

When the direct and immediate expressions of the libidinal energies are checked by the ego and the superego, the child experiences frustrations, conflicts and anxieties. This is the basis for the early negativism in the child. He, as it were, put up a fight with his parents who impulse limitations on his pleasure seeking and on his demands for immediate gratification. According to the Freud, the child reduced these frustrations and anxieties through the process of "identification" and "displacement".

The Unconscious and Repression

Besides the id, ego, and superego, Freud assumed that there are three stages of consciousness: the conscious, the preconscious, and the unconscious. In the conscious state, we are aware of things around us and our thoughts. In other words, the conscious state consists of everything we are aware of at the moment. The preconscious state consists of memories or thoughts that are easily made conscious. If, for example, you ask me the name of my college professor in psychology, I may not have thought of her for some time, but after a moment's reflection I can recall it. All memories of this sort—memories that are easily tapped—are said to lie in the preconscious. In contrast, the unconscious contains memories which we cannot easily tap because we have pushed them from consciousness (repressed them) or have never allowed them to reach consciousness. There are several different ways in which memories may be repressed. These are defense mechanisms, described in the last section.

Repression takes place because of a conflict between the conscious portions of the ego and superego and the unconscious id. The motives of the id constantly seek expression. Many of the id urges, however, would arouse a great deal of anxiety if they were openly expressed, because they are in conflict with ego and superego forces. When disguised (by means of defense mechanisms), however, they may find expression without causing so much anxiety. Thus, because of repression, we are often not aware of id motives, and for this reason they are called unconscious motives. Unconscious motivation is the underlying dynamic force in Freudian psychoanalytic theory.

The Freudian interpretation of dreams, for example, is based on the idea of unconscious urges. Dreams are supposed to be disguised manifestations, sometimes called "wish fulfillment" of id motives. In every day life the existence of id urges may be revealed by slips of the tongue and by selective forgetting. In this book *The Psychopathology of Everyday Life*, Freud analyzed the disguised manifestations of id motives. The following examples are from the edition translated by A.A. Brill : A woman wrote to her sister, felicitating her on the occasion of taking possession of a new and spacious residence. A friend who was present noticed that the writer put the wrong address on the letter, and what was still more remarkable was the fact that she did not address it to the previous residence, but to one long ago given up, but which her sister had occupied when she first married. When the friend called her attention to it, the writer remarked. "You are right; but what in the world made me do this?" to which her friend replied : "Perhaps you begrudge her the nice big apartment into which she has just moved because you yourself are cramped for space, and for that reason you put her back into her first residence, where she was no better off than yourself." "Of course I begrudge her the new apartment," she honestly admitted. As an afterthought she added, "It is a pity that one is so mean in such matters."

Ernest Jones reports the following example given to him by Dr. A.A. Brill. In a letter to Dr. Brill, a patient tried to attribute his nervousness to worries and excitement during the cotton crisis. He went on to say: "May trouble is all due to that d—frigid wave: there isn't even any seed to obtained for new crops." He referred to a cold wave which had destroyed the cotton crops, but instead of writing "wave", he wrote "wife". In the bottom of his heart, he entertained reproaches against his wife on account of her marital frigidity and childlessness, and he was not far from the cognition that the enforced abstinence played no little part in the causation of his malady.

Psychosexual Development

As you probably know, Freud put a heavy emphasis on biological motive in general and on sexual motivation in particular. He believed that such motives play an important part in personality development. This development he divided into three general stages: a pregenital stage, a latency period, and a genital stage. In turn he divided the pregenital stage into three sub-stages: oral, anal, and phallic.

Pregenital Stage. In the oral stage occupying much of the first year, the infant obtains pleasure by sucking and other oral activities. A baby who is prevented from sucking, or is made anxious about it, may acquire an oral fixation. Later in life such a fixation sometimes takes the form of an oral syndrome, which may include excessive oral behaviour, greediness, dependence, and passivity.

The *anal stage* is most prominent during the second and third years, a period when parents are toilet-training their children and teaching them to avoid "naughty" behaviour connected with excretion. In our society this is ordinarily the child's first encounter with authority and the first time he or she must bring the id under the control of the ego. In fact, it is during the anal period that the ego is beginning to develop. Psychoanalytic theory says that if the training is too strict and arouses too much anxiety, the child may develop the anal syndrome. In adulthood the syndrome may appear as excessive compulsiveness, over conformity, and exaggerated self-control.

After they master toilet training, children's interest turns to their sexual organs. In the phallic stage a child typically develops "romantic" feelings toward the parent of the opposite sex. Freud called these feelings in boys the Oedipus complex after the mythical story of Oedipus, who unwittingly killed his father and married his mother. According to Freud, the phallic stage is a crucial one. Boys, for example, feel threatened by a jealous father, and they begin to construct psychic defenses against anxiety. The defense that normally emerges is identification with the threatening parent; the boy tries to become like his father, taking on the father's behavioural patterns and ideas—especially ideas of right and wrong, which usually are characteristic not only of his father but of the culture. Thus the superego begins to form.

Latency Period. Following the pregenital stage, the latency period begins at about age 6 and extends approximately to the onset of puberty. During this period nothing much new happens. The defense mechanisms which emerged in the pregenital stage are strengthened and elaborated, and the ego expands as the child learns more about the world.

Genital Stage. At puberty the child enters the genital stage, when normal heterosexual interests appear. The person begins to focus more and more on others instead of centering on the self. People who have reached the genital stage become interested in playing the normal roles of adults in society.

Jung's Analytic Psychology

Freud himself had a dominant personality that both attracted and repelled people. He attracted many disciples, or his theory would not have made such an impression on the western world. But some of his prominent disciples found themselves unable to agree with all his teachings, and they split off to found their own schools. Two of these were Jung, whose theory is called analytic psychology, and Adler who emphasized individual psychology.

The theory formulated by Carl Gustav Jung is not easy to summarize. It is not a complete theory, as Freud's was, and it is sometimes shrouded in mysticism. One point about it is that Jung did not subscribe to Freud's emphasis on sexual motivation. Another is that he gave more weight to people's aims and plans and less to instinct.

Perhaps the concept for which Jung is best known is the collective unconscious. He broke down Freud's general idea of an unconscious into a personal unconscious and a collective unconscious, which consists of primitive and ancestral experiences. According to Jung, all people throughout history have shared the experiences which form the collective unconscious. It is humanity's storehouse of myth and memory concerning such universal realities as mothers and fathers, the sun and storms, caves and rivers, and so on. Jung believed that this collective unconscious interacts with the personal unconscious in the development of personality.

Another idea of Jung's is that healthy personality development consists of a balance between conscious and unconscious forces in which all part of a personality grow into a fully realized self. In this respect his theory is similar to the self-theories to be discussed a little later. Finally, Jung formulated the concepts of introvert and extravert--terms that have found their way into common use.

Adler's Individual Psychology

Alfred Adler, like Jung, rejected Freud's heavy emphasis on biological drives and sex in particular. His theory, like most theories after Freud, put more emphasis on social factors in personality development. It is Adler who originated the concept of the inferiority complex, a phrase now part of everyday speech. Because we strive for power, argued Adler, we are always seeing ways in which we fall sort of our aspirations, and hence ways in which we are inferior. This itself is healthy, for feeling our weakness in first one respect and then another provides things for us "to work on." We are forever striving to overcome our inferiorities. But an inferiority complex develops when a person regularly fails to overcome his or her weaknesses, or for any reason comes to put too much emphasis on any particular inferiority.

From Adler, too, we have the concept of compensation (a defense mechanism). Being aware of a weakness, we may strive especially hard to overcome it. The person who, like Theodore Roosevelt, is fragile and sickly as a child may throw himself into physical activities and overcompensate for handicaps or inferiorities. In many instances, because of overcompensation, people ultimately become superior in areas where they were originally inferior. In addition, people may compensate for inferiority by achieving distinction in some other area. For example, a frail boy may become superior in academic things when he fails in athletics. This kind of compensation resembles Freud's idea of displacement; the difference lies in the motivation. Freud's displacement is an outlet for libidinal motives; Adler's compensation is a means of satisfying the striving for superiority.

Anxiety Theory by Karen Horney

Most theories give anxiety an important place in their scheme of things. Freud considered anxiety the outcome of conflicts between the id, ego, and superego. Another theorist, Karen Horney, made the concept of basic anxiety central to her theory (1937). She believed that this anxiety arises from important influences in the development of the child, rather than from the conflict between biological motives and the ego or superego.

According to Horney, basic anxiety is first aroused in children by any social situation which tends to make them fearful. It can be instigated by threats or domination by a parent, by tension and conflict between the parents, by being required to do too much, by being mistrusted, by criticism, coldness, or indifference, and so on. Once anxiety is aroused, the child attempts to alleviate it by trial-and-error behaviour, as any organism might try to solve a problem. In this way children learn certain methods of dealing with anxiety; these in turn form a pattern of "neurotic needs".

A neurotic need is thus a learned need. If children learn to cope with anxiety by running to mother for affection and approval, they may develop a neurotic need for affection and approval. If they manage to cope with some anxiety-producing situations by obtaining prestige or personal admiration, they may acquire a neurotic need for these things. There can be any number of neurotic needs, depending on the things the child earned to need in order to reduce anxiety. In any given culture, however, certain patterns of needs can be expected to arise. This is because the sources of anxiety tend to form a repetitive pattern from one family to another and from one child to another. Horney has formulated a list of 10 needs, which include needs for such things as affection, dependency, power, prestige, achievement and self-sufficiency.

Horney's theory, like Freud's and most others, has a place in it for conflict. To Horney, however, the major conflict is between needs, simply because some needs are incompatible. If a person develops both a need to have someone to depend on and a need to be self-sufficient and independent, these needs will often conflict. According to her, almost everyone possesses neurotic needs in some degree, but when a person is unable to resolve conflicts between them, some needs tend to dominate his or her life. The person then becomes a "neurotic".

Self Theories

Several theories make the self their central concept and emphasize motivation related to the self. One called Hall and Lindzey, 1970, self-actualization theory, distinguishes between basic needs and meta needs–"meta" means "after", "in addition to" (Maslow, 1968). In this theory, the basic needs are such motives as hunger, sex, affection, security, and self-esteem. They tend to form a hierarchy, so that physiological needs like hunger must be satisfied before the person attempts to fulfill needs like self-esteem. The basic needs are also called deficiency needs, for they are needs to remedy something a person lacks. The meta needs, by contrast, are growth needs—needs for such things as justice, beauty, order, goodness. These are not arranged in a hierarchy, because one may take the place of another. If people manage to fill their basic deficiency needs and go on to satisfy their meta growth needs, they are said to be self-actualizing. They are actualizing their growth potential.

Another theory called self-theory, also uses the concept of self-actualization, but assumes that people have two major needs: a need for positive regard by others, and a need for self-regard (Rogers, 1961). Self-theory also assumes that each person has a perceived self and an ideal self. If a child does not receive positive regard from others, that individual's self-regard is impaired, creating a discrepancy between the ideal self and the perceived self. Such a disagreement—called incongruence by Rogers—makes the person anxious and uncomfortable. But as a normal person grows, he or she can learn ways of reducing the incongruence (although never eliminating it entirely), and of bringing the ideal self and the perceived self closer together. This growth is self-actualizing.

Personality as Traits

Of course, personality theorists of all schools would agree that most human adult behaviour is learned. They would also agree that it is motivated. They differ, however, in where they put the emphasis. The motivational theories just described concentrate on motives. Other focus on behaviour, but even these differ about how to measure or characterize behaviour.

Trait theorists try to find a limited number of traits and measure them, ordinarily with tests or ratings of behaviour. They attempt to describe a person by measuring *distinctive characteristics* of his behaviour (Allport, 1961). The two italicized words are important. First, for any bit of behaviour to be meaningful, it should be *characteristic*, that is, relatively consistent over time. Second, the aspects of personality that we choose for study should be *distinctive*.

Confining ourselves to those aspects of personality which are characteristic, consistent and distinctive simplifies the problem of studying personality. Even so, the possible number of distinctive characteristics is enormous. Moreover, they are not always easily separated from each other. Is there a clear-cut distinction, for example, between honesty on the one hand, and conscientiousness, integrity, or dependability on the other hand? In this and many other instances, we find that personality characteristics often overlap and are highly correlated with each other. Hence several possible sets of characteristics may not be clearly different from one another. Each set, however, may serve some particular purpose in describing personality.

Traits and Types

When we talk about aspects of personality that are reasonable characteristic, consistent, and distinctive, we are talking about traits. As constructs, or ideas, that bring order to the many observations of human behaviour, traits provide a useful means of characterizing a person. Types based on patterns of inter-related traits that are known as syndromes are sometimes useful in characterizing people; it is the types based on extremes of one or a few traits that are misleading.

Notions of personality types based on these extremes arise on several ways. They can stem from observations of a few dramatic instances of somebody's behaviour, from contact with relatively rare personalities, or from exposure to fictional characters who have purposely been overdrawn to make them interesting. We then unthinkingly use these are instances as models for people in everyday life. The big bully who beats up all the kids on the neighbouring becomes a model for an "aggressive type". The relatively rare person who is the life of the party may be the model for the "extraverted type". And distinctive fictional characters like Hamlet, Pollyanna, and Scrooge serve as models for their types. Actually, such models are so rare that they are hardly valid in describing real people.

Another objection to typing people is that it lumps together a number of different personality traits. The "introverted type" is supposed to be withdrawn, sensitive to criticism, and inhibited in emotional expression; the "extraverted type", is supposed to be outgoing, thick-skinned about personal features, and spontaneous in emotional expression. It happens more often, though that a person is as sensitive as the introvert, yet as sociable as the extravert. Another person may be as thick-skinned as the extravert, but as ill-humoured and unfriendly as the introvert. A personality is not simple enough to be put into a single basket; people are characterized by a number of traits. Some of these may be introvertive and some extravertive: they seldom all fit the pattern of any one type. Even in the rare case where they do, it is very unlikely that all of them will be so extreme. Most people are not extreme types, nor do they exhibit extreme traits; they fall somewhere in between.

Factor Analysis

A scientific way of selecting and measuring a limited number of traits is called factor analysis. A mathematical procedure that is essentially a correlational technique, it shows how the items on a personality test correlate with each other. Suppose the experimenter starts with several hundred questions designed to describe a person. In each question is a key adjective or phrase that means a trait.

A typical factor analysis of items on personality tests or rating scales produces a number of factors–often 12 or more. But usually several of the factors are not very significant; they refer to correlations among a small number of items. Much of the time, about 5 factors all account for virtually all the correlations among items. Such a case in illustrated. This example is based on 20 trait-rating scales which factor analysis reduced to the 5 factors listed. The names of the factors given in the first column did not come from the factor analysis; they were devised by the psychologist doing the study (Norman, 1963). After he identified a factor, he looked at the trait-rating scales that measured it and decided from the nature of the items what the factor should be called: "extraversion", "agreeableness", and so on.

Weaknesses of Trait Theory: Problems of Measurement

When psychologists have performed a factor analysis and identified, say, five factors, they are tempted to think they have isolated "the" traits that can be used to measure characteristic and distinctive ways of behaving. As it turns out, the five factors, or very similar ones, are founded in many different studies, so long as the items on the scales are very similar. This fact increases the experimenter's temptation to think that primary traits have been discovered. But are primary traits really revealed by such a method? There are problems, it seems, with this way of con-structing traits.

One problem which psychologists have long been aware of is that the factors identified depend on the items in the test. Factor analysis only gives out what has been put into it. If the experimenter changes the kinds of items, or the number of items of a particular kind, the best yields a different set of factors. This dependency of traits on the items used to measure them leads to the suspicion that the traits are in the heads of the test makers rather than in the personalities of the groups being listed.

And the suspicion is confirmed by research in one study, judges rated fellow college students who were complete strangers (Passini and Norman, 1966). The judges were in the same room with the persons being judged for only fifteen minutes, and no verbal communication was permitted. The five main factors that emerged from their ratings were very similar, which was obtained on subjects well known to the judges. This is strong evidence that the traits represent established ways of thinking about personality characteristics—factors that judges used whether they know the individuals or not. Put another way, such results suggest that "personality factors" are concepts which most of us share about the way to judge people rather than characteristics of people's behaviour.

There are other weaknesses of personality traits as ways of measuring traits (Mischel, 1968). One, is a tendency of the person taking the test to respond with socially desirable choices—he gives the answer he thinks he should, rather than describing how he actually behaves. As the Edwards Personal Preference Schedule attempts to overcome this weakness by pairing items in such a way that the alternatives are equally desirable. Thus the person is forced to choose between alternatives on some other basis—on his actual way of behaving, the testers hope. But most personality tests do not attempts to compensate for the bias of social desirability.

Personality tests are also vulnerable to people's tendency to agree with statements—sometimes called the tendency toward acquiescence. People who are inclined to go along with whatever statements are on the test help produce not their own personality traits, but traits that were imagined by the test maker.

Probably the greatest weakness of the trait approach, based on personality tests or rating scales, is that the traits measured do not correlate well, if at all, with actual behaviour. Experiments that objectively measure some bit of behaviour—say, a sample of honesty—show that this behaviour does not have much to do with the trait of "honesty" as measured on a personality test. The reason, psychologists now know, is that the behaviour of people is not very consistent, even if their responses to paper-and-pencil tests of personality are. The significance of one classical study of honesty has become clear only in recent year (Hartsborne and May, 1928).

These criticisms of personality measures are not meant to damn them. Personality test do have predictive value in some situations. The point here is that they are not good ways to get at primary traits, partly because of biases in the making and taking of tests, and partly because primary traits of actual behaviour are not measured well by such tests.

Trait Theories

One way in which we can analyze personality is by systematically studying the individual characteristics that make up personality. We can simply describe the individual as they are. We can describe the various dimensions of their personalities in terms of certain characteristics called traits.

Traits are relatively enduring behaviours or characteristics that distinguish two or more people from each other. The list of traits by which we can describe people is practically limitless. The aim of the trait theorist, therefore, is to reduce traits to their common denomination and formulate a series of dimensions on which all individual can be characterized. The trait theorist defines behaviour as a function of certain number of predispositions that manifest themselves in many different situations. The theorist's task is to identify each person's position on these personality dimensions by comparing that individual with others.

Trait theory involves a battery of tests that are supposed to measure a person's tendency to have various traits. By generating many different questions and analyzing the responses to these Qs, researchers believe they have found an objective way (within limits) to measure the basic personality traits. The limitations of such test are in the wording of questions, the reliability of the person's answers, and the interpretation given to the answers. For instance, in asking whether a subject enjoys going to parties, it is only on asking him and not on established fact that a yes answer indicates the trait of sociability.

Kinds of Traits

We can divide traits into many different kinds according to our interest. For example, traits can be differentiate into physical and mental traits, individual and universal traits and ability and preference traits.

Gordon Allport (1961), a leading proponent of trait theory, stresses the uniqueness of each individual. He has identified three kinds of traits according to the generality of their influence: cardinal, central, secondary. Allport believes that people have generalized dispositions that guide most of their behaviour. He calls this disposition a *cardinal trait*. A women who organizes her whole life around home and family may have a cardinal trait of domesticity. A women who goes for a professional degree and whose primary source of satisfaction is her work may have a cardinal trait of achievement. Central traits are the pervasive than cardinal traits, although they too influence a wide variety of behaviour. Most people display a few (8-10) important central trait or interest patterns. Lastly, Allport calls traits that are situation specific and less consistently, present secondary. Quick anger suggest a secondary trait of being short tempered

Raymond B. Cattell (1965), another leading trait theorist, also clusters *common traits*, which are universal and *unique*, which belong to a particular individual. In addition this theorist talks about surface and source traits, *surface traits* are commonly found together in cluster, and *source traits* are underlying factors. For example, a person may be idealistic, imaginative, and grateful. These surface traits suggest the underlying source trait of buy sensitive. Cattell divides source traits into what he calls environmental—mold traits and constitutional traits. Both of these sources can be either general or specific, according to the range of their influence.

3

Methods of Studying Personality

Methods: Ratings and Observations

Since there are so many different definitions of personality, inevitably there must be diverse approaches to the study of personality. Some methods stress the personality as stimulus for others; some stress patterns of response. If a psychologist conceives of the personality as "the organism as a whole" in all its functioning, then obviously almost any total organismic function can be treated as a method for studying personality–and this has been done.

The formal statement of principles and procedures for measuring personality by scientific devices is a recent development; but the practical study and estimation of personality traits dates far back into human history. The customs of primitive tribes today reveal practices which have the status of pragmatic tests of personality. Before a boy is accepted into the status of manhood, he must have proved his fortitude, his emotional control, and other traits, to the satisfaction of the elders of the tribe. The history of early religions and other movements indicates that great stress was laid on the personality qualifications of new initiates and that they were required to pass strenuous tests before being accepted into full membership.

The tests employed in these rites were not tests as we shall use the term. They were actual situations. We ordinarily speak of a test when the subject goes through some brief performance which enables us to infer some related quality or ability. In those days the procedure was simpler. Daniel's courage was tested by his being tossed into a den of lions. Adolescent boys are tested in many primitive cultures, even today, by painful skin lacerations. Reactions to such situations are not mere token manifestations of traits, but heroic, full-scale performances.

From some points of view, perhaps, it is to be regretted that such methods are not permissible in our culture. Certainly it is a more valid procedure to test a man's honesty or courage in these ways than simply to ask him questions. On the other hand, psychologists would have great difficulty in getting experimental subjects after the first one escaped!

Scientific Method and Personality Theory. These primitive devices for eliciting evidence about personality were based upon the crude theory of some shrewd individual. Today, we have developed far more extensive and precise statements about the presumed fundamentals of personality; yet, for some reason, there is relatively little attempt to devise methods of investigation which derive directly from these theories.

In the following pages we shall take a intermediate course between a tight theoretical classification of methods and a simple practical arrangement. This compromise is in part necessitated by the fact that much of the work done in this field is still based on the philosophy of "Let's try this and see how it works." Systematic thinking, however, is emerging as new methods are developed, and we shall call attention to these in their proper places.

Natural of the Recording Instrument. One of the significant problems which faces every scientist is that of deciding what recording instrument is to be employed. The chemist may use colorimeters, balances, radiation meters, and other instruments. The psychologist does not have so extensive an array of technical devices, although gadgetry in the field is increasing rapidly. We have represented, in a way generally approved by research psychologists, some of the relationships between the object being studied and the conception, the comprehension, which is sought.

The object of study is some human being who is engaged in a course of action. John Jones may be observing and responding to "natural" stimuli (not under the control of the experimenter); more often, he is receiving and reacting to standard stimuli, since this makes possible a more rigorous analysis of the observed behaviour. The diagram suggests that there are basically four different kinds of "recording instruments" used to make this material available for scientific analysis and theorizing.

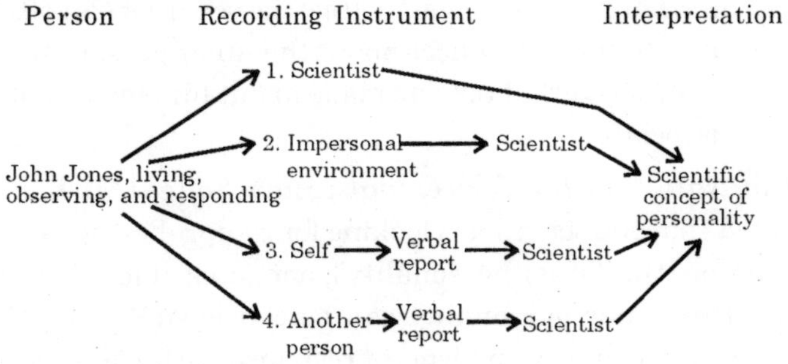

Fig. 1 : A scheme for gathering data relevant to personality. The scientist's understanding of a specific personality, or of personalities in general, may be derived from a variety of clues.

1. **The Scientist Himself.** A psychologist may directly observe John's actions; or he may make photographs or tape-recordings; he may obtain graphs showing pulse rate, blood pressure, galvanic skin response, brain waves, and the like. All these data are then subject to analysis and integration to produce a concept, a theory about personality.
2. **The Impersonal Environment.** John also leaves traces of his personality on the environment and these can be studied. Literary critics infer personality characteristics of an author from his production, and to some extent this is feasible also for artists and musicians. Indeed, it is now becoming common practice for the scientist to ask his subject to produce something (e.g., a painting) which can then be analyzed according to certain rules to elicit inferences about personality.
3. **The Self.** John may be asked to explain why he did something, to describe "what the situation looked like to him." He may report moods, fantasies, impulses which are completely inaccessible to the scientist. Whether or not these reports correspond to "reality" as others see it, they constitute important data about the person.
4. **Another Person.** Sometimes it is equally important to ascertain how John is perceived by Mary or by Tom. None

of us has the gift "to see ourselves as others see us," partly because the personality of the other becomes a component of what he sees. Nevertheless, the scientist can often arrive at valuable inferences about the inner personality of John from the verbal reports made about him by his friends and associates.

The Nature of the Conceptualization Sought. It has already been noted that the scientist is looking for comprehension of a hidden phenomenon, the "inner personality", not accessible to direct study. Further, this inner personality can be conceptualized in terms of social stimulus value, or in terms of response patterns, or in terms of intervening variables patterns of perception, and belief. The choice among the recording instruments described above will be influenced by the theoretical preference of the psychologist for one or another conceptualization of personality.

The behaviouristic psychologist will prefer to make his own observations, generally using equipment which reduces his own judgment and personal bias to a minimum. Thus he may count the number of times a child initiates a conversation with others, or record the response of blood pressure to a pistol shot, or determine the visual threshold for accurate report of emotionally charged words. Whereas his personal interests determine both the kinds of stimuli he present and the kinds of responses he records, the observations themselves acquire greater objectivity than if he simply watched and made notes. The instrumental data can later be examined by investigators with different prejudices, if this seems important in order to rule out any effect of his theoretical preconceptions.

Less has been done with the analysis of traces on the environment. Some work is now being done with paintings, and social psychologists have begun analyzing documents to get at insights regarding public figures. In industry, there is speculation about the study of organizational events to reveal the personality of the leader, although this obviously gets very complicated.

Most extensive use has been made of the "self" as a source of data. Many important events occur in a fashion which renders them inaccessible to recording otherwise; there is probably much visceral activity of significance which we cannot study by instrumentation, and there are tremendously complex perceptual and imaginative process, regarding which we have not the slightest idea as to physical methods of recording. Hence, much of the personality research going on today utilizes the person's own verbal report to obtain data for analysis. These methods are used extensively by psychoanalysts and by psychologists who are looking for a conception of personality in terms of intervening variables.

Finally, the use of "other persons" as recording instruments is directly tied to the conception of personality as social stimulus value. If we wish to know John's effect on Mary, there is virtually no method of study which does not involve using Mary as the recording instrument. Generally, we obtain the verbal report of the second person as to the perceived qualities of the first. These reports can then be processed to obtain insight into the social stimulus value of the subject person. This class of methods will be examined first.

Personality as Stimulus

When we speak of the personality in terms of its social stimulus value, we imply that the appropriate "recording instrument" to be used in research will be another person. The psychologist may himself watch and record what he perceives to be the personality of the subject; or he may induce others to record their perceptions and provide him with these records for analysis.

Since our perceptions of others are notoriously in error, at least a fair share of the time, the problem of method here is that of devising ways of recording observations which will minimize these errors. This is a crucial problem, of course, in all research: how to minimize errors of observation.

Since the specific devices to be mentioned here are subject to certain errors in common, we shall simply describe the techniques which have been employed and then discuss the problem of reducing error in relation to all of them.

The Guess Who Test. Hartshorne and May (1928) asked school children to give their impressions of each other in an ingenious way. A description was read to the class, such as "a boy who gets into fights a lot on the playground"; they were asked to write down the name of the boy. Obviously this gets an aspect of social stimulus value; unfortunately, sometimes it only produces an indication of dislike, not of the specific kind of personality described.

A more sophisticated use of the Guess Who technique is described by Mitchell (1955). In this case, resort to factor analysis makes possible a rather precise determination of the attributes which influenced the children making the judgments.

Sociometry. Moreno (1934) suggested that it would be possible to measure an individual's social status by a somewhat similar method. Nursery school children may be asked, "Whom do you like to play with?" Air Force cadets have been asked, "What men do you think will make the best officers?" Fraternity men have been asked to choose prospective room-mates, study partners, buddies for a beer party, and so on. Where members of the group have had a good chance to become acquainted, this method has obvious values in terms of the recording of social stimulus value.

The number of times a person is chosen for a particular role indicates his positive or attraction value; a person who gets many choices obviously has some attribute which causes him to be perceptually distinctive. As noted above, this may not be the attribute defined by the instructions. Some studies (e.g., Mouton, Blake, and Fruchter, 1955) have found sociometric judgments to have substantial validity; other studies have found that they do not. Much depends on the criterion of validity employed. Apparently cadets, after four or five weeks together, can, with considerable accuracy, pick the men who will make the grade as officers.

Similarity Scaling. Although the problem of perceiving persons is essentially similar to that of perceiving objects, surprisingly little has been done in applying the techniques of psychophysical scaling in this area. One exception is the study by Jackson, Messick, and Solley (1957a), in which fraternity men took their fellow members in groups of three and chose the two who were most similar. Statistical techniques were then applied to determine what the men meant by "similar". It was found that two sets of standards were obviously involved: first, a dimension from "intelligent-studious" the opposite (some men were similar because they were close together on this dimension); second, a dimension of general liking. The intelligence dimension might, of course, be replaced by some other or others, if a college context were not involved. One can imagine, for example, that in a factory groups, a dimension might be skill, or attitude to the union, or even conflict with the foreman. Unfortunately, the scaling technique does not automatically identify these dimensions; their identification depends on the ingenuity of the investigator.

Identification of Attributes. A second broad category of devices for studying social stimulus value seeks to determine the extent to which a person manifests given attributes. Mostly these are called "rating scales," and a rating scales is simply a device for recording the extent to which a person is perceived as possessing the defined attribute.

Each of us finds it necessary at times to make judgments about the extent to which a friend possesses some quality. In occupational, political, and social situations we are not necessarily interested his all-round "goodness"; we want to know if he is vigorous, or shy, or practical in his judgments. The psychologist needs the same kind of evaluation, for the same reasons. He differs from the amateur chiefly in the controls that he imposes on the task. He defines more precisely the characteristics that he wants to study; he uses a standard scale for recording his impressions; and he sets up uniform conditions in an attempt to reduce the effect of irrelevant factors. Further, he introduces statistical checks, to determine the freedom from prejudice, and from inconsistency, of his judgments.

Graphic Scales. Much effort has gone in to the development of forms which will facilitate the recording of impressions in an accurate manner. An example is shown. The attribute to be observed here is not defined by a single word, such as "appearance", but a question is asked which defines more precisely what to look for. The response is made by checking along a linear scale; it is believed that this induces in the rater an attitude of measuring differences. The degrees of possession of this characteristic are defined by a series of phrases below the line; this means that different judges, using the same scale, will be more likely to have the same meaning in mind.

Graphic scales are extensively used in personnel work, e.g., by interviewers who wish to record their impressions of an applicant, by supervisors making merit appraisals of workers under their supervision, and so on. They are also used widely by the armed services and by civil service.

Numerical Scales. Instead of checking on a line, the rater may be asked to assign a number between 1 and 10, or between 0 and 100, to indicate the degree of a certain attribute. These scales do not differ in principle from the graphic scale. Whereas there is a spurious appearance of greater precision in a scale of 100 points, numerous studies have demonstrated that the average observer cannot use effectively more than 11 steps on such a scale, and this only after training. For untrained rates, 5 or 7 steps would be the maximum usable.

Sources of Error: Reliability. The problem of methodology is the problem of reducing error. Everyone makes judgments of personality; the task of the psychologist is to develop techniques which are more consistent and more dependable, in short, which accomplish the purposes for which they are made. The discussion of these sources of error traditionally centers around two concepts: reliability and validity.

One source of error is revealed when we find that the same person, evaluated by the same rater on two occasions, gets quite a different rating. Let us suppose that on one instance the rater was suffering from indigestion, had not slept on the train the night before, and was in a strange office. On the second occasion he felt well, was fresh and rested, and was in familiar surroundings. The influence of these irrelevant factors upsets the consistency of the ratings. Chance errors, then, represent a problem in making judgment of persons.

The term "reliability" refers to freedom from chance errors, and in a positive sense means that a measuring device renders substantially similar results when applied to the same person. A yardstick made of rubber would be an excellent example of an unreliable measuring device. While physics does not use such instruments, the importance of increasing reliability by ruling out chance errors is stressed in all physics research. In quantitative chemical analysis, it is standard practice to take 10 readings of the microbalance to reduce these chance errors. Psychologists could profit by this example.

Reliability is commonly divided into two aspects, consistency and stability. Consistency of an estimate may be determined by splitting our observations in half, and correlating one against the other set. Thus if we observe Johnny for two minutes each day, for ten days, we may add all the odd-numbered days together, add the even-numbered days together, and so determine whether the attribute we are recording is consistent. Or we may have two judges observe Johnny and correlate their ratings to show consistency.

"Stability" refers to consistency over time. Johnny's behaviour in January may be related to his behaviour in June. Reliability in this case means high predictability from one time to another. (It is obvious that stability figures will tend to be lower than consistency figures; some real change in Johnny, besides chance factors affecting the judgment, may occur in six months.) Stability figures based on the same judge, however, may be spuriously high; the judge may recall his rating on the second occasion.

Even among skilled judges the range of reliability measures may be very great. Stern, Stein, and Bloom (1956) report on a study of school children in which pairs of clinicians gave reliabilities ranging from –48 to +.73, after very careful study of the children. We suspect that the negative correlation was an accident, since even untrained judges rarely disagree that much, but it is obvious that ratings are often unreliable. Such interviewers as those in industrial personnel offices are likely to give reliabilities around +.50, which would mean that many chance errors are affecting the results.

Validity of Ratings. It is clear that unreliability of a rating will also affect its validity–i.e., the success with which it identifies the person "really" possessing a given attribute. However, realiability is of high and yet validity is low. For example, ratings of the intelligence of a beautiful woman, made by male observers, might all agree (hence, meet the standard of reliability), yet be grossly in error which checked against her score on an objective test of mental ability.

Such errors are endemic in all sorts of judgments of personality. It should be remembered, that personality is always inferred. Certain cues come from the person being observed; the judge takes these in, compares them with his mental yardsticks (frames of reference), and arrives at a percept. Since these frames of reference will never be identical from one judge to another; differences in rating will ensure. Analysis indicates some sources of difference, and appropriate steps for their reduction.

Errors of Definition. Judgments of personality must be made in terms of trait names, but not all people use the same terms and, even when two individuals use the same descriptive adjective, they may not have the same meaning in mind. Nervousness to one judge is primarily a physical phenomenon, including trembling, jumpiness, tics, and stammering; whereas a second interprets it in terms of mood, depression, worries, and other emotional upsets. The defect can be remedied by providing a uniform list of all terms for all judges, preparing detailed operational definitions for these terms, or having conferences at which the judges agree on definitions. Murray (1938) reports that many lengthy debates were held before his group of experts came to use trait name in a uniform fashion.

Errors of Destribution. Judges are often found to differ on their concepts of high, low, and average for a given trait. One may be lenient, putting all his judgments above the theoretical neutral point, while another is severe. One judge uses extreme ratings often, while a second avoids extreme marks. Either deviation will introduce inaccuracies into the ratings.

A statistical technique for correcting this difficulty involves converting ratings to standard scores. It is arbitrarily assumed that each judge should come out with the same average and the same scatter of ratings. The standard score method enforces this requirement. Thus it avoids errors in validity of the type described.

Errors Due to Unequal Units. Ratings are made on the assumption that units of judgment are equal–that the jump from 2 to 4 on the scale is as large as that from 4 to 6. Some judges do not, for one reason or another, stick to this rule. A very conservative judge, for example, will be unable to distinguish units on the radical end of the scale. Socialists, communists, and Trotskyites may all look alike to him.

There is some evidence (cf. Murray, 1938) that this is a general problem in judging human nature. Men generally rate most accurately the personalities of those most resembling themselves; judgment of those markedly different is less accurate. It is difficult to correct such a basic distortion; we can only suggest (1) that judges should be carefully selected to exclude extremists, particularly in the field being studied, and (2) that the individual who is often called upon to make judgments of personality ought to cultivate a middle-of-the-road position and make a special attempt to understand people who are quite different from himself.

Halo Effect. Perhaps the most persistent and most annoying of all errors in personal judgment is the halo effect. This term relates to the following type of mistake. Because Sam is excellent in schoolwork, his teacher rates him high on character. Because Dick is rebellious and disobedient, she rates him low on general intelligence. The term "halo" means that from some central fact–friendship, high intelligence, beauty, or some other trait of importance to the judge–an influence radiates out to change the ratings on other traits.

The halo effect has so far proved to be the most troublesome of all problems in rating. It is particularly operative when a judge is asked to estimate several different traits of the same person in succession. The perception of personality tends toward a gestalt, an integrated pattern. It thus becomes difficult to make independent judgments about specific aspect of an individual. This may explain the fact that long acquaintance does not automatically make for valid judgments. We may simply become more and more confirmed in our incorrect judgments of a person.

The principle of perceptual closure, regarding which we shall say a great deal more in later chapters, may operate to interfere with accurate ratings. As Luft (1950) and Dailey (1952) have demonstrated, if the observer arrives at a premature hypothesis as to "what this person is really like," this hypothesis may interfere with the use of additional information about the personality being studied.

Stereotypes. Another type of error results from the fact that the judge identifies the person being observed as a member of a certain group, and then imputes to the individual those attributes which he believes pertain to the group. In its extreme form this kind of error is manifested in the stereotype of a racial, national, or religious minority. A person who sees all Negroes as lazy, ignorant, and dirty can scarcely give an accurate evaluation of a Negro who has earned a Ph.D. degree in nuclear physics. The judge sees only his mental picture, not the real person.

Gage and Cronbach (1955) have shown that the stereotyping phenomenon is almost ubiquitous; the example given is only one instance of it. They found that their observers, making judgment of grade school and high school students, were actually employing stereotyped belief of the form, "All ten-year-old boys are..." Differences in accuracy of judgment of specific children, surprisingly enough, turned out to be due in large part of differences in the accuracy of these stereotypes. Their results suggest that all perception of other persons may utilize this process, and that the training of judges is in part a matter of giving them a larger number of categories (e.g., in clinical psychology the student must study many different kinds of abnormal personalities) and of teaching sensitivity to the cues identifying these groups. Obviously it is also helpful for the judge to be aware of his own stereotypes and to watch for signs that the individual in question deviates from the stereotype.

It should perhaps be noted in conclusion that there is a semantic problem of considerable size involved in validity studies of social stimulus value. This problem arises because only the judge can report on his own perceptions. If he says, "Mary looks lazy to me", no one can challenge this. His percept of Mary is a uniquely private event. But if he says, "Mary is lazy", he is committing himself to a judgment which is open to consensual validation by other observers. It is only in this latter sense that we can speak of validity of ratings. But, after all, the over-whelming majority of judgments of others are framed in exactly this fashion.

Personality as Response

We have already suggested that, while the psychologist starts with the notion of personality as the social stimulus value one individual has for another, he soon shifts to an interest in the responses which give rise to this stimulus value. After all, a percept does not arise without cues. The person being observed must give off information which, received by the judge, elicits in him the awareness of certain attributes. (His awareness, as noted above, may be in "error" in the sense of not agreeing with other observers, but within his own phenomenal field it is an unquestionable fact). The primary mode of emitting information which serves as a basis for such judgments is, of course, behaviour. Gestures, words, vocal inflections, facial expression–not to mention the organized activities of the individual–give clues to the observer as to "what manner of man is this?"

As Cattell (1957) has noted, progress in the study of personality seems to be correlated with a shift for man interest in overall judgments of attributes to a more precise determination of units of behaviour, through questionnaires and through experiments. For systematic reasons we defer the consideration of questionnaires to the following chapter. The other points will be taken up here.

Behaviour Ratings. Cattell (1950) has particularly favoured a mode of investigation which he calls "behaviour rating" to distinguish it from attribute rating. He notes however, that the making of such ratings for personality studies is a somewhat tricky proposition. First of all, the behaviour should be very carefully defined: "Thus the judges are not asked to rate 'sociability' but. 'How often does the person speak to a fellow worker spontaneously, without practical need?' 'Does he speak to strangers first?' and so on". Secondly, the judges must be trained in observing these units of behaviour. Often there is a marked increase in reliability after the judge has practiced making these observations.

On the other hand, it must be noted that these behaviour ratings encounter their own characteristic difficulties. For example, a young man may not speak to his fellow workers because his work place is too noisy. The interest may be present, but the opportunity to manifest the specific behaviour is not. Hence Cattell must use a number of behaviour ratings, all of which bear upon the attribute in which he is interested, and count on probabilities to rule out these interfering effects.

Time Sampling. An extension of the same idea is found in the sampling of observed behaviour for specific time units. Time sampling has been used especially often with young children, for whom verbal report is likely to be quite unsatisfactory anyway; their significant behaviours are likely to occur in the open, in play groups, and easily observed interactions. This has led to sample studies of thumb-sucking, fighting, competition and rivalry, and similar behaviour. A particular exponent of the sampling technique is Roger Barker, who has gone to the extreme of following a specific child throughout an entire day, sampling all of his interactions with significant people and social roles (see, for example, Barker and Wright 1951; Barker and Wright, 1954).

Many early time-sampling studies deteriorated into trivia of counting without meaning. Barker and Wright (1954) avoid this criticism by dealing with what they call "behaviour episodes," recognizable by the observer as a unified piece of action by the subject, directed toward a certain end. Thus, when a boy spies an old crate, works it free from entanglements, and drags it across to a preferred play spot, this is clearly identifiable as an episode which is unified as far as the boy is concerned. Such behaviour sampling enables the researcher to deal with meaningful units, and makes possible significant generalizations about the personality under observation.

Problems with Behaviour Sampling. Behaviour sampling generally attains a much higher reliability than the judgments of attributes described earlier. Reliabilities as high as +.90 have been reported in well-planned studies; this means that the records are about as accurate as any but the most refined physical measurements.

Validity is, of course, more difficult to ascertain. In a sense one can say that if a person executed a certain kind of act six times in a specified number of opportunities, this is a valid fact in itself. However the psychologist always has more in mind than a simple census of behaviour. He wants to know what further inferences can be made about the personality from this behaviour sample. Cattell (1957) reports that in many instances he gets loadings as high as +.70 for a particular behaviour rating on a "source trait" or common factor in a set of data. However, it is not yet clear that this figure really indicates ability to make valid predictions about any significant aspect of the personality; a factor loading tells how well the behaviour rating agrees with the entire factor, but this need not mean agreement with an observable and significant attribute of the personality being studied.

Laboratory Situations. Behaviour rating and behaviour sampling are attempts to get significant material about the person within a normal environment (There is some doubt that this holds perfectly; certainly an observer, following a child all day long, is bound to have some significant effects in modifying the latter's actions. In general, however, the total context of behaviour is reasonably normal). Behaviour sampling in a laboratory situation is inevitably artificial, since the subject may be responding out of curiosity, or to do the examiner a favour, rather than expression of his normal impulses.

Laboratory situations, on the other hand, may be so devised that the results are of value regardless of these factors. One method, of course, is to make the laboratory a part of the life situation; Voas, Bair, and Ambler (1956) put Air Force cadets into a decompression chamber, representing it as a simulated "high altitude" test, and noted the evidences of anxiety shown by each cadet. A later check of men washed out of flight training for psychiatric reasons showed that most of them could have been predicted ahead of time by these records. Hence, whatever underlying personality attribute caused the psychiatric failure was rather well-sampled by this laboratory test.

The foregoing example illustrates what has been called the "miniature-situation" approach to testing. In the Office of Strategic

Services' work on assessment of agents during World War II (see OSS Staff, 1948) miniature situations were used extensively. For instance, the candidate was told to build a small wooden structure; he was assigned two helpers (members of the assessment them). One of the "helpers" was incredibly clumsy; the other, critical and sarcastic. Observer rated the candidate on how he tolerated and dealt with these helpers.

Crutchfield's Conformity Test. It is possible to miniaturize the situation even more, and thus get more complete control of all possible variables. One must assume, for example, that the two frustrating assistants did not perform in exactly identical fashion at all times, hence some candidates got more stress than others.

Crutchfield (1951) has developed an artificial group situation which gives the experimenter complete control over the stimuli which apparently emanate from the members of the group. This makes it possible for him to study differences in conformity tendencies. Each S has a panel of lights, the flashing of which purports to show judgments made by other members of the group. For example, he may be asked to judge the relative sizes of rectangles; he is told that the lights show which rectangle is judged longest by each of the group members. Actually, the experimenter feeds the same cues to all members, but records the judgments made by each. At a critical point S is given "information" that everyone else considers a rectangle largest which, he can plainly see, is not. He is then under pressure to agree with the group. Yielding to a "majority" judgment which opposes his own views shows conforming behaviour on the part of S.

Another version of this technique uses tape recordings, with each S wearing earphones (cf. Blake, Helson, and Mouton, 1957). S believes that he is hearing the voices of his fellow subjects, giving their judgments in a certain order, his own coming last. Thus all subjects are under the same pressure to conform. Results of these studies. We mention here only that these kinds of controlled situations offer exciting promise for advance in personality study and may ultimately provide high validity diagnoses of underlying trends on truly significant variables.

Expressive Movements. Finally, we may mention another category of responses which are revealing of personality. Gestures and expressive movements have been objects of interest to psychologists for many years. The manner of executing a perfectly ordinary task may be very useful as an index of underlying trends. In speaking, for example, two men may use the same words to deliver messages which are identical in intellectual content, yet by their manner they may convey quite different impressions. Speed, hesitation change of tone, accenting words, and other cues are involved.

Handwriting, too, is often expressive. Not only letter form, but linkages of letters, spacing, curved or angular style, and similar bits of information may be relevant. The results of scientific research on handwriting are far less exciting than the often fantastic claims of commercial graphologists, but it is clear that some information can be gotten from a study of handwriting. Reliabilities of specific data about script are high, but the reported validities, when these are checked against ratings or tests of personality, are rather low.

Everyone studies personality. As opposed to popular devices, the scientific study of personality is distinguished by consideration of reliability, validity, and objectivity. In accordance with the three approaches to a definition of personality, techniques can be divided into three groups. Two of these have been considered in the present chapter.

Personality as stimulus is investigated chiefly by the rating technique. Ratings are useful, but subject to numerous errors. Both reliability and validity of ratings can be appreciably increased by due consideration of (1) characteristics of the rater, and (2) technique of making and summarizing ratings.

Personality as response may be studied by behaviour samples and miniature situations. The miniature-situation technique is hopeful, although it is difficult to find such tests which will adequately predict the individual's behaviour in life situations. Behaviour samples are useful in young children, and samples of functions such as gesture and handwriting may yet be found useful in the analysis of the adult personality.

Methods: Inventories and Projective Tests

We seek greater precision in our estimates of a person's social stimulus value by developing better rating scales. We may also sharpen our understanding of an individual by obtaining samples of his behaviour under standardized conditions. But our long-run purpose is to get a more satisfactory method for studying his inner personality the structure of perceptions, expectancies, desires, and ideals, which accounts both for his behaviour and for his stimulus value.

There are, broadly speaking, two classes of devices which have become pre-eminent in studying personality as an intervening variable. One class includes the personality questionnaires and inventories which have multiplied so rapidly in the United States and are now proliferating in other parts of the world. Essentially, these devices assume that we can infer the nature of the person's inner organization from his answers to questions–not directly, in many cases, since what he will give us is his "mask" or the picture he wants us to have of him. Indirectly, however, we should be able to make inferences from combinations of items and by including correction factors of various kinds.

The second broad category of methods relevant here includes the so-called "projective tests". Essentially these tests involve facing the subject with an ambiguous stimulus and requiring him to respond. Since he cannot figure out what the examiner wants, he must "project" his own meanings into the situation and behave accordingly. Obviously it should be necessary for him to reveal something of his concealed self in this operation.

The research publications dealing with these techniques–inventories and projective–fill several volumes annually. The following treatment can do no more than identify some examples and try to outline the key problems relevant to their application in the study of personality.

Inventories and Questionnaires

The first questionnaire designed to obtain a self-description of personality seems to have been that devised by Woodworth (See Hollingworth, 1920).

This was used with draftees in World War I, in an effort to locate psychiatric risks before they broke down under stress of combat. The items, samples of which are shown in above table, were essentially symptoms taken from psychiatric notes on patients. It was assumed that if a soldier reported more than some minimum number of these symptoms, there was a high probability that he possessed a "neurotic personality" and would be incapable of functioning under combat conditions.

Questions Intended to Test "Emotional Instability"

1.	Do you usually feel well and strong?	(No)
2.	Do you usually sleep well?	(No)
3.	Do you frightened in the middle of the night?	(Yes)
4.	Do you troubled with dreams about your work?	(Yes)
5.	Do you have nightmares?	(Yes)
6.	Do you have too many sexual dreams?	(Yes)
7.	Do you ever walk in your sleep?	(Yes)
8.	Do you ever have the sensation of falling when going to sleep?	(Yes)
9.	Does your heart ever thump in your ears so that you cannot sleep?	(Yes)

Source: Hollingworth (1920).

In the period between the two wars, psychologists in the United States produced a wide variety of inventories and questionnaires calculated to measure many different aspects of personality. Important contributions are associated with the names of Bernreuter, Cattell, Guilford, Bell, and Thurstone. A good summary of developments in this area can be obtained from Ferguson (1952).

Assumptions of the Inventory Technique. Any technique which purports to measure some aspect of personality starts from certain assumptions about the relation of this aspect to an observable act. Thus, inventories depend upon assumptions about the relation of the postulated underlying "trait" of personality to the act of answering questions about oneself.

Common Traits. All inventories, and indeed, all measurement techniques which can be used to make quantitative comparisons between individuals, assume the existence of common traits. Although this point will be elaborated, we note here that common traits are assumed to be essentially similar structures in all personalities, scalable in the same units (Height, for example, is a common physical trait; it can be measured in the same units for all individuals). Thus, it is assumed that sociability, emotional stability, self-sufficiency, manifest anxiety, and other traits are common to the population being studied; one may therefore make numerical comparisons within this population.

Quantitative Nature of Traits. It is further assumed by most inventories that traits can be estimated quantitatively by simply adding the number of indicators. For example, a given scale may include 55 items (the Minnesota Multiphasic Personality Inventory–MMPI–scale for hypochondriasis, described below). John answers 11 of these in a "hypochondriacal" manner, and Sam also gets a score of 11. The test user holds that John and Sam are equally characterized as average on this aspect of personality, even though the 11 items scored for John are not the same as the 11 scored for Sam. This approach assumes that the trait is simply a kind of quantitative sum of specific acts, and that these are equally diagnostic for the trait. Critics of the questionnaire approach reject this view; however, one has difficulty in avoiding it, even when dealing with the more subtle projective tests.

Relation to Inner Pattern. Finally, developers of these tests assume that there is some kind of dependable relation between the act of answering the questions and the existence of some unknown inner pattern (the "real" trait). This does not necessarily mean that the person is assumed to be giving an accurate description of himself in the ordinary sense. Such an item as "I would never tell a lie under any circumstances" is not interpreted as meaning that this individual possesses a truthful personality. Rather, it is scored in terms of a desire to make a good impression, to deny the presence of disapproved attributes. Thus, psychologists assume a predictable relationship of a response to some inner pattern, but not necessarily the one manifestly involved in the item content.

The Minnesota Multiphasic Personality Inventory. Only one example of a personality inventory can be analyzed carefully in our limited space. The Minnesota Multiphasic Personality Inventory (MMPI) has been chosen for this purpose because of its wide use in clinical and research work by psychologists.

Hathaway and McKinley (1940) set out to develop an inventory which could be used for estimating the extent to which a person showed a variety of personality traits. Their procedures will be listed in some detail, since these same steps have been followed in most scale construction of this type.

(1) The authors collected about one thousand items of a self-descriptive form, such a "I often feel as if things about me are not

real". These items were collected from earlier tests, from clinical case histories, from autobiographies, and from conversations with patients. (2) Ambiguous and duplicate items were eliminated; thus the total number was cut down to 504. (3) These items were administered to various groups of persons, selected in some fashion to exemplify the extreme of some alleged personality pattern; e.g., to a group of hypochondriacs (persons who show an "abnormal, psychoneurotic concern over bodily health"). The answers to all 504 items were tabulated for the 50 patients who showed a fairly pure kind of hypochondriacal reaction pattern, and for normal control subjects (4) By statistical means, 55 items were selected which differentiated the hypochondriacs from the normal at a suitable level of significance. These 55 items thus constituted the MMPI scale for hypochondriasis.

The procedure thus far is similar to that used by various other investigators. Hathaway and McKinley, however, took steps to avoid one criticism leveled at such standardization. This criticism is: The hypochondriacs used to select the item key were also psychiatric patients; isn't your "trait" confused with sheer abnormality without any specific patter? To avert this possibility, the MMPI was administered to a large group of patients who were not hypochondriacs, and a "correction key" was prepared. This key shows the typical answers of abnormals who are not hypochondriacal. In use, the hypochondriasis score is determined, and this correction score is subtracted from it to give the final trait score.

The MMPI has such a large reservoir of items, many of which are still unscored, that investigators regularly choose new groups and set up new scoring keys. Keys are now widely used for schizophrenic tendency, mania, "psychopathic deviation", paranoid tendency, anxiety, depression, "ego strength", and an assortment of other variables. The test is used extensively in clinical practice, and also in research when an investigator wishes to select subjects who can be presumed to be extreme on a specific personality trait.

Special Validating Scales. Hathaway and McKinley have also attempted to build into the test some safeguards against criticisms of inventories in general. These safeguards take the form of three special validating scores which can be used to decide how far a given person's diagnostic scores should be trusted.

1. The question score is simply the number of times he has checked "cannot say" instead of giving a "yes" or "no" answer.

A question score above 30 casts doubt on the subject's scores, since it is assumed that he is being excessively evasive.

2. The lie score represents the person's tendency to give socially desirable answers even if they are untrue. The items scored are of such an ideal character that very few of us can truthfully give an affirmative answer; the individual who feels that he must make a good impression on the examiner, however, will give such answers.
3. The validity score is composed of 64 items which are very rarely answered in a given manner by normal subjects. Hathaway and McKinley allege that a high score on these items indicates that the items were marked carelessly or that the person could not understand what he was doing.

These three validation scores undoubtedly represent a significant methodological improvement over previous questionnaire construction, in that they attempt to forestall certain kinds of criticisms. However, the authors have given us little evidence to support their claim that these three scores actually serve the purpose claimed for them.

Reliability. On a test-retest basis, the reliabilities of the various subscales of MMPI run from +.46 to +.93. Repeated retesting of a small group indicates that though specific scores change, the profile (relatively strong and weak points in an individual's pattern) remains rather constant. The reliabilities are probably satisfactory, particularly for the more widely used scales such as the Manifest Anxiety Scale.

Validity. Studies of validity of the psychiatric scales have given widely varying results. Some investigators find that the scales select patients and predict their diagnostic categories with marked accuracy. Others are more critical. Apparently psychiatrists differ markedly in their use of certain diagnostic terms, so that a test which is valid in Minnesota may not work so well in California. This raises the problem of choosing a validating criterion for any kind of personality measure; we shall return to it at the close of this chapter.

Cattell's 16 PF Scales. The MMPI has been attacked on other grounds. One is that its basis is purely empirical; there is no rationale behind the various scores, except that a criterion group could be found which was presumably extreme on some dimension. A second is that the scales are not independent of one another; many items are scored for more than one trait. Thus, a person taking the inventory who receives a valid high score on the trait may get an unjustified high score on another because of these questions which are scored for both.

One attempt to deal with these problems is that offered by Cattell (1957) with his 16 PF test. This test evolved out of a long series of researches. Starting with behaviour ratings, Cattell identified 131 clusters of ratings, which were then reduced to 50 "nuclear clusters." These 50, in turn, were arranged to identify 20 "sectors of the personality sphere", independent traits which rather thoroughly covered the social stimulus aspects of personality.

In a later study Cattell attempt to develop inventory items which would measure these 20 aspects by self-description. Using the method of factor analysis, he succeeded in locating 16 groups of items which could be paired modestly well with the earlier data. The procedure of factor-analyzing the relationships among items assures the unity and independence of the 16 scales; and the general procedure gives some theoretical groundwork for this grouping, although there is no way of being sure that the entire "personality sphere" is being covered.

Grygier's Dynamic Personality Inventory. A few attempts have recently been made to construct personality scales based directly on some theory of personality. Sigmund Freud suggested, many years ago, the importance of studying personality in developmental terms. The child, he said, goes through oral, anal, phallic, and genital stages, and the adult personality usually bears the marks of fixations and frustrations at each of these stages. Krout and Tabin (1954) prepared an inventory (PPS) based on this theory. Grygier (1957) started with their test, but greatly expanded it. He also took the step of intercorrelating and factor-analyzing his items, thus assuring unity and independence of his various scores. His Dynamic Personality Inventory looks promising, but is too new for any substantial evidence to have accumulated as to its value.

Edwards's Personal Preference Schedule. Edwards (1954) likewise attempted to develop an inventory based on a theory: in this case, Murray's theory of needs, such as the need for achievement, the need for change, the need for affiliation, heterosexual needs, and other impulses.

Edwards made use of another recent development in test methodology, the forced-choice technique. The subject is presented with two items, and must say which is more descriptive of himself.

Edwards experimented with items worded in different ways, and matched his pairs of items for "social desirability", i.e., each member of the pair sounded just as good as the other. It is now generally conceded that social desirability of items must be controlled, and that the Edwards procedure is probably superior to the "validity scores" developed for the MMPI. The forced-choice procedure is also considered desirable for many kinds of personality measurement tasks.

The Semantic Differential. Although it does not take the form of a questionnaire, the semantic differential developed by Osgood (Osgood, Suci, and Tannenbaum, 1957) is basically a way of asking questions and getting quick responses. The form used is a graphic rating scale similar. The subject responds by making a check mark somewhere along the line to indicate how he perceives the concept presented.

The differential so far has been used to provide two kinds of data. Obviously, it gives the qualitative attributes of the percepts held by this particular person. A woman, for example, may describe father, husband, boss, and other male figures as weak, dirty, small, etc. This provides highly significant information about her orientation toward males.

Secondly, the differential makes possible a unique determination of organization for this person. A young man may cluster his responses in such a way that father, God, power, and security are all close together in his "semantic space", i.e., his meaning structure; whereas another cluster includes mother, sin, fraud, and sickness. Although it cannot be assumed, without further evidence, that these data are valid representations of his personality organization, it does seem highly probable that he has problems in relation to his mother.

Life	Sad .... Happy
My Father	Strong .... Weak
Sex	Good .... Bad

The simple format of the differential makes it easy to introduce new concepts which may be significant for a specific person. This is in contrast to structured inventories such as MMPI, where new items cannot be introduced. On the other hand, if an investigator wishes to classify subjects as hypochondriacal, paranoid, manic, etc., the MMPI would be much more useful than the differential.

What is a Good Personality Inventory? What are the characteristics which identify a personality inventory as good or poor? The criteria most often stressed are reliability and validity.

Reliability. We have noted earlier, in connection with ratings, that an unreliable measure is one which fluctuates in an unpredictable sort of way, and hence is of little value for any kind of research. Specifically, a personality inventory on which chance is a major determinant of scores will not be very useful in diagnosing anyone's personality.

Reliability is usually broken down into two components: consistency and stability. Consistency refers to the degree of agreement inside the measuring device; for example, all of the inventories described above have been tested for internal consistency. Half the items are scored and compared with the other half, to show that the person's score agrees fairly well on the two halves. Stability refers to reliability measured over time; thus, a person tested at six-month intervals should presumably get comparable scores on successive tests. This assumes, on the other hand, that personality does not change, and we know that it does. Hence, psychologists do not demand that reliability over time be as high as reliability (consistency) at a point in time. Although any figure chosen is arbitrary and subject to criticism, a common opinion among psychologists is that consistency should be not less than .80 and stability around .70, for a test to be useful.

Validity. A more difficult question is that of validity. A test is said to be valid if it "measures what it is supposed to measure." This means, inevitably, that any single test may have high validity, low validity, or no validity at all, depending on how it is being used. For example, a test of "neurotic tendency" may successfully pick out people who worry and experience a lot of emotional disturbance, but it may not pick out people who make nervous movements. Is the test valid or not? Much depends on what is claimed for it, or what the test user is trying to accomplish.

Validity is also affected by the circumstances under which the test is administered. Some personality tests have proved useful in counseling and guidance situations, in helping young people choose the type of work they want; but if such tests are used in a personnel office, in selecting applicants for that same kind of job, they are not valid (cf. Heron, 1956). Why? The reason seems to be that in the guidance centre respondents are more likely to tell the truth; in the employment office they are more likely to say what they think the employer wants.

Cross-validation. One way of determining validity is simply to repeat the procedure used in the original validation. Hathaway and McKinley, for example, developed their hypochondriasis key; then they gave the MMPI to a new set of hyochondriacs, and demonstrated that the key assigned scores to this group which were significantly above those obtained by a group of normals. If a test is developed around a group chosen by such an external criterion, a new group of the same kind can be chosen for cross-validation.

Predictive Validity. An even more severe test of validity is that of showing that the test can predict future personality developments. The original inventories were devised in an attempt to preselect soldiers likely to become psychiatric casualties in wartime. During the World War II several such tests were administered to military personnel, and later follow-ups were conducted to see if the scores were valid. For example, Jennings (1948) studied MMPI profiles of 516 Air Force officers. Of these, 33 had psychiatric breakdowns in service. When they were compared with those who completed tours of duty without breakdown, highly significant differences appeared. Thus the MMPI seems valid when tested for predicting breakdown under stress. By contrast, it has proved invalid for predicting failure in flight training (a relatively less stressful situation).

There are several reasons why such test of validity encounter difficulties:

1. If an individual is trying to get into a desired situation (employment, the Air Force, officers' training school, etc.), he will be tempted to distort his answers, whenever possible, in the direction he believes to be acceptable. Thus many of the military studies may have failed because the individual falsified the inventory–from the best of motives, of course.
2. Another difficulty lies in the fallibility of the criterion. If psychiatric breakdown is used, we assume that the judgment of a military psychiatrist is a safe criterion. But numerous studies indicate that psychiatrists often disagree with each other, that a given psychiatrist changes his mind

about a specific patient, and so on. Hence the low validity of the test may be an artifact produced by a poor criterion.

Peer Ratings. In the preceding chapter behaviour ratings and attribute ratings by peer groups were described as ways of identifying certain kinds of personalities. Obviously, then, these can be used as criteria for inventories. Questionnaires for children have often been related to judgments by classmates of each other, using either defined scales, sociometric choices, or the Guess Who technique. The assumption here is that an inventory should be able to differentiate among children who are perceptibly different from their classmates. If this is verified, then the psychologist can use the test in dealing with children for whom such ratings are not available; and he may be able to ascertain ways in which the child's personality can be modified to improve his acceptability or to reduce the amount of friction he has in his group.

Self-ratings. Finally, we may mention efforts to demonstrate the validity of a test by checking it against self-ratings of the corresponding trait. Since, it may be argued, no one knows this person better than he knows himself, agreement with a self-rating should be good evidence of validity. There are two sound objections to this; one is that many people do not know themselves indeed, they avoid observing their own weak points. Secondly, people are notoriously gullible about descriptions of their own personalities. The author has often used a set of glittering generalities, collected by Forer (1949), to demonstrate this fallacy. Persons who have taken a personality inventory are handed a sheet with these glowing statements checked in such a way as to make it appear that the sheet is different of each person. They are asked to report how valid the description is. About 90 per cent of a college student or businessman's group (Stagner, 1958) will check either "amazingly accurate" or "fairly good". Since everyone received identical "diagnoses", it is clear that the average person cannot be trusted to judge whether a given test score is an accurate reflection of his inner make-up.

A Survey of Validity Studies. The problems involved in arriving at an overall assessment of the validity of inventories can be illustrated by reference to the survey by Ellis (1953). A critic of the inventory approach, Ellis shows that of 499 articles published between 1946 and 1951, 290 reported significant evidence of test validity, while

209 did not. This looks rather poor for the inventories. What Ellis does not do, however, is very important. (1) He does not eliminate studies in which no theory would have predicted a difference; indeed, in some cases it could be argued that the groups compared should not differ, e.g., age,

Table : Summary by Ellis of Validity Studies on Inventories, 1946-1951

Type of validation	*Studies in which significant differences were found*	*Studies in which no significant different were found*	*Total*
Inventory scores vs. diagnostic examinations (psychiatric, therapeutic, delinquent)	114	52	166
Inventory scores vs. rungs (by associates, Instructor etc.)	13	13	26
Inventory scores vs. behavioural characteristics (usually objectively measured	53	41	94
Inventory scores vs. vacational and academic test and performance results	45	56	101
Inventory scores vs. rmp differences (age, sex, socioeconomic, etc.)	65	47	112
Total	**290**	**209**	**499**

Source: Ellis (1953), Table 1, p. 40. By permission of the American Psychological Association. Inc.

sex, and socio-economic groups. And he includes some studies for which no rationale is apparent; for example, should inventories reveal differences in extrasensory perception when the phenomenon itself is still of dubious reliability? (2) He does not differentiate between inventories, some of which give more satisfactory results than others. (3) He fails to consider the fallibility of the criteria used (see our discussion above). These criticisms do not justify reversing Ellis's conclusion and deciding that inventories are valid; rather, they suggest that some inventories are valid some of the time, and should be selective about inventories and also about the criteria we expect them to meet.

Criterion Validity versus Construct Validity. The foregoing discussion assumes the existence of an external criterion for the trait or a criterion performance which the inventory seeks to predict. In such a case one can compute a validity coefficient a correlation shown the degree of confidence we can adopt with respect to the rest as a predictor. Such validity coefficients are widely used in connection with aptitude and ability tests, where it is fairly easy to obtain a criterion performance or criterion group to use as a standard of success.

In the field of personality measurement, on the other hand, it is often difficult to locate a suitable external criterion. Suppose we postulate there a personality variable called "anxiety", which refers not to a momentary state but to a recurrent pattern. Criterion groups may be located by psychiatric judgment, or by peer judgment, or by self-evaluation, but in each case we may question whether the basis of selection is satisfactory.

The developer of a test for anxiety, then, may fallback on evidence that the test picks people who behave as they would be expected to terms of a theory. Thus, the Manifest Anxiety Scale (Taylor, 1953) has been shown to relate to amount of palmar sweating in stress situations, to loss of efficiency of problem solving under shock threat, and so on. Since these are "reasonable" predictions in terms of a hypothesized trait of anxiety proneness, the test may be said to have validity even though no criterion group was tested.

This kind of validation is referred to as "construct validity". It means that a personality measure may be judged valid if its relations with other variables fit a theory in which the assumed personality trait is a "hypothetical construct". The trait cannot be defined observationally but the theory holds that such a trait must exist in order to explain behaviour which is observable. Validating criterion groups cannot be identified in such cases. Consequently, much work is now being done using construct validity as the logical basis for justifying the value of the test. This holds also for projective devices, to which we now turn.

SECTION B
PARENTS AND CHILDREN

4

Theoretical Background of Parenting-Patterns Study

For many years, the socialization influences of parents were thought to mould the behaviour pattern of the children, until Bell (1968, 1977) studies drew attention to the fact that children themselves can make the ongoing interchanges between parents and themselves as well as the development of their own characteristics. This revolutionary viewpoint of Bell has now become the modern-day orthodoxy (Belsky, 1981; Lerner and Busch 1981; Rossnagel, 1981). By manipulating children's behaviour, several researchers have experimentally demonstrated that children's behaviour affects their parent's responses (Osofsky and O'Connel, 1972; Stevens-Long, 1973 ; Bell, 1972; Lytton, 1982). Whereby, (Sameroff, 1975) found from his study that the outcome in the child is determined by the reciprocal influences between the parents and the children. No doubt, the writings of early and modern philosophers have certainly helped a lot in understanding the scientific study of parent-child relationship, but the speculations offered by them have get to be tested on psychological grounds. As a scientific discipline, Child Psychology is less than a century old, but even centuries ago, some of the problems of the field, which are now investigated by systematic research were the subjects of discussion and literary easy. Many of the prominent classical philosophers have written about the characteristics of children and factors affecting their development.

Plato (427-327 B.C.) recognized that to some extent, individual differences in ability are inborn but he also claimed that early childhood training and teaching help in determining the later vocational voice and adjustment. The early socialization process starts from the family and the home. The family acts as a socializing agent for the child. It is within a family, the basic unit of society, that a child learns the fundamentals of social interactions and acquires the behaviour patterns and basic personality structure. The family also functions as a system in which each component part acts on the others, so that circular reactions such as the following occur—

Actually parenting incorporates both potentiality and effectiveness in rearing the child for the development of his/her personality and 'Self'. It exhibits a unique relationship with the socio-genic need-satisfaction of the child.

Before delving into the matter further, it is important to have an overview of the ideas and theories about child development that have been propounded in the past, since these ideas have influenced a lot of research and paved way for better parent-child relationship. Indeed, Scientists welcome theories, hypotheses and hunches, for in science one attempts to test such propositions with the measuring instruments, available and then as a result of experimentation assign them a proper place in the expanding body of knowledge. Theories are important because they are useful in integrating and abstracting the interrelatedness of natural phenomena. They serve as a lure and a spur to the scientist's curiosity. Like the treasure map, they encourage quest of the unknow. They satisfy his desire for understanding the forces of nature.

Plato (427-347 B.C.) is considered as a philosophical Godfather of modern child psychology. He devoted considerable thought to finding more appropriate and effective ways of guiding children's education and training. He encouraged discovering and developing children's unique talents. Every child is an individual with an unique blend of traits. From his observations he concluded that children are born with different types of abilities and each child should be guided into the type of service for which his particular aptitudes best apply. He saw child as a future citizen.

With the coming of Christianity, another viewpoint appeared. As a result of Adam's fall, all mankind is born in sin. A conception of the child as innately depraved arose. The warning 'spare the rod and spoil the child' exemplifies the attitude that was considered appropriate under these circumstances. Thinkers as recently as 1920s believed children to be endowed by nature with perverse tendencies that must be eradicated. Nowadays, we believe that child is born amoral-basically not good nor bad and that best way to ensure proper behaviour is to reinforce that which is good.

Locke (1632-1704) who considered the mind of a new born as '*tabula rasa*', stressed the need for training directed toward the formation of desirable habits in the child by curbing the child's natural impulses. Locke (1693) believed that children by nature are perverted by their wild, native instincts, which are not adaptive to social living. He proposed that rigid controls be applied to children to alter their baseness. Society could not afford the luxury of allowing children to run wild. Modern behaviourism tends to follow his philosophy.

Rousseau (1762-1778) stressed an opposite point of view that child should be permitted freedom to express his natural impulses and to develop without restricting the abilities endowed on him by nature. He opposed the doctrine of innate sin and argued that civilization, not the child's basic nature, was the source of moral pollution. He held the view that child was inherently good. He was unspoiled until corrupted through contact with adults and society. Rousseau (1762) declared 'God makes all things good; man meddles with them and they become evil.' He proposed that children should grow up in a free, unstructured environment that allows open expression, exploration and experimentation and that makes no demands regarding the control of behaviour other than minimum conformity. He also opposed the view that child is a miniature adult and believed that child should by all means be a child.

Dewey (1959-1952) through his pragmatic functionalism aroused interest in man's natural curiosity about the behaviour and psychological development of children. He emphasized learning by doing and education through activity. He believed that children's need must be met and they should be allowed to do as they liked. Darwin (1809-1882) in his principle of natural evolution focused the Psychologist's attention on human development. He emphasized the importance of adjustment to the continuing survival of an organism and thus laid the groundwork for the concept of psychological adjustment in contemporary child psychology. He regarded baby as a link between animal and man. The crawling of the infant replicated the swimming movement of a fish, creeping the locomotion of mammals and running the stage of man's movement. Children's love for scrapping and climbing trees corresponded to the cave man era. The infant's grasping reflex was his heritage from the branch-grasping days of his ancestors, the monkeys. His theory of recapulation, erroneous though it may be, was rooted in the biology of the day. Hence, in it a scientific interest in the child was apparent. This helped to pave way for the advance of modern child psychology, suggesting concepts which lent themselves to experimental test instead of providing merely a loose philosophical scaffolding. Systematic observation is basic to all scientific investigation. Systematic observations of children reached a position of importance and significance in the later decades of past century. The first observational procedure used was the so-called baby biography. The pioneer biography of child was written by Darwin (1877) of his infant son.

Pavlov (1849-1936), a notable Russian physiologist contributed significantly to child psychology by developing the experimental technique of the conditioned response. His work influenced research on learning at all levels of human development, but especially aided child psychology by providing experimental procedure which made children suitable subjects for psychological investigation. Watson (1878-1958) as a result of his work on emotional conditioning in infants prepared a treatise (1928) on the psychological care of infants that had a potent effect on earlier child care and training. He was, an exponent of objectivity and scaffed at the experimental. He wrote 'Treat children as though they were young adults. Never hug or kiss them, never let them sit on your lap. If you must kiss them, kiss them once on the forehead when you say good night. Shake hands with them in the morning.'

Tiedemann (1787) was one of the first psychologists to observe systematically the psychological development of children in a biographical form. He studied the infant's sensory, language, motor and conceptual growth by conceptual growth by systematic observations made at fairly regular intervals of time. This biographical approach pointed out the way toward modern longitudinal studies of child development. Preyar (1888), a physiologist, recorded a careful and detailed account of his son's mental development during the first four years. He observed the development of reflexes from birth and the influence of experience and learning. His book, The Mind of the Child, resulting from his labours is one of the great classics of child psychology.

Galton (1869, 1874, 1889), founded and greatly influenced the psychometric movement. He began with a strong conviction that human intelligence is biologically determined. Although, his instruments generated a great deal of interest in research and theory buildings, they have little practical utility, since the major problem relating to intelligence in children was the prediction of academic success. Hall (1891, 1904) is one of the foremost psychologists in early experimental work with children. Stimulated by the theories of biological evolution, he adopted and used a new research approach to the study of children. He theorized that the normal growth of the mind is to be seen as a series of stages more or less corresponding to those which early man and his ancestors went through in the history of the race. With the aid of questionnaire he and his students collected vast quantities of data about children's interests and activities at various age levels. Some of his students including *Conklin, Gessell, Goddard, Kuhlmann, Mateer* and *Terman*—made classic contributions to methodology and knowledge in the area of child development, Hall's findings are exemplified in his paper on children published in 1882 and his study of the content of children's mind published in 1891.

Binet and Simon (1905-1908, 1916) were first to take on the task of relating intelligence tests to the actual prediction of intelligence and thereby school performance. Their work began with a simple notion of developmental task, that is, what does a child have to do to succeed in school? By skillful observations and careful analysis, they identified several pre-requisite skills for academic success. They found that the children in the first grade must have a certain level of small muscle/visual motor co-ordination, they must have both short-term and long-term memory, etc. The Binet instrument proved an immediate success, it was a classic.

Goddard (1991), a student of Hall, worked at the Vineland Training School, the first modern training school for the retarded. He became interested in classifying retarded children on the basis of their disability. He devised a questionnaire, now refined into Vineland Social Maturity Scale (Doll, 1953). This method survives today in the form of personality inventories and sociograms, initiated through the work of Moreno (1953), a social psychologist interested in group structure and social position of children. Terman (1961), a doctoral student of Hall at Clark University, standardized Binet's test on Americans. Beginning in 1916 and continuing for the rest of his life, he conveyed the Binet Test from an obsure, hand-tooled, modest instrument to the benchmark of intelligence testing, the Stanford-Binet Intelligence Scale (Terman, 1916 ; Terman and Merrill, 1937, 1960).

Gesell (1928, 1934), another doctoral student of Hall, attempted to develop an instrument at Yale Medical School to measure biological intelligence. Like Galton, he believed intelligence was inherent in the geneses and functional in survival, but he felt that the key to the mystery of biological intelligence was the developmental rate of nervous system. Gesell provided the model and encouragement for the infant tests of intelligence, such as those development by Cattell, P. (1960) and Bayley, N. (1969). He developed a photographic dome and photographic techniques with movie cameras that enabled him to study in slow motion the development of motor sequence in children.

Psychoanalytic Theories: Freud (1909, 1910, 1933, 1936, 1938) was first to recognize the psychological significance of the family and its members for the child development. On the basis of the free association of his patients undergoing psychoanalytic treatment, he described the roles of the mother and father in relation to the child and also of the child in relation to the parents during the early stages of development. Freud believed that both boys and girls formed their first and most important relationship with their mothers, though he did not acknowledge that the infant preoedipally cathected and identified with both mother and father. At around to 3 to 5 years of age, the boy realized that his mother also loved his father, who is consequently seen as a rival for her affections. Further, the son, become cognizant of the anatomical differences between the sexes and assuming that girls once had penises, feared that his father might castrate him in retaliation just as, presumably, his mother and other females were punished for their transgressions. To avert the possibility of this occurring, he repressed his affection for his mother and identified with his father. Not only is this supposed to diminish the father's aggression but also it is supposed to ensure the affection of the mother. The identification with the father is crucial for the boy's sex-role adoption and also prestages the formation of the superego. Freud became convinced that these experiences exerted a profound and heretofore unrecognized influence upon subsequent adult behaviour and experience. Although the principles and techniques of psychoanalysis were developed from work on adult patients, his findings indicated the crucial role of childhood experiences. Freud, thus forcibly called attention to childhood as a critical period of development. He emphasized that adult neurotic symptons were the outcome of childhood experiences, therefore these incidents were studies intensively in order to explain present behaviour. Freud's influence is to be found not only in the direct utilization of psychoanalytic concepts and findings in child psychology today, but also in the subtle, indirect and sometimes unnoticed after upon child training practices. Bearing the imprint his thinking are present day practices concerning the child's experiences in his motivated strivings, parent-child relationships, effect of unconscious influences and our understanding of the disturbed children.

Adler (1927, 1929) emphasized, in his point of view, the initial weakness and helplessness of his child. Although child is aware of his comparative inferiority, he possesses an inherent urge to grow, to dominate, to be superior and to compensate. One of the neurotic solutions to this feeling of inferiority is compensation through striving for power. Healthy, non-neurotic solutions involved striving for superiority, perfection and self-actualization. Adler also stressed the child's position in the family constellation and his relationships to parents. Like Freud, Adler stressed the family situation and the early years as the critical factors in the development of the child's personality structure. Both the over-pampered and the rejected child are in danger of becoming maladjusted. The pampered child cannot develop confidence in himself, excepts too much from others and attempts to dominate them just as he dominated his mother. The rejected child becomes insecure, anxious or in some instances hostile and rebellious. In any event, both over protected and rejected children never acquire the spirit of co-operation that makes for sound, productive human relationship. By the age of four or five, the life-style of the child is being established, the creative self emerges through which the person solves the basic emotional problems of early life. Life-style grows out of the efforts to deal with life problems and his unique method of having transactions with the world. The creative self is the organizer of the personality into a unique from on the basis of the hereditary capabilities and life experiences.

Jung (1923, 1931, 1933) held that Freud's conception of infantile sexuality was incorrect and that the child's libido expressed itself in terms of growth and the urge to excel. Although his conceptions are complex and too extensive, one of his basic idea was that the goal of development is self-actualization. By this, he meant a harmonious union of all the conflicting and diverse aspects of personality. Although self-actualization was not regarded as the only force in behaviour, it played an important role in personality development. Jung's view of the self and the transcendent function can thus be regarded as one of the forerunners of principle of self actualization as described by Rogers and Maslow.

Rank (1945, 1952) also emphasized the constructive strivings of the person, his efforts to break with the past in order to live independently in the present. He conceived of life as a struggle between the 'life-fear' and the 'death-fear.' The life fear begins with the trauma of birth in which the person is forcefully and harshly separated from the protective and benign confines of his mother's womb. This separation is the prototype of later anxiety, the universal problem of mankind. At the moment of birth, human individualism begins to emerge, and the individual establishes a separate identity and relationship with the environment. Just as separation itself is threatening, so the loss of this budding individuality is also a key threat which Rank called the 'death-fear', literally the psychic death of the individual. As the person struggles to reinstates the unity between himself and the protection of the mother, every advance toward independence is perceived as a threat. On the other hand, any dependency on the part of the person also becomes a threat because the reinstatement of the union represents a loss of individuality.

The person goes through life attempting to produce a balance between these conflicting forces by an act of creative will. There are three basic solutions to this conflict situation illustrated by three types, the average man, the neurotic and the artist or creative man. Rogers acknowledge Rank above all others as the grandfather of his personality theory. Rank saw the tendency to move toward the actualization of man's highest nature as a force of its own, rather than a derivative of the inevitable thwarting of innate primary drives.

Anna Freud (1949) in her analysis of parent-child relationship in psychoanalytic theory draws attention to the current trend toward the emphasis on the early years as crucial to personality development. She has discussed the role of both parents in the early years of child-life. She has been concerned with the qualitative differences between the mother and father-child relationship. She also notes the importance of psychoanalysis in seeing the father important by virtue of his role in the family system. Anna, Freud, like Adler shifted the focus of psychological inquiry from Id and Superego toward ego but within the theoretical framework of psychoanalysis. Her father, Sigmund Freud himself accepted her ideas and incorporated them in this theory of personality. Main contribution of Anna Freud to the psychoanalytic theory was her volume on the defense mechanisms of the ego. Horney (1937, 1939, 1945, 1950) is the outstanding exponent of the neo-Freudian point of view. Genuine lack of love and affection in childhood generates 'basic anxiety.' Child needs to be accepted, but basic anxiety is child's reaction to lack of acceptances. The child develops 'compensatory trends' in striving to overcome this anxiety and to gain security. If the child's dominant compensatory trend is 'moving toward people,' he is attempting to overcome anxiety and insecurity through his excess demands on others for love and affection. If the child's predominant bend is 'moving against people,' he seeks to overcome insecurity by the excessive development of power prestige and dominance. Finally 'moving away from people' implies a search for security through withdrawal. The child who is hurt or rejected, retreats from the source of pain and eventually refuses to try at all lest he fail.

Horney admits after Freud that character develops in early childhood, but she recognizes that the connection between later peculiarities and early experiences is more complicated than Freud assumed; there is no such things as an isolated experience; but the entire infantile experiences combine to form a certain character structure. Horney contends that the development of the child depends upon how the child is treated. The child's needs can be dealt within a satisfactory way by the parents, who thus contribute to his mental health. His needs may, indeed, be thwarted and frustrated. He may be bullied about, severely punished, or even entirely rejected by his parents. He may perceive his home environment and his parent-child relationship as unfair, unjust, begruding and merciless, and this will influence his actual behaviour and future development as well. She believed that the child has the capacity as well as the desire to develop his potentialities and become a decent human being. He can change and go on changing as long as he lives.

Fromm (1941, 1947, 1948, 1955) extended the idea that man's strivings were not exclusively tied to the animal instincts. He drew attention toward the fate of psychological man as a produce of society in which he lived. Thus, he showed interest in the role of society in facilitating or undermining health personality development. He emphasized less the individual character of the person and more social character, that is, the values and behaviour patterns that are shared by most of the members of a society. Formm believed that as the child develops, he grows apart from his family.Losing some of his dependence upon parents and other persons, he becomes free to express his own individuality. This movement toward individuality is one of the inherent needs of man. However, in the process of individualisation, one feels more isolated and helpless. This places the person in conflict between loneliness and fear, on the one hand and the striving to become individualated, on the other. This conflict is distinctively human situation. One of the solutions to the sense of isolation and loneliness to escape the frightening condition of freedom and to submit to social authority. Like Rogers and Maslow, Fromm sees man's failures of adjustment largely as a result of the inadequacy of society in meeting his basic needs. Although, no society has yet fully succeeded, he remains optimistic that a successful one can be created. Such a society would have to be one in which man is rooted in bonds of brotherliness, yet is also able creatively to transcend nature by achieving a sense of self-identity.

Sullivan (1938, 1947, 1953, 1954) believed that early childhood plays a very important role in the development of a child's feeling of security. The infant feels somehow, by empathy, whether he is accepted or not by his parents. The accepted and loved child develops a feeling of well-being and euphoria. From the very first days of life, the infant shows a curious relationship with his mother. If the mother is seriously disturbed around the time of feeding then on that occasion there will be feeding difficulty, or the infant will have indigestion. Empathy between the child and his parents is strongest from the age of six months to that of twenty-five months. The child responds to the emotions of his mother or father or any significant adult and they produce in him an impathized comfort or discomfort, in accordance with their friendly or unfriendly attitude to him. The child learns how to adjust his behaviour to his environment. This process of adjustment is a result of his striving toward security. His activities are influenced by what the environment has to offer him in terms of being accepted and loved by others. The attitude of significant others toward the child produces in him the feeling of security or insecurity.

Sullivan conceived the stages of development, in part, as three modes of thinking which characterize the person as he moves from primitive or infantile to more advanced, adult forms of thought. The first and most primitive is the prototaxic mode or stage. This is the form of thought of the infant in early months of life and is the precursor of later mode of thinking. The second, parataxic mode beings to evolve through experience and involves conception of cause and effect. For the young child, this magical conception based on physical or temporal proximity of events is the predominant way of thinking that sometimes continues in adulthood. The third, syntaxic thought is the highest stage. It permits us to introduce logical order and reality testing into our experiences.

Sullivan also identified six general eras of life which represented the main points of transition in psychological development. These included infancy, childhood, the juvenile era, pre-adolescence, early adolescence and late adolescence. Such periods correspond in part to those listed by Erikson. Sullivan tried to identify the social psychological features characteristics of each of these periods of life.

Erikson (1950, 1951) proposed 'the resolution theory of crisis' according to which each stage of psychological growth is characterized by a particular conflict which must be resolved in a positive way, if future conflicts are also to be resolved. One is never wholly successful in this task and carries with oneself through life some residue—small or large—of failure at each developmental stage. If the residue is large, it limits one's ability to cope successfully with the next conflict, just as shallow foundation limits the height of a building.

Erikson has expanded the Freudian *description* of the psychosexual stages to include what is implicit in Freud, but not alway fully clarified, the social meanings that accompany each stage and shape the impact of each stage on the social features of personality. The social conflict that characterizes the oral stage in Erikson's analysis is that of 'trust versus mistrust.' The manner in which the mother responds to the biological needs of the infant during the oral stage determines the trust or mistrust the child will acquire concerning the social environment. The social issue associated with the anal stage is 'autonomy versus shame and doubt.' At the phallic stage it is 'initiative versus guilt.' During the latency period when the child is struggling with the preparatory phase of establishing a work role in the society, 'industry versus inferiority' are the conflicting polarities. In puberty, with the return of oedipal urges and the evolution of psychosexual maturity, the basic issue is the establishment of an 'ego identity versus role diffusion.'

Erikson has described the social modalities of each psychosexual stage, or more accurately the intertwining of the psychological impulses and methods of discharge at each stage with the objects of an attitudes toward the child's social world. Social attitudes are, in effect, interdependent with the management of the libido, influencing his management and in turn, being influenced by it. In Erikson, one can observe modifications of the Freudian psychosexual theory in the form of supplements or shifts in emphasis rather than abandonment of the theory.

Meerloo (1956, 1968) Von Der Heyat (1964) and other psychoanalysts have stressed the importance of the role of father in breaking the infantile, symbolic mother-child relationship and thus 'cutting the cord' between the two. They presume, of course, absence of an early father-infant relationship, indeed in so far as this may involve the father in feminine interaction.

Other Approaches to *PCR:* Piaget (1952, 1954, 1960, 1961, 1969) became interested in the development of logical thinking. Using a kindergarten as his laboratory and a relatively small number of children, he began to study the origin of certain logical principles, such as conservation of mass, weight and space. Much of Piaget's work involved skillful, insightful observation of children from which he developed a theroy of developmental stages of thinking that resembles the motor-development theory of Gesell and psychosexual theory Freud. In marked contrast with Freud, he dealt strictly with cognitive development, completely ignoring the motivational and emotional life of the person.

Piaget feels that maturational clock controls the personality development. The logical thinking follows a critical period schedule just as do the motor activities upon which, it is based. Just as a child cannot be taught to walk until the neurological development necessary for walking is complete, so a child cannot learn to perform mental combinations until a similar development in the brain is complete. Until the hereditary sequence of readiness is passed, specific development is not possible; conversely, if the hereditary stage arrives and is not used, the opportunity is lost almost irretrievably. It is probably true that intellectual ability particularly in the middle range of intelligence, can be significantly manipulated by the heightening of experience in childhood. The development of logical thinking represents the application of a set of operations that either are used or not used. But once they are placed it use, the whole cognitive style of the child is altered permanently.

There are three major stages of intellectual development. The first is the sensory-motor stage,' in which the child first acquires a knowledge of the object of his environment through concrete sensory-motor manipulations. This stage extends roughly from birth to the age of eighteen months. It is divided further into six developmental periods: namely, reflex exercises, primary circular reactions, secondary circular reactions, co-ordination of secondary reactions, tertiary circular reactions and invention of new reactions. The second major stage of cognitive development is 'concrete operations stage.' Prior to this, the child did not use symbols or language extensively. This stage extends from eighteen months to twelve years and is subdivided into three developmental periods: namely, pre-conceptual, intuitive, concrete operations. The final stage of cognitive development is the stage of 'formal operations' which is the type of conceptual thought characteristic of the mature adults. The distinctive feature of this stage is the ability of the person to reason without the manipulation of concrete objects. Events can be imagined, manipulated symbolically, reasoned out, critically evaluated and planned for the future.

White (1956, 1960) proposes a new drive, 'effectance,' the desire to have an effect on the environment. He suggests this drive is an inherent property of the child at birth. It leads to the motivation to be competent, to effectively manipulate the environment, to person's advantage, to use the environment in achieving ends. Striving for competence, however, is not merely the tool of adjustment the means of gratifying primary drives such as hunger, thirst and sex, but is based on an inherent property of man, the basic drive of effectance.

White appears to belong to the school of theorists which regards primary drives as relatively unimportant or at least uninteresting in civilized man compared with the drive for effectance. The behaviour directed by the traditional primary drives is rather a small addition or supplement to the main part of behaviour which is driven by the drive for effectance. Furthermore, this drive is innates as are the other primary drives; that is, our most important motivated behaviours are not derivative from sexual or erotic interests, as in the Freudian view, but have independent biological status.

For Rogers (1942, 1952) and Maslow (1954, 1964), the basic motivational force in the personality is the effort at 'self-actualization.' This single life goal or motivating force involves a tendency toward positive growth. Positive growth is difficult to define, but it is perhaps best seen in Maslow's hierarchy of needs. Some needs such as those dealing with safety and survival—are very primitive and basic. Some are considered as higher needs in the sense that they are found only in man who has evolved from lower forms of life to the higher form. Man needs to think, to have esteem and to enjoy beauty, because his brain makes such activity natural and pleasurable. Maslow believes that only if the more primitive needs are blocked or threatened, will the higher needs fail to express themselves. In short, the higher needs, being less crucial for survival, cannot be actualized unless the more primitive ones are satisfied.

A person is willing to experience pain in this effort toward self-actualization because the innate urge to grow is so strong. The adolescent, for example, seeks independence or autonomy in spite of the fact it is frightening to leave the protective custody of the parental home. Under moderately this self-actualization or growth process leads him to independence. It is an inherent part of the man's make-up. Rogers suggests that if a person can discriminate between forward and progressive growth and regressive and backward looking ways of behaving, he will choose progression rather than regression.

Bandura (1963, 1966-1968) serves as an introduction to a contemporary thrust of experimental child psychology. One of the dimensions lacking both in the operant strategy proposed by Skinner (1956, 1959, 1971) and the classic strategy proposed by Watson (1913, 1919, 1925) and Pavlov (1927) was the principle of modeling and imprinting. Bandura called attention to the combination of a good model and conditioning as an efficient and parsimonious method of teaching, most of the behaviour needed in children. One of the major strengths of the approach suggested by Bandura is his emphasis on vicarious training. They point out that not only can various social-training procedures be employed in the modification of a single childs behaviour, but that they also have a predictable effect on other children who watch. In the area of social limitation and modeling Bandura has made his greatest contribution to the prediction and control of group behaviour of children in situations typical of the classroom,where so much of a child's training takes place today.

Actually, Bandura is concerned with how children learn. Are operant conditioning and classical conditioning sufficient to explain the child maturing to adulthood ? Bandura felt not and his research has centered around the importance of modeling for the maturing child. He begins his presentation with the notation that the effectiveness of modeling depends upon the ability of observer to identify the emotion and to identify the cues that produce the emotion. The more vivid the encounter, the easier the vicarious learning is.

Bandura makes a distinction between removal of positive reward, non-reward and aversive conditioning, or punishment. The major difference between the effectiveness of non-reward and aversive conditioning is that non-reward usually results in the extinction of responses, aversive suppresses rather than eliminate them, and may, in fact, result in a general decrease in performance. Aversive stimulation should be used with children only a circumstances wherein desirable behaviours are being elicited and rewarded at the same time, such the direction of change is under the control of the therapist and not left to chance.

Child Rearing Practices and its Effects on Child's Personality

Child rearing practices is an area of divergent and confusing evidence. There are opinion that, similar child rearing practices lead invariably to similar adult personality. But similar adult character types may be found in societies having different child rearing techniques and that similar child rearing method may lead to different types of adult personality.

Child rearing is not a technical term with precise significance. It refers generally to all the interactions between parents and their children. These interactions include the parents' expression of attitudes, values, interests and beliefs as well as their care taking and training behaviour. Child rearing is a continuous process. Each moment of a child's life that he spends in contact with his parents has some effect on both of his present behaviour and his potentialities for future action.

Child rearing practices can be defined as idea, beliefs and attitudes widely held in a community on how to bring up children. These practices are likely to change as the time advances. Thus the idea prevalent on this subject a hundred years ago, may appear remote and alien to us. However the attitudes of the post generation may retain more of a hold on us than we realise. Ideas we are not conscious of may continue to exert influence on the levels of conceives feelings, which are transmitted from one generation to the other through the process of child rearing itself. This process of child rearing is generally influenced by the characteristic ways of thinking, feeling and acting, prevalent in the cultural group to which the family belongs.

Child-Oriented Parental Attitudes and Resulting Behaviour in Children

Modern dynamic psychology lays heavy emphasis on the socialization process, the process, by which an individual grows from a dependent infant into an independent and dependable adult. There is accumulating evidence that all manner of behaviour deviations can be often accounted for the subtitles of home relationship. Much of the phenomenology of behaviour disorder and personality deviation can be linked directly with motivation's resulting from parents attitudes towards their children. In the first phase of infant's life after death, it is clearly recognized that the mother is the prime parents. The first source of nutrition and the child's security comfort and survival depend upon the mother's care. Thus the role of the mother reflects a factor of biological as well as social indispensibility in the life of the child. Several investigators like symonds (1938), Levy (1942), Baldwin (1945), Fanner (194B), Shoben (1949) and Sear (1953), Hess (1970), Faizunnisa (1965, 1967), Iffat Unnisa (1965), Nalini Devi (1967), Atit Rama (1967), Warty, M.S. (1970), Paricra and Tirtha (1972), Patel, K. (1965), Victor, F. (1975), Sidana (1973), Lytton, H. (1974) have pointed out the effects of different maternal attitudes on the personality development of the child.

Studies of authoritarian, democratic and permissive child training methods have revealed what different effects they have on the child's developing personality pattern. Studies show that authoritarian training method produce a child who is quiet, well behaved, non resistant, socially unaggressive and restricted in curiosity, originality and fancifulness. These methods are characterised by the use of strict rules and regulations to enforce the desired behaviour. In these methods parent foster control through external force in the form of punishment.

Many studies have found that authoritarian parents tend to adopt highly conventional goals for their children and look at the child's behaviour in terms of their own needs, rather than in terms of needs of the child. Such type of strict treatment and demands for rigid confirmity in the early years of life often lead to the development of an 'authoritarian personality syndrome'.

Overstrictness can make the child so submissive that he is less competitive and socially successful than other children. It may make him compulsively obedient but inwardly definite. In addition, it undermines his confidence in his ability to make decisions and be independent. Restrictive parents impose many rules in children, insist on supervising their children closely and have quite definite standards of behaviour to which their children are expected to conform but they do not necessarily punish often or severly. A successful restrictive parent has a child who usually complies with rules and does not require frequent punishment.

Democratic child rearing practices result in greater independence in thinking, acting and in a healthy, positive confident self-concept This leads to better personal and social adjustments and to more outgoing active and spontaneous behaviour. Children from democratic homes are more active in their relations with peers, show more initiative, produce creative ideas and tend to be more enterprising freer to express their feelings and less conforming.

In the homes where parents are permissive the children learn more by trials and errors than by guidance. They mould their personality pattern without the guidance and help from the others. Permissive parents have few rules and made few demands on their children, for mature behaviour the tend to view aggression as natural, they allow their children considerable freedom to play without adult supervision or intervention.

Jersild, stressed that when too little control is exercised on the child he becomes insecure and confused. He feels unprepared to meet life's problems. These children become selfish and self-centered and show little compassion for others. Children brought up by permissive parents, who indulge them and permit to do much as they please develop feelings of inadequacy about their abilities and tend to become inactive and to withdraw from social situations. Also these children become dependent on adults.

Parental Attitude and Home Atmospheres

Parental attitudes are already familiar; home atmospheres, a new concept are phases of the familial situation that have been isolated for study, such as the democratic atmosphere of the home, or the presence of unharmonious family relationships. The home atmospheres appear to be somewhat more general in nature than attitude. Although these two approaches are distinguished methodologically both have often been used in the same study. Hence the natural term, patterns will be used to refer them collectively.

Baldwin's Approach to Patterns

On the most significant research programmes concerning parent behaviour came from the Fels Research Institute. The investigators utilized the Fels Parent Behaviour. Rating scales as their major instrument. There carefully continued rating scales were designed to measure 30 variables of parental attitudes, parental behaviour and home atmospheres. Each scale was concerned with something considered important for its psychological impact on the child. The scale ranges from such global, all inclusive judgement as 'adjustment of the home to such specific variables as "restrictiveness of regulations."

Baldwin correlated the interrelationship among the 30 variable. The subjects they used were drawn from 124 home, a major portion of the institute's permanent cooperating population. The parents in the main were about in intelligence, economic students and education. A visitor observe both mother and child in the home made the rating on the scales.

Knowing that homes fall into these three syndromes does not tell into which category a specific home would fall. It would be too much to expect that the three categories describing home in general would be suitable for classification of the individual homes. In specific homes we would expect varying position from high to low on each syndrome. Consequently, the investigator first subdivided each of the three syndromes into regions of "Wigh', low and "widdling" and then classified the homes into these terms. A given home might be placed in any one of the three subdivisions for each of the syndromes. This allows emergence of 27 combinations. Actually, a considerably smaller number of patterns accounted for all but a few of the homes. It was possible to classify the majority of the homes into three major patterns, rejectant, acceptant, and casual.

Rejectant Patterns. The rejectant patterns characterized the homes of figure. These were the parents who more or less consistently received ratings at the low or rejectants end of the variables in the acceptance syndrome. Basically, they were consistently hostile, unaffectionate and disapproving. These attitudes were so pervasive as to prevent them from being genuinely solicitous or democratic in dealing with their children. Instead they were autocractic toward them. Although having these attributes in common, rejectant parents did fall into groups. One group was non-chalant, with general atmosphere of unconcern the other was dominant with hostility very prominent. General similarity of the rejectant pattern to instanced described in earlier chapters makes further comment unnecessary.

Acceptant Patterns. Acceptance characterized a little more than an other quarter of homes of the parents. Although they had acceptance in common, there were three major groups: indulgent, but not democratic; democratic, but not indulgent; and democratic—indulgent In this home the parents were especially prone to be very high indulgence and acceptance items, but only about average for almost all the items in the democracy syndrome. The acceptant, indulgent non-democratic home bears considerable resemblance to the overprotective home. The acceptant home, democratic but not indulgent, would appear to be related to acceptance within normal limits on psychosocial development in infancy. The finding by Baldwin and his associates that these two belong in separate groups serves to strengthen the contention made earlier that acceptance and overprotection should be distinguished.

Although having the acceptant pattern in common, three sub patterns of democratic homes were found (1) pseudo-democratic–th parents allow the child to participate in some decisions, but at the same time give no freedom concerning anything fundamental or important; (2) Scientifically democratic–The parent, although fond of their children, tend not to show it, but conscientiously apply and even force democracy because they know it is "right". (3) Warm democratic–the child is treated warmly, accepted in his own right, and treated democratically.

Casual Patterns. The casual pattern behaviour included nearly 50 per cent of the homes in the sample. These homes could not be as neatly categorized as those either the acceptant or the rejectant patterns. They were united only by being mild and casual, not being either acceptant or rejectant. Along with other lesser groupings, there were two which the investigators thought deserved particular mention—the causal autocratic and casual indulgent.

Results of Factor Analysis. Another approach to the patterns of data obtained by Baldwin and his collaborators is through factor analysis of the Fels Behaviour Rating Scales. For the 30 scales Roff found seven factors (1) concern for the child (2) democratic guidance (3) permissiveness (4) parent-child harmony (5) sociability—adjustment of parent (6) activeness of home and (7) non-readiness of suggestion.

Since there was substantial correlation among these factors, Corr and Jenkins used Roff's matrix to perform so called second order factor analysis. This was an attempt to eliminate this correlation and to reduce further the number of factors. They reported three second order factors which they labeled (x) dependency encouraging (y) democracy of child training and (z) organizations and effectiveness of control in the home.

The largest correlations with the x factor among the original scales were child-centeredness, solicitousness for the child, protectiveness, intensity of contact, duration of contact and acceptance of the child that is devotion rather than rejection. Overall, the x factor seemed to represent encouragement of the child's emotional dependence on the parents.

The second factor 'y' is best described by the scales for democracy of policy, non-coerciveness of policy, non-restrictiveness, non-readiness of criticism, readiness of explanation and clarify of policy. Clearly democratic value in child training are being upheld in the y factor.

The third factor 'z' is characterized by the scales for vigilance of enforcement, severity of penalties, attempts and accelerating and coordination of the household. The z factor seems to be concerned with organization and effectiveness of control ranging from strict orderliness at one extreme to chaos at the other.

Radke's Approach to Patterns

Another approach to the patterns of parent behaviour and attitudes in relation to their children's behaviour is that of Radke. Behavioural data on the pre-school children were obtained through teacher's ratings, interviews with the children, and several experimental and projective situations. Her subjects, mother and fathers of 43 pre-school children, completed questionnaires and were interviewed concerning disciplinary practices and ways in which they carried on authority functions of the family. He investigated the effects of parental attitudes and practices on pre-school aged children's behaviour by a variety of research technique. The items in the questionnaire were grouped into scales which made it possible for the investigation to make judgements concerning (1) Philosophy of authority, from autocratic to democratic. (2) Parental restriction from strict and firm to lax and easy going. (3) Severity of punishment, getting along well with schoolmates are logical outcomes. In general, the patterns from the restrictive homes and those were severe discipleness is used give the same picture as that from autocratic homes.

Children from more democratic homes were found to show an opposite constellation of behaviour characteristics to those of the autocratically controlled children. Thus, they are more popular, non-quarrelsome, considerate, compliant, emotionally stable, sensitive to the opinions of others and non-leaders.

Sears Approach to Patterns

A factor analysis of the ratings on the sears, Maccoby, Levin child rearing scales performed by Milton isolated five major factors: (1) permissiveness-strictness, (2) general family adjustment, (3) warmth of mother-child relationship, (4) responsible child training orientation and (5) aggressiveness and punitiveness. In discussing the effects of child rearing on the children sears and his colleagues close to emphasize the mother's warmth and the effects of punishment and of permissiveness.

The other end of the warmth continuum from severe to mild and parent-child rapport, from good to poor.

What are some of the characteristics of the children who come from homes characterized as autocratic, democratic, restrictive or severely disciplined? A summary answer to this question may be obtained from information Radke had collected about the children and the home.

Children from relatively autocratic homes compared with children from more democratic homes were found to rate as more unpopular with other children, as more given to fighting and quarreling, as more inconsiderate, as more emotionally unstable, as more daring uninhibited, and as more insensitive to praise or blame. Radke suggests in explaining these results that they come about from the shift of setting which such a child experiences.

A child coming from an autocratic home to the presumably less autocratic atmosphere of the schools finds himself in the midst of contemporaries whose powers are not as strong as those of his parents.

As a consequence, he assumes the behaviour of his parents towards the other children, acting without sensitivity or consideration for others. Unpopularity and not maternal coldness, associated in their research with the development of feeding problems and persistent bed wetting, contributed to high aggression and was an important background condition for emotional, upset during severe toilet training and for the slowing of conscience development. The second factor, punishment, and the third, permissiveness, were related primarily to the first factor of permissiveness—strictness and secondarily to the fifth factor, aggression and punitiveness.

Punishment was important—mother punishing severely for toilet accidents or punishing dependency severely tended to have bed-wetting children in the first instance and dependent children in the second. The children who were punished severely for aggressiveness were apt to be more aggressive than those who were punished lightly.

Permissiveness, the third quality, had no discernible relation to dependent behaviour. But permissiveness for aggression was an important source of continuing aggression and was associated with a low frequency of feeding problem. Permissiveness about sexual matters was less associated with a low frequency of enuresis.

A Comparison among the Patterns

The studies of Baldwin, Radke and Sears, although derived by different methods, with different population, and with varying scope of content and direction of interest, permit comparison of their major findings on parental factors. Another source in the search for patterns of attitudes is the factor analysis of the questions concerned with attitudes the towards child rearing and family presented by the Parent Attitude Research Investigations (PARI). Answers in one study came from 100 unmarried student, nurses, in another study 100 mothers, and still another from a large heterogeneous sample of mother.

The Major Dimensions of Parent Attitudes Found by Various Investigations

Fels (Lorr and Jenkins)

Dependency encouraging

Democracy of child training

Organization and effectiveness of control

Radke

Autocratic—democratic

Parental restriction

Severity of punishment

Parent-Child rapport

Pattern (Sears)

Strictness

General family adjustment

Warmth

Responsible orientation

Aggressiveness and punitivenss

PARI (Schaefer and Bell)

Interpersonal distance

Hostile rejection home-making role

Excessive demand for striving

Over possessiveness

Hostile Punitive control

PARI (Schaefer)

Approval of maternal control

Approval of expression of hostility

Approval of positive attitudes toward child rearing

PARI (Zuckerman)

Authoritarian control

Hostility rejection

Democratic attitudes

Originally Schaefer and Bell found five relatively independent factors: (1) Suppressive and interpersonal distance—which has to do with a close to distance relationship, and seems to be related to warmth. (2) hostile rejection of home-making role—adequately defined in itself. (3) excessive demand for striving—a need for conformity and achievement on the part of the child (4) Over possessiveness—keeping the child indebted to the mother, and dependent and immature (5) hostile primitive control—parental dominance and submission of the child.

However, in the subsequent factor analysis using 100 multipural woman (mother of more than one child) only three factors where found (1) approval of maternal control (2) approval of repression of hostility and (3) approval of positive attitudes towards child rearing.

Schaefer tends to place greater emphasis on the results of his second factor analysis, not only because it was carried out with experienced mother but also because it agrees with the results found by Zuckerman and his associates. These latter investigators obtained result on PARI from a large heterogeneous sample of mothers. Factor analysis revealed three factors: authoritarian control that has to do with authoritarian, suppressive primitive and restrictive kinds of attitudes: hostility-rejection that has to do both with hostility towards children and rejection of maternal role, and democratic attitudes which involves encouraging verbalization, equalitarianism comradeship and sharing.

Using some of the data of the earlier studies, Schaefer applied a quite different method of analysis, the so-called circumplex model, which is said to have the advantage of isolating more molar social emotional interactions of mother and child. His practice of referring to the results as "dimensions", rather than as factors, will be followed here to signalize the shift in intent and in statistical method. He isolated two major dimensions, love versus hostility and autonomy versus control. Thereafter the proceeded to analysis of the literature and finally arrived at a hypothetical circumplex model.

Dimension of Parent Behaviour

Parent behaviour is not unidimensional, it does not consist simply of variations along a single axis, as popular over simplifications sometimes seem to imply. Parents may love their children, or they may reject them. They may also, however, be loving and controlling, or living and permissive, rejecting and controlling, or rejecting and permissive. The response of the child will not depend simply on one aspect of the parent's behaviour and personality, but rather on the combined effect of many aspect.

There are number of theoretical model and schemes that prove extremely helpful both in conceptualizing variation in parent behaviour in an orderly manner, and in permitting to design meaningful research and to interpret its findings. Two dimensions that consistently emerge in such theoretical schemes (or model) are love-hostility (or warmth hostility) and control-autonomy one such hypothetical model, formulated by Schaefer is as follows:

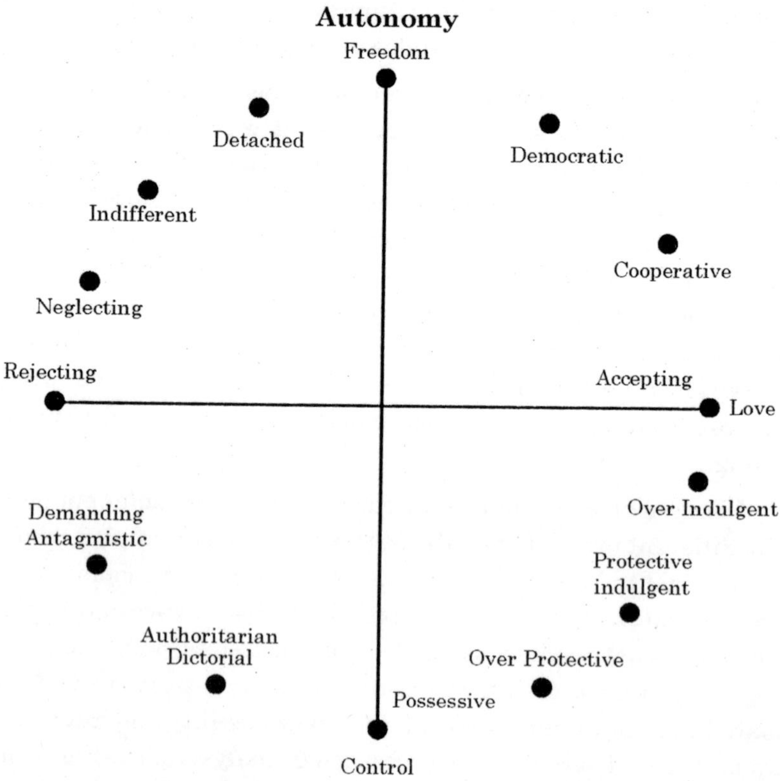

A Hypothetical Circumplex of Maternal Behaviour Concept

Parents relationships with their children have frequently been conceptualized in terms of the interaction between two dimensions of parental behaviour. The first deals with the emotional relationship with the child and ranges from warm, responsive, child-centered behaviour to rejecting, unresponsive behavour towards on the head and wishes of the parents.

(1) **Warmth-Hostility.** This dimension of parental behaviour is defined at the warm end by such characteristic as "accepting" affectionate approving, understanding, child-centered, frequent use of explanations, positive response to dependency behaviour, high use of reason in discipline, high use of praise in discipline, low use of physical punishment. The hostility end of this dimension is defined, in general by the opposite of these characteristics.

Parental warmth is regarded as important in the socialization process for several reasons. First, the child is likely to wish to maintain the approval, and be distressed at any prospect of the loss of love of a warm parent and therefore, the need for harsh form of discipline to gain compliance is often unnecessary. In contrast, the threat of withdrawal of love is unlikely to be an effective mechanism of socialization when used by hostile parents who have little demonstrable affection to rescind.

Second, the frequent use by warm parents of reasoning and explanation permits the child to internalize social rules and to identify and discriminate situations in which given behaviour is appropriate. It is easier to learn the rules of the game if someone tells you what they are and why you should play the way.

Third, warmth and nurturance by parents are likely to be associated with responsiveness to the child's needs. Loving, responsive parents make children feel good about themselves and this lead to security, low anxiety and high self esteem in the children. Such attitude and emotions are more likely to be conducive to learning and lead to acceptance and internalization of parental standards than the high anxiety and tension associated with hostility or physical punishment by rejecting parents. The high stress associated with a hostile, unresponsive family situation may interfere with the child's learning the rules of the 'socialization game' that the parent is attempting to teach.

(2) **Parental Control Control-Autonomy (i.e. Restrictiveness-Permissiveness).** This dimension is defined at

the restrictive end by many restrictions and strict enforcement of demands in the area of sex play, modesty behaviour, table manner...neatness, orderliness, care of household furniture, noise, obedience, aggression to sibs, aggression to peers and aggression to parents". These parental behaviours can be carried out in a rather calm, detached fashion or in an excitable, emotionally over involved manner.

Parental love alone is not enough to lead to positive social development in children. Some degree of parental control is necessary if children are to develop into socially and intellectually competent individuals. However, it should be kept in mind that the goal of socialization is socially responsible self-regulation by the child, not control externally based on the behaviour of the parent. Socialization involves a process of mutual influence between parent and children, the parent usually has more control than the child in their interactions. If parents are not in charge, the family is likely to be dysfunctional. Parents beliefs about their children's behaviour is largely shaped by experience in contrast to those who think problems in the child are due to the child's disposition, are more likely to try to change the child's negative behaviour. However, it is not surprising that most parents accept greater responsibility for desired than undesired behaviour in their children.

When parent use suggestions and reasoning, and when they present possible alternative course of action the child is more likely to comply with the parent's wishes. If parents are consistent in their discipline, use the minimum amount of pressure necessary to change the child's behaviour and encourage the child to view this compliance as self-initiated, children are more likely to cooperate and to adopt or internalize the standards of the parents.

(3) **Warm-Permissive Parent.** The parent who is both warm and permissive probably comes closet to the popular stereotype of the recommendations of child-rearing specialists, whether this stereotype serves as a sources of assurance or outraged alarm. The child of sum parents is likely to be rather active, outgoing, socially assertive and independent as well as friendly, creative and lacking in hostility towards others or himself. He may also be somewhat aggressive and bossy and on occasion, somewhat disobedient and disrespectful, particularly at home. However, these kinds of aggressive manifestations appear to emerge largely because of feelings of security

and a lack of severe punitive responses from parents and to be "more easily turned on and off in response to reinforcing conditions, rather than reflecting chronic anger frustration or uncontrollable explosions of deep seated but demand-up feeling of hostility.

(4) **The Warm-Restrictive Parent.** A parent who is warm may nevertheless be restrictive in child-rearing practices, particularly if the restrictiveness is not extreme. It has been found that children reared in warm-restrictive homes, as compared with those reared in warm-permissive homes, were likely to be more dependent, Less friendly, less creative, more hostile in their tentasies, and ether very high or very low in persistence. Restrictiveness was defined as the degree to which the mother attempted to force the child-through punishment or threat to adhere to her standards, and the degree to which deviations from these standards were punished. In general it was found that early maternal restrictiveness particularly during the first three years tended to have lasting effects upon the child. Children of restrictive parents were more confirming, less aggressive, less dominant and competitive with their ears and less likely to display mastery behaviour.

(5) **The Hostile-Restrictive Parent.** The parent who is both hostile and restrictive tend to promote counter-hostility within the child without allowing to be expressed in behaviour. Sometime the child may not even be able to admit his hostile feelings to conscious awareness. Under such conditions, it is perhaps not surprising that the parental behaviour pattern is often found among neurotic children. The combination of low permissiveness and high punishment (restrictive hostile) leads to self-punishment, suicidal tendencies and accident process as well as to shyness and social withdrawal, difficulties in relating to peers, and little confidence in or motivation toward adult role taking.

(6) **The Hostile-Permissive Parent.** While restrictiveness combined with hostility tends to maximize self-aggression social withdrawal, and symptoms of internal conflict (particularly when parental hostility is covert and difficult for the child to label), permissiveness combined with hostility appears to maximize "aggressive, poorly controlled behaviour".

Pattern of parental behaviour expressed in attitude and home atmospheres have been found with a certain degree of consistency in different studies using different subjects and procedures. These patterns may be related to characteristic behaviour in the children exposed to thee patterns. When the patterns of different studies are compares by factor analysis and other means of study, authoritarianism, love hostility and democracy seems to be recurrent themes. A final summary in terms of a circumplex model with the dimensions of love hostility and extraversion introversion is technology suggested.

Parent Typologies

Family systems theorists would argue that it is not the sum of individual dimensions of parenting but the configurations or combinations of dimensions that are important. Present a classification of four types of parenting based on combinations of the warm/responsive, unresponsive/rejecting dimension and the restrictive/demanding, permissive/undemanding dimension. This yields a classification of four types of parenting authoritative authoritarian, indulgent, and neglecting. A critical question is whether these variations in parenting style relate in any systematic way to differences in social, emotional and cognitive development in children.

Two-Dimensional Classification of Parenting Patterns

	Accepting Responsive Child Centered	*Rejecting Unresponsive Parent Centered*
Demanding	Authoritative-reciprocal	Authoritarian
Controlling	High in bi-directional	Power-assertive
Restrictive	Communication	
Undemanding	Indulgent	Neglecting
Low in control		indifferent
Attempts		uninvolved
Permissive		

A classic study by Baumrind was one of the earliest systematic studies attempting to relate parenting typologies to children's behaviour. On the basis of fourteen weeks of behavioural observation in the nursery school. Baumrind identified three groups of children who had widely varying pattern of behaviour. She called these groups energetic—friendly children, conflicted irritable children and impulsive aggressive children. She then interviewed the parents of these children in the home and the laboratory. As it can be seen in the table distinctive patterns of behaviour were related to the patterns of child behaviour. She found that authoritative but not authoritarian or overly permissive behaviour by parents led to positive emotional, social and cognitive development in children.

Authoritative Parents were not intrusive and did permit their children considerable freedom within reasonable limits, but were firm and willing to impose restrictions in areas in which they had greater knowledge or insight. They did not yield to their children's attempts to coerce them into acquiescing to their demands. Such discipline gives children the opportunity to explore their environment and gain interpersonal competence without the anxiety and neurotic inhibition, associated with hostile, restrictive, power assertive discipline practices or the inexperience in conforming to the demand and needs of other associated with extreme permissiveness. In general, high warmth and moderate restrictiveness, with the parents expecting appropriately mature behaviour from their children and setting reasonable limits but being responsive and attractive to their children needs, are associated with the development of self esteem, adaptability, competence, internalized control, popularity with peers and low level of antisocial behaviour.

In contrast, the *authoritarian parents* of the conflicted—irritable children were rigid, power-assertive, harsh and unresponsive to the children's needs. In such family, children have little control over their environment and receive few gratifications. They may feel trapped and angry but fearful of asserting themselves in a hostile environment. This result in the unhappy conflicted, neurotic behaviour often found in these children. Finally, in spite of the *permissive parents* reasonably affectionate relationship with their children, their excessively tax and inconsistent discipline and encouragement of the free expression of their children's impulses were associated with the development of uncontrolled impulsive behaviour in their children. Both authoritarian and permissive parents thought that free expression of these impulses was healthy and desirable, whereas the authoritarian parents perceived them as something to be suppressed or stamped out.

Baumrind has followed her authoritarian, authoritative and permissive parents and their children from the preschool period through adolescence in a longitudinal study (Baumrind, 1991) she found that authoritative parenting continued to be associative with positive outcome for adolescents as with younger children and the responsive, firm parent-child relationships were especially important in the development of competence in sons. Moreover authoritarian child rearing had more negative long-term outcomes for boys than for girls. Son of authoritarian parents were low in both cognitive and social competence. Their academic and intellectual performance was poor. In addition they were unfriendly and lacking in initiative, leadership and self-confidence in their relations with their peers.

It can be seen that only three of the parenting types presented in table were identified by Baumrind in her preschool children. The fourth parenting style (in the lower right-hand quadrant) which is characterized by neglect and lack of involvement. These are *disengaged parents* who are motivated to do whatever is necessary to minimize the costs in time and effort of interaction with the child (Maccoby and Martin, 1983). Such parents are motivated to keep the child at a distance and focus on their own needs rather than the need of the child. They are parent centered rather than child centered. With older children this is associated with the parents failure to monitor the child's activity, to know where the child is, what the child is doing, and who the child's companions are. This pattern of parenting has been related to several different types of personality characteristics in parents and to social change and stressful life events.

In infant such a lack of parental involvement is associated with disruptions in attachment in older children it is associated with impulsitivity, aggression, non-compliance, moodiness and low self-esteem. Adolescent and young adult from *neglecting* homes are more likely to have drinking problems, be trauant, spend time on the streets with friends who are disliked by the parents, be parcociously sexually active and have a record of arrests. Lack of parental monitoring is strongly associated with the risk of delinquent behaviour. It is not just that children with disengaged parents are socially incompetent, irresponsible, immature and alienated from their families. They also show disruptions in peer relations and in cognitive development, achievement and school performance.

Parenting Styles and Children's Behaviour

Parental Type	*Children Behaviour*
Permissive-indulgent parent	Impulsive-aggressive children
Rules not enforced	Resistive, non-compliant to adults
Rules not clearly communicated	Low in self-reliance
Yields in coercion, whining nagging, crying by the child	Low in achievement orientation, lacking in self-control.
Inconsistent discipline	Aggressive
Few demands or expectations for mature, independent behaviour	Quick to anger but fast to recover cheerful
Ignores a accepts bad behaviour	Impulsive
Hides impatience, anger and annoyance	Aimless, love reciprocal directed activities domineering
Authoritarian parent	Conflicted insane children
Rigid enforcement of rules	Fearful, apprehensive
Confronts and punishes bad behaviour	Moody
Shows anger and displeasure	Easily annoyed
Rules not clearly explained	Passively harsh and guileful
View of child as dominated by uncontrolled antisocial impulses	Vulnerable to stress
Child's desires and opinions not considered or solicited	Alternates between aggressive unfriendly behaviour and sulky withdrawal
Persistent in enforcement of rules in the face of opposition and coercion	Aimless
Harsh, punitive discipline	
Low in warmth and positive involvement	
No cultural events or mutual activities planned	
No educational demands or standards	
Authoritative parent	Energetic—friend children
Firm enforcement of rules	Self relient
Does not yield to child coercion	Self complex
Confronts disobedient child	High energy level

Contd.

Table Contd.

Parental Type	*Children Behaviour*
Shows displeasure and annoyance in response to child's bad behaviour	Friendly with peers
Shows pleasure and support of child's constructive behaviour	Copes well with stress
Rules clearly communicated	Interested and curiosity in novel situations
Considers child's wishes and solicits child's opinions	Cooperative with adults tractable
Alternative offered	Purpose
Warm involved responsive	Achievement-oriented
Expects mature, independent behaviour appropriate for the child's age	Achievement oriented
Cultural events and joint activities planned educational standards set and enforced.	

5

Effect of Parental Personality, Parental Attitude and Behaviour on Children

Parents and their Children

The parent-child system is a complex and intricate interaction pattern rather than one in which particular child behaviour result from particular parental behaviour.

During the early years of middle childhood, children seem to be interested in pleasing adults, first parents, and then teachers. However, with physical growth, increasing skills, and more contact with other children pleasing adult become less pressing. Fitting in with and winning the approval of other children assume greater and greater importance. While adult are necessary, children have achieved enough trust, autonomy and initiative that they want to become involved in a private world of their own where adults are usually not welcome. Withdrawal into the society of children occur at a time children are least attractive to adult. Children rebel against cuddling, are more restless, usually are dirty, snaggle-toothed and speak a language adult find too difficult to understand.

At home, vocalization assumes new patterns—children talk back and accuse parents of unfairness. Chores are foregotten, they fail to show up in time for dinner, embark enthusiastically on projects, only to have to be prodded to finish them. Children are not interested in the social amenities, greeting their mother's friends or explaining some project on which they are working. During elementary school years, children spend about six to seven hours a day away from home.

This is in contrast to one hour a day during the preschool years and eight hours a day during adolescence.

All of this–but at the same time, a keen awareness of feeling and relationship within the family is present. Family values are internalized. Parents might be surprised to hear their sixth-graders handing out parental admonitions to their friends. This on and off behaviour of children is the result of rejection of adult standard. In the fourth, fifth and sixth grades, problem behaviour reaches a peak, teasing, discourtesy, scuffling, rebelliousness, carelessness, untidiness and disobedience. These children are frequently irritable, easily offended, and often discourage. Physical aspects of problem behaviour include facial ties, restlessness nail-biting and scratching.

While the children pushing away from the family, they still need the pull of the family to give security and allow them to try out new ways of acting and relating. Sometimes behaviour of children leads parents to be somewhat rejecting of them. Parents cannot allow this to happen. Children need their families as much or more during the middle childhood years than any other time. In spite of the change in family patterns and styles and the child's growing interest people and things outside the family, the family is still the most significant influence in the life of the child.

So, what is it about the family that makes a difference to the children of school age? The overall climate of the home seems to be the major factor in the total development of its children, at any age (Sears, Maccoby and Levin, 1957). During the preschool years, it is not the isolated routines, such as toilet-training, bottle or breast-feeding, which make a child develop 'properly' or not. Likewise, during the middle years, it is not whether a child has home chores, shares a room, has a specific bedtime or is an only child which solely determine his development. It is total atmosphere and attitude of the family which becomes the major force in shaping behaviour and guiding development.

Basic in family adjustment and success is the relationship of the parents to each other. Children keenly sense how parents get along and are not often fooled when things are not as they should be. Children draw their first impressions of the adult world, including marriage, from their parents. They unconsciously absorb attitudes and ways of behaving from parental models. They learn through observation far more than they may ever be formally taught in the area of relationship.

Parents are the life or death of a society, for more than any other single factor, they determine the traits, the personality structure and the adjustment of it member. Parents influence the six attitude and behaviour of their children, their emotional stability, their flexibility, their self confidence, their interest and values, their ambitious and their acceptance or rejection of others. Poor parent-child relationship are a major source of neuroses. Also, parents control what their children learn in school, how they work, whom they marry and the success they make of their marriage, and the kind of parents that they, in turn, will become.

The ideal parents have superior personalities, themselves, love and accept their children, are rewarding rather than punitive and place realistic restrict ons and make reasonable demands of, their children. Of course, the average parents is far from such an ideal, and it is difficult to break into the vicious circle by which poor parents raise children who become poor parents. However, there is no want of effort in our child-centered society, parents are almost too anxious to make use of the flood of articles, books, television programmes, discussion groups, courses, school psychologists and choices available to help them in task. The massive attack is probably producing better parents.

It is not possible to prescribe a precise formula, the use of which by parents will insure the child's optimal personality development. By reason of genetic constitution and developmental history, no two children are identical in all respect; situations in which children live and develop are varied and dynamic. A few general principles an positive side can, however, be stated, indicating that rejection and over protection are, of course, not the only alternatives. It has already been pointed out elsewhere that children need to have the feeling of security which can be provided by parents; a feeling that they belong, that they count, that they "can do". *A child requires the help of someone to assist them in organizing his increasingly widening variety of experiences*: and it is the parents, more than anyone else, who are in the position to provide a child with that essential from month to month, year to year.

Part of the feeling of organization and security can come from *parental supervision and guidance*, which, if wisely administered unable the child later to use his own freedom with more confidence and to determine his own course behaviour more adequately. Parental support, supervision and guidance, obviously, imply the necessity of certain restraints, but these child should know are neither capricious nor autocratic.

The desirable alternative to the extremes of rejecting or over protecting parent then is the parents who is the child's affectionate companion, sharing this interest, providing supervision and guidance on a basis as nearly democratic as the child's development permits.

Three Principal Parent Variables

More important than how individuals model their behaviour affect perceptions, of their parents' behaviour is the influence parents exert on the adjustment and personality of their children, which determine the kind of adult and, in turn, the kind of parents they will be. If mother spanks her five-year-old son if he flaunts her command in obey instantly when an order is given. Her choice of disciplinary tactic may be related to her belief or attitude that physical punishment is necessary when children do not submit readily to parental authority. This belief may emanate from her authoritarian personality structure, a vestige from her parents. It is one of three main parent variables—*parent behaviour, parent attitudes*, and *parent personality*. Although it may seem obvious that the three variables are closely related—that is, a parent behaves toward his child in accord with his attitudes toward child rearing, which are an aspect of his personality structure relatively little research has been undertaken to find the nature of their relationships.

Parent Personality

If personality is the sum of an individual's character traits, attitudes, and values, the personality of a parent may be expected to influence the personality development of his child. Although not much is known about he precise operation of this influence. We can get some idea of how the parent's personality affects the atmosphere and emotional tone of the home and the child's development by categorizing parental personality as either healthy or neurotic. In addition, there are many other aspects of personality that psychologists have described.

Various studies have sought to learn whether parental attitudes and parental behaviour are tied in with parent personality. One factor analytic study (Becker, Peterson, Hellmer, Shoemaker and Quay, 1959) found no close connection between parental behaviour and personality as these affected problem behaviour in children. But, inspired by publication of *The Authoritarian Personality* (Adorno, Frenkel-Brunswik Levinson, and Sanford, 1950) considerable research has been undertaken to uncover the relation between authoritarian attitudes and personality structure. In the original investigation, the research team found persons having authoritarian attitudes to be rigid, inflexible, and concrete in their thinking, conforming and conventional in their values, excessive in their respect for authority and prejudiced or ethnocentric in their view toward others who differed form them, racially or in national origin.

Parents and their Children

Sometimes a mother may notice that the children's grand-parents are more relaxed, affectionate and indulgent than she is herself. She may comment, 'Mother and Father spoil them.' Such a comment contains a note both of envy and fear; envy because of the continuing sense of responsibility she feels for the children and for their good behaviour (a responsibility the grand-parents do not feel to nearly the same extent) which prevents her from relaxing control and from being indulgent and affectionate; fear because she feels that the grand-parents' 'spoiling' may upset the control she imposes.

The main responsibilities of parents to their children may be summarized as follows, and the way parents fulfil these responsibilities may be expressed at one of the extremes or somewhere between the extremes suggested by the terms in the brackets:

- to provide food, clothes, shelter, toys (over-indulgent/ neglectful);
- to give affection (over-affectionate/rejecting);
- to protect—from physical and psychological harm (over-protective/indifferent);
- to encourage the development of skills (over-demanding/ unconcerned);
- to control (authoritarian/over-permissive).

It is proposed now to show the varying ways in which parents carry out these responsibilities and what, according to the research findings, their differing effects on children's personalities are. Many sources will be drawn upon, but more especially the work of Baldwin and of Schaefer, both of whom have rated parents on or between such extremes as those given above.

Over-possessive Parents

Possessive parents combine over-affection with the tendency to over-protect and, maybe, to over-indulge their children. They become too involved and there is a suggestion that one parent, if not both, is using the children to compensate for some deficiency. Many of these parents had an unhappy childhood and, in reflecting upon this, say that they had been deprived of parental affection or not been given the opportunity to develop because of household and family responsibilities imposed upon them too early. In their determination that the same would not happen to their own children, they become over-affectionate or over-indulgent.

Steinbeck's Shark, illustrates a typically possessive parent. His daughter's beauty and her femininity contrast with the drab toughness of his own life. She affords him an opportunity to cherish, to express tenderness, to be gentle—to demonstrate qualities which at other times he has severely suppressed. Besides, she is a source of great pride to him.

Parents may not be consciously aware of this fierce involvement, but they do reveal it by excessive fondling and a general anxiety about the child's safety that prevents them from allowing him to be independent, to explore alone, to adventure with other children.

Children of possessive parents are generally apprehensive, as if the world were a dangerous place. In the Nursery School they are afraid to abandon themselves to free and expansive bodily activity which involves the use of large muscles, as in swinging and in climbing ropes and frames. On the average they show less originality and less desire to explore new situations and new places. This is understandable, for to be original and to explore means to move into the unknown; to be freely active physically means taking risks. The anxiety which these children have acquired from their parents and the confusion they feel make them unable to do this.

In Primary School, children of over-protective parents tend to be well-behaved and to be prodigious readers, but they find difficulty in making friends and in participating in regular social activities with other children. This behaviour at school often contrasts with behaviour at home, where the child may have tantrums and be disobedient, impudent and demanding. Because he is so good at school, his teacher, if she hears about this, is surprised and puzzled by the inconsistency which the child shows. The misbehaviour at home may perhaps be explained as an attempt on the child's part to free himself from the subtly confining effect of his parents' over-protection. On the other hand, the school provides contact with adults which does not constrict him in this way and so he feels less anxious, and is therefore happy to conform.

Rejecting Parents

Not only do these parents reject their children, but they show, too, a general indifference to their children's safety, and a lack of real concern for their personal and social development. In this sense, they are quite the reverse of over-possessive parents. They may also neglect their children physically. But the extent to which they do so will vary, according to the particular economic and social circumstances of the parent.

A wealthy mother may employ a nurse and dutifully visit the nursery at breakfast and at bed-time. When the child asks for a kiss the mother says, pointing to her cheek, 'Just a peck there, or you will smudge Mummy's lipstick.' A working mother, with academic or vocational aspirations, may do much the same.

Much the same may happen in a very poor home; here, a parent may not establish any routine of child care, and the child may be physically as well as emotionally neglected.

Children of rejecting parents show characteristics similar to those who are brought up in an institution where the staff is too small to give individual and personal care and encouragement. Thus, the children tend to be retarded in the development of their bodily, language and social skills, and often show an inordinate desire for affection and approval. In the Nursery School they are less physically active, sometimes clinging to the teacher and refusing to leave her. They often sit and do nothing, and are less curious about the many activities going on around them. When they do start an activity of their own, they lack the tenacity to continue at the task for any appreciable length of time. These findings are understandable. Because these children receive little affection, they are hungry for it. Further, as children mature and being to acquire the rudiments of many simple skills, they need the individual encouragement which a mother can give. Without this, progress is slow and there is no stimulus to persist.

In school, the lack of persistence may continue and the teacher may speak of 'poor work habits'. On the other hand, a child may be so eager to gain the teacher's affection and so sensitive to any loss of the teacher's goodwill that he is a well-behaved pupil who works well.

But he is somewhat insecure which makes him timid when at play with his companions.

Authoritarian Parents

Parents who are authoritarian combine over-control with lack of warm affection. The control may be obtained through moral precepts with little or no physical punishment. An extreme approach of this sort may be based upon religious convictions of a fundamentalist kind—that a child is born depraved and that complete obedience and submission is necessary if the child is to be kept from sin and evil. Such attitudes are relatively rare in modern times. They were, however, prevalent during the eighteenth and nineteenth centuries, as Sundley has illustrated by drawing upon original early nineteenth-century sources, including writings on child-rearing practices in parent and family magazines, and medical and religious books.

The moral precepts may not necessarily be so based, and other authoritarian parents, themselves convinced of the value of obedience, orderliness and control, seek to imbue their children with similar virtues. They adopt a philosophy of strict upbringing involving mandatory routines and unquestioning obedience which they may justify as a determination not to spoil their children. Often they are themselves over-controlled and their control of their children is a reflection of this.

There are other forms of control, such as by excessive physical punishment. In this case, parents are cold, hostile and punitive, and they make no attempt to invoke moral judgment. Again, authoritarian parents may not be as consistent, either in a moral or punitive way, as is implied in the foregoing descriptions. The authoritarianism may then be expressed as continuous nagging with an occasional resort to physical punishment.

There are two main effects on children of authoritarian parents: where control is predominantly by moral precept, the child becomes socially timid and non-assertive; when it is imposed by means of severe physical punishment, the child is the opposite—socially outgoing and aggressive.

In the Nursery School, children of parents whose chief mode of control is through moral precepts are less curious, explore and play less and are less sociable than the average child. The over-control and the demands for absolute obedience seem to suppress children's spontaneity, originality, creativity, and the growth of social skills.

The parents are so concerned with conformity that all else is sacrificed to this end. At school, these children are generally obedient and submissive, polite and dependable, but somewhat inhibited and unable, for example, to be expansive in their play, to answer up in class. They tend to be somewhat withdrawn from other children.

Such behaviour may arise because the predominance of moral precepts, understandable only to an adult, creates a universe which a child cannot comprehend, and he is confused and anxious because of this. This over-control and the resulting anxious confusion seem to impair the development of initiative, independence and the ability to hold his own with his companions.

When the environment is unequivocally cold, hostile and punitive, a child tends to be other than obedient, submissive, polite and so on; at Nursery School he tends to be aggressive, to have frequent temper tantrums, and to be a little rebel, refusing to accept the restrictions necessary in such a social environment. At school age he is disobedient, unruly, coldly aggressive and sadistic towards his companions. He may use dictatorial methods to control and dominate other children. This contrasts with his behaviour at home where he is generally submissive and subdued Perhaps this inconsistency in his behaviour can be understood in terms of the following comparison: it is well-known that a class of children who have had a very strict authoritarian teacher for a long time become quite out of hand immediately they have a new and permissive teacher. Similarly, a child of punitive authoritarian parents is unable to the atmosphere at school which, relative to that at home, is benign and permissive.

In that he is without warm affection, the authoritarian parent is like the rejecting parent. One could, therefore, following Baldwin, describe both as 'rejecting' parents, the one, as he says, 'passively rejecting' and the other 'actively rejecting'. For both, a child interferes with an established way of life: in the examples given, a mother's social or professional aspirations, work in the store, a noiselessly quiet existence, a rigid set of principles. In a very poor home a child may be resented because he increases a poverty that is already crippling.

Over-permissive Parents

These parents allow a child to do more or less exactly as he wishes. Usually, they are over-indulgent so that the child is given far more possessions than he reasonably needs. The mother may appear indifferent about the child's safety because she does not stop him from behaving in an uncontrolled way—throwing stones, swinging a bat, speeding on a tricycle, with possible danger to himself and others. But the child is allowed to do these things not because the mother is unconcerned (such a mother may be very anxious about his safety) but because she is unable to assert herself, to make a stand and say, 'No!' Occasionally, a mother may for a moment realize, and then over-compensate for, this inability. To the surprise, consternation and confusion of the child, she suddenly gives vent to an outburst of scolding and screaming because of his continued rowdy and uncontrolled behaviour.

It is sometimes difficult to distinguish between the over-permissive and the over-possessive parent. Both tend to be indulgent and unassertive. But there is a difference. The over-possessive parent is anxious and her anxiety causes her to be hyper-sensitive about, and to fear, overt assertion: that is, physically punishing or admonishing her child (though such a mother may use more subtle forms of control, by demanding affection, by a pained and silent admonishment, or by saying, 'How could you do this and hurt Mummy so?'). The main problem which the over-permissive parent experiences in bringing up her children is this inability to assert herself. It causes her to feel personally inadequate in coping with the many difficult situations which inevitably rise with children; and the uncertainty she feels may cause her many moments of anxiety.

This uncertainty is reflected in the children. They tend, for example, to be unstable and to show swings of mood and of behaviour—from confidence to lack of confidence, from independence to dependence, from control to lack of control, from friendliness and sociability to hostility and aggression. In short, children of over-permissive parents present the picture of the typically 'spoilt' child—disobedient, rebellious, given to frequent temper tantrums, excessive in their demands on other people, domineering over other children. They misbehave in these ways partly because they have no external control to protect them from their own impulsiveness. Such behaviour may also be an implicit plea to their parents to make a stand, not to give way to their every whim, and so to set limits to what they, the children, are allowed to do.

These children may show the same kind of inconsistency as do the children of possessive parents, being model children at school and terrors at home. The reason for this could be that the school, in contrast to the home, provides an ordered and controlled environment which makes such children feel less anxious. This is then reflected in more stable behaviour.

Democratic Parents

The nearer parents approach to a mean between the extremes of which we have spoken, the nearer they approach to the democratic parent. Baldwin makes a distinction between the cold democratic and the warm democratic parent. Cold democratic parents approach a mean between all extremes except that they do not express warm affection; they are direct, rational, unemotional. The child is given reasons why he should do this and should not do that; if he is in the way, he is told quite dispassionately that this concerns adults only and is of no interest or importance to him. He is given freedom to express his own ideas; he is given materials and is encouraged to develop his maturing skills. But about it all there is a lack of warmth, a scientific detachment from the child. He is not cuddled when he comes crying to his mother because he has been hurt. Instead, the wound is attended to in a precise, medically prescribed way and that's the end of the matter. And there is no 'nonsense' about Santa Claus. Such parents suppress expression of spontaneous affection. Behaviour is controlled and rational. There is a 'taboo on tenderness'.

Such parents may show over-concern with the child's progress and attempt to accelerate this. In the pre-school years the child may be given special puzzle-type toys, or problem situations may be devised, such as placing a treasured object in an unusual place and getting him to find it. He is encouraged to do things not usual for a very young child, such as a little shopping in the local store, answering the telephone, receiving and taking messages. This persistent encouragement of his independence and mastery usually continues during the school years and parents may have high aspirations for their child and will watch his progress with concern and interest, assessing this progress relative to the rest of his classmates. In this way, they imbue the child with a sense of the importance of scholastic achievement.

The warm democratic parent has many of the characteristics of the cold democratic parent—giving the child freedom to express his own ideas; materials, opportunities and encouragement to develop skills. But these parents are warm. They are able to be tender or sympathetic as occasion demands, and to be affectionate without that excess of fondling which confuses and embarrasses a child. They are able to view their children objectively, to assess their good and not-so-good qualities. With an admonition or humourous reminder a mother will convey to one of her children that she knows he's up to some tricks to score one over his brother. There is a balancing of extremes—for the very young child, chances to explore, yet the realization that an eye must be kept on possible hazards; for older children, freedom of choice wherever possible, yet the realization that they need help, support and advice on many issues that are important to them. Such parents are not obsessed with their children's progress, although they are happy to have them succeed and encourage them to do so.

It is difficult to review the results of investigations of warm and cold democratic parents because most investigators speak of the democratic home without making the distinction made by Baldwin. However, from the descriptions they give and the assessments they make, it would seem that when these writers speak of the democratic home they are including the idea of warmth. It is the effect of such a home that will be considered in what immediately follows.

Radke presents a rather idealized picture of the behaviour of children of democratic parents in the nursery and kindergarten. She speaks of them as being emotionally stable, popular, sensitive to the opinions of others and less quarrelsome than other children. Baldwin does not report such ideal social relations and finds that these children are not particularly sociable although he does find them to be intellectually curious, original, constructive and able to plan their own activities. In other words, he finds that their social development is not so advanced as their intellectual development. This is understandable. At home they have been encouraged to develop maturing skills, but, because the home is 'warm and cosy', the child finds the many children, the bustle and noise of the Nursery School, hard to take. He is content, therefore, to make use of the toys and apparatus available and to explore and to play alone. Such behaviour should not be interpreted as neurotic withdrawal; the child is happy and actively busy.

At school, children of democratic parents are independent, responsible and co-operative. Baldwin himself says that the picture presented above is now different. The democratic group are sociable, not in a dominant, but in a good-natured way. They are often precocious and able to converse with grown-ups on a surprisingly adult level.

Children of cold democratic parents show many similar characteristics. In the Nursery School they are active, curious, original, but socially uninhibited and aggressive, exuberant in an extraverted kind of way, always ready to join in a social activity and more than able to look after themselves in competition for toys and for the notice of the teacher. At school they are also socially active, prepared to take part in competitive games and in competitive strivings within the classroom. They show the same precociousness when conversing with adults as do the children of warm democratic parents. Because of the continued pressure put on them for high achievement and independence, these children 'excel in planning ability and performance'. This planning ability may be seen in their play, for here we may have the 'bossy' child who tells all the others what to do.

Their determination to excel may become a compulsive 'search for glory', such as Horney describes, and be accompanied by a vindictive drive to triumph over other children.

So far it has been assumed that both parents are, or at least the parent who plays the dominant part in brining up the child, is possessive or authoritarian and so on. But it is important to look for a moment at the effect on boys and girls of the respective disciplinary roles of mother and father. It would appear that a mother who is extremely dominating—strict, cold, punitive—has a detrimental influence on a boy. To be dominated and controlled by a woman, even his mother, is such an indignity for him that he develops feelings of dejection and inferiority, and in the presence of his companion, he feels ashamed. Further, physical punishment by the mother paralyses a boy's powers of assertion. He 'swallows' (introjects', as Freud would say) the aggression he feels towards her and is unable to displace it on to others. Consequently, he is unable to assert himself even in a legitimate way, as in standing up for himself while at play with his companions.

Similarly treated, a daughter tends to become like her mother, somewhat hard and lacking tenderness, suggesting that such a mother is not an appropriate model for the development of feminine behaviour in a daughter.

When it is the father who is very strict, cold and punitive, the son does not introject the aggression he feels but gets rid of it on others ('displaces' it, as Freud would say). He behaves in a manner generally characteristic of children of cold, authoritarian parents which has already been described, being aggressive and using physical force in getting his own way with his companions. He may become the dominating leader of a 'gang', but, if he has not the qualities of leadership necessary for this, he becomes instead a typical bully and takes it out on younger children. His aggressive behaviour, especially if he is the leader of a 'gang', may become delinquent.

The effect is somewhat the same on a daughter, who also tends to become hard and aggressive. She may, for example, become the leader of a group of children who make scapegoats of weaker children.

By contrast, a father who is warm and companionable yet firm, and who imposes discipline only if necessary, is likely to have sons who are self-confident, positively assertive, use little physical force, and are able to make friends and to accept such frustrating situations as inevitably occur. Hoffman sums up the research findings in this way: 'It would appear that a mother's love makes a boy feel warm and cosy, but a father's love equips him to face the world.' The daughters of such fathers are also confident, sociable, able to assert themselves in a positive way.

All this suggests that while each parents needs to combine both warmth and control, it is more appropriate in our own culture for the mother to be the main source of warmth and affection, and for the father to be the main source of control. Thereby each parent provides an appropriate model which accords with the accepted views of most members of our society on what is a predominantly feminine and what is a predominantly masculine role.

In concluding this study parents and their children, it will be useful to look for a moment at control through the consistent use of physical punishment, since effects here are somewhat complex and confusing (one is not thinking of the occasional slap). As has been seen, physical punishment can increase a child's aggressiveness: the more severe it is, the more aggressive he becomes, and when it is coldly punitive, the child will tend to become viciously aggressive and sadistic. On the other hand, over-permissiveness may also lead to aggressive behaviour—that of the spoilt child—although here the aggression is more impulsive, as in a temper tantrum. The answer to this apparent paradox probably lies in the fact that neither environment allows inner controls to develop as they do in an environment combining reasonable restraints with warm affection.

When outer control is itself aggressive, an eye is taken for an eye, a tooth for a tooth and parents provide a cold, aggressive model for the child to follow. He does not then generate feelings of guilt and therefore inner controls are not developed. In short, severe physical punishment leaves him free to be aggressive, his only fear being of the outer control, of being caught and punished.

On the other hand, the over-permissive parent provides no external control over aggressive tendencies, despite the fact that anger is a powerful emotion and the urge to be aggressive hard for a child to restrain. Further, there are no inner controls because, to develop, these must be preceded by reasonable external controls. Consequently, over-permissiveness again leaves a child free to be aggressive. In short, in the over-permissive environment the absence of external controls hinders the development of inner ones; in the punitive environment it is the lack of warmth and the severity and quality of the restraint that hinders their development.

It may be well at this stage to pause and utter a word of caution. Parent-child relationships are complex and it has not yet been found possible experimentally to isolate all the nuances within the kinds and degrees of affection shown, control exercised, demands made, and so on. It is only the broad categories that have been described. The danger is that, in doing this, an impression may be given that the complex is, after all, simple. This would be erroneous. The complexity remains. Thus, not all parents by any means 'fit' into the categories described above. Although differing from the more detailed combinations suggested by Baldwin, these categories are partly based on his findings. And even using his more detailed combinations, he was unable to classify 25 per cent of the parents whom he studied.

Following an earlier inquiry, the Newsons made a detailed study of what actually happens between four-years old children and their mothers. The Newsons studied seven hundred mothers and children who lived in an English urban environment, and their results demonstrate most clearly the complexity of mother-child relationships and the difficulty of classifying parents. The actual number of occasions which led the mothers to take issue with their children were numerous: meal times and eating, sex play and physical modesty, jumping on beds or disarranging furniture, uncleanliness, untidiness, and so on. But the importance the mothers attached to these issues varied considerably.

Most parents demanded obedience, but in differing ways. For example, one mother, corresponding more nearly to cold democratic parent, demanded the independence of her child; she expected him to dress himself, to run errands, to keep himself occupied independently of her, and to stand up for himself. Another mother, corresponding more to our morally authoritarian parent, demanded controlled behaviour; she expected her child to stand or sit perfectly still while she washed or dressed him, to play in a quiet orderly way, stay in the garden, and come indoors when neighbouring children began quarrelling.

Some mothers were both permissive and authoritarian, according to the issue involved. To take two examples: one of the mothers of the study allowed her children to play messily with paint, earth or water, and to make a noise; she ignored genital play, and satisfied her children's curiosity about where babies come from. Yet this same mother said, 'We do not have many rules, but one is that you do as you're told, when you're told and how you're told.' Another parent allowed her child a dummy and showed considerable tenderness, cuddling the child to sleep each night; yet she would not allow him to jump on the bed, smacked him for touching his genitals, and insisted that 'babies come from the sweet shop'.

Further, while the effects of the behaviour and attitudes of parents on their children are, in general, much as has been indicated in the course of this chapter, the investigations also show that there are exceptions. A particular child may or may not respond in one of the various ways described and summarized immediately below, depending upon other social circumstances and upon his particular temperament. It would be unfortunate if a teacher over-simplified the position and interpreted the results in an absolute sense—for example, in thinking about a particular child, reasoned as follows: 'He's nasty, aggressive and a bully in school, and must have authoritarian parents.' In many cases such a judgment will be found to be true. But human beings are generally for too complex to fit within the simple formula 'one cause, one effect' and it is necessary to beware of making snap judgments.

Despite this, certain broad principles are suggested namely:

Extreme attitudes on the part of parents tend to result in extreme behviour of some kind in their children.

A balancing of extremes tends to produce a balanced child.

In some respects children's personalities are a reflection of the personalities of their parents. The following summary of what has already been said illustrates this:

Anxious and apprehensive	— Over-possessive parents and their children
Unstable	— Over-permissive parents and their children
Over-controlled	— Morally authoritarian parents and their children
Aggressively cruel	— Punitive authoritarian parents and their children
Drivingly ambitious	— Cold democratic parents and their children
Stable, balanced	— Warm democratic parents and their children

From the point of view of a child's 'creative becoming', the most beneficial ingredients of child care are freedom (to enable him happily to explore or to adventure); warmth, shared relationships with, and genuine affection of, a trusted adult (to give security); encouragement (to stimulate the development of maturing skills). These broad principles are very much in accord with the commonsense judgments we make from our everyday observations of children and their parents.

Parent Attitudes

How the adult conceives of the parental role in relation to the child influences his attitudes as a parent. Does he see the parent's primary function as one of restricting and controlling child behaviour? Does he view the socialization process as essentially a taming of the young child's uncivilized nature? Or does he regard the parental role as mainly one of guidance and setting the proper example for the child to emulate? The conception of the responsibilities, functions, and obligations of a role mold the individual's attitudes in the role which, in turn, presumably engender his behaviour in it. The interest of the child psychologist in parental attitudes stems, therefore, from the notion that a basic, understanding attitude influences many behaviours of parenthood that are assumed to affect the personality development of the child.

According to Symonds, the essence of parent-child relations lies in how a parent *feels* than in what a parent *does*," In this respect Symonds's concern lay with parental attitudes towards the child. Subsequent research has also been conceived with attitudes towards child rearing.

The assessment of parent attitude poses a number of problems (Bell, 1958), most of them arising from attempts of psychologist to find a cause-and-effect relationship between these attitudes and child behaviour. The *first* problem results from changes in parental attitudes. It is extremely hazardous to maintain in the assessment of parent attitudes that certain ones cause particular child behaviours when the measurement is made after the appearance of the behaviour. One cannot know the attitude of the parent before the onset of the behaviour, whether it be schizophrenia, stuttering, delinquency, or anything else. More important, one must be aware of the possibility of changes in parent attitudes. For example, a large percentage of parents can readily name the age level of children that they prefer and the level that they regard least endurable. Since one age level is more satisfying and rewarding than another, it might be assumed that the parent-child relationship is most conducive at that period to healthy personality development in the child.

The *second* problem relates to the first. It is the impact on the parent's attitudes of the feedback provided by a certain kind of child. That children at birth differ in many ways is obvious and that these differences affect the parent's attitudes toward a child must be considered. Since parental attitudes condition the child's further development of personality, the point is especially important in relation to the effect of such attitudes on the personality growth of the handicapped, the chronically ill, or the extremely sensitive child. This brings up the matter of the "vicious circle" phenomenon which has such dreadfully harmful consequences for the youngster. Two examples will suffice. That a child's intellectual capacities are below his parent's expectations may first come to parental attention when the youngster experiences some difficulty in learning to read in the first grade, or when he is placed in a reading group that the parents consider beneath his level. The child must thus face the frustration flowing from reading difficulties as well as the equally bitter torn of parental rejection. At a time when the child most needs parents acceptance and reassurance to bolster his self-confidence and sense of security, he is met with criticism and disapproval. This changed parental attitude only serves to handicap the child further in the efforts to improve his reading. Or, to cite the other example, perhaps for deep-seated reasons rooted in his own psychological past, a parent may find himself unable to accept fully one of his children. From this non-acceptance may emerge undesirable school behaviour such as attention and seeking. When the teacher or other school officer expresses concern over this behaviour, the non-acceptance may increase. Here again the change in parental attitude may aggravate rather than ameliorate the child's disturbance.

Third among these problems is the necessity for identifying the attitudes of the parent toward a particular child. It is well-known that an individual views each of his children differently. Not only does a parent's attitudes vary according to the age of the child but also, undoubtedly, on the basis of such factors as sex, intelligence, personality, and appearance.

The *fourth* problem is that the emphasis is psychological literature on the crucial significance of parental attitudes for child adjustment has made parents highly sensitive and defensive about revealing their attitudes. Tapping a parent's attitudes directly is no simple task. How difficult this may be through a paper-and-pencil test may be judged from the failure of the Parent Attitude Research Instrument (PARI) to distinguish among the attitudes of various groups of mothers. For example, the PARI cannot differentiate significantly between the attitudes of parents of well-adjusted and poorly adjusted first-grade children (Medinnus, 1961), nor among the attitudes of mothers of children with speech articulation problems, delayed speech development, or lack of speech (Moll and Darley, 1960), nor among mothers of asthmatic, chronically ill, or healthy children (Margolis, 1961).

Authoritarian Attitudes. To understand fully the effects of a parent's authoritarian attitudes on the personality development of a child requires a knowledge of their source. Several possibilities have been raised: the personality structure of the individual, his own upbringing and his parent's pattern of authority, his conception of both parent and child roles. Regardless of the cause, an authoritarian attitude implies an emphasis on authority and a belief in the value and efficacy of an autocratic approach to child rearing. Control is pre-eminent. The parent is dominant, the child subordinate. Insufficient respect is shown for the youngster as an individual, for his rights, his wishes, and his individuality. Hoffman (1963) found some evidence for a relation between parental authoritarian attitudes and power-assertive behaviour toward the child. A parent who attempts to control his child's behaviour in a direct and physical way without using explanation or reasoning may be expressing a more general attitude of authoritarianism that pervades his social relations.

From this it would seem possible to predict that authoritarian parental attitudes would lead to a child who is submissive, lacking in security and independence, and who is, therefore, less popular with his companions. In general such predictions have been borne out by research (Read, 1945; Radke, 1946; Miles, 1946). Yet Radke discovered that children from autocratic homes were rated by preschool teachers as most likely to fight and quarrel with other children, as more inconsideration to others, and as more insensitive to praise or blame than those from democratic homes. A child from a home in which the notion of power is highly important assumes a role similar to his parent's when he find himself in a relatively permissive nursery-school environment.

In general, children of autocratic parents are seen as emotionally stable. This may be ascribed to a number of reasons. The different in approach between autocratic parents and more permissive teachers leads to uncertainty and confusion for the child. Having little opportunity for choice and decision in the home, the child finds the freedom of nursery school fearsome. Harsh paternal attitudes have also been to relate to personality problems of shyness and withdrawal and to conduct problems of truancy and stealing among kindergarteners (Peter Becker, Shoemaker, Luria, and Hellmer, 1961). Such attitudes are reflected in demands for instant and unquestioning obedience, in inability to tolerate the "annoyance value" of children, and in the preference for a quiet, cautious child rather than a noisy, daring one. A relation has been found between the authoritarian attitudes of mothers and their adolescent daughters, although low correlations were obtained between the authoritarian attitudes (Mosher and Mosher, 1965). This suggests that although the child-rearing practices employed in the home are not unimportant, certain attitudes may be transmitted fairly directly from parent to child.

Parental Acceptance-Rejection Attitudes. A 40-item scale specifically designed to measure parental acceptance of children consisting posted four traits in the accepting parent by porter in 1954. Parent who (a) "Regards his child as a person with feelings and respects the child's right need to express these feelings"; (b) "Values the unique makeup of his child and does what he can to foster that uniqueness within the limits the healthy personal and social adjustment"; (c) "Recognizes the child's need to differentiate and separate himself from his parents to become an autonomous individual"; and (d) "Loves his child unconditionally." However, the results obtained from relating parents' scores on the Porter to the adjustment of children have been negative (Burchinal, Howkes and Gardner, 1957; Burchinal, 1958a). No significant tie has been made between the two.

Because of the emphasis in Western culture on maternal love and the affectional obligations of motherhood, strong feelings of guilt arise in a parent who, for one reason or another, cannot fully accept his child. Any attempt to assess this sensitive area on an objective, paper-and-pencil level is therefore almost doomed to failure. What is needed is a subtle disguised, projective-type instrument that does not arouse the parent's defense system. Psychologists have long shown concern over acceptance and rejection. Yet not much research has been directed toward creating an instrument for tapping these vital parental attitudes. Medinnus and Curtis (1963) defined maternal acceptance on the basis of the discrepancy between a mother's rating of her child on a series of traits and her description of how she wanted the child to measure up on them. A significant correlation was obtained between self-acceptance scores of a group of mothers and their acceptance of their children. Presumably the psychological adage that one can accept others only to the extent that one firsts accepts oneself applies to the mother-child relationship.

There is undoubtedly a wide margin of safety in parent attitudes (Ausubel, 1958). Only when they deviate markedly from the typical do these attitudes exert harmful influences on child adjustment. In such cases, it is more likely the attitudes toward the child, relative the acceptance or rejection, rather than toward child rearing that are significant.

Parent Behaviour

From what has been seen of parent behaviours apparent that an isolated examination of them is not likely to bear fruit. At this point in man's knowledge more is to be learned from exploring the characteristics that describe the general behavioural atmosphere of the home. Table contains some of the principal characteristics identified over several decades of research activity.

Two characteristics recur throughout the studies; these are acceptance versus rejection and autonomy versus control, depicted. In theory, the psychological atmosphere of a home many fall into any of the four quadrants, each of which represents one of four general combinations: acceptance-autonomy, acceptance-control, rejection-autonomy, rejection-control.

Acceptance versus Rejection. The most significant aspect of the home warmth of the relationship between parent and child. Both the Pattern Study (Sears, Maccoby, and Levin, 1957) and the Fels research be considered presently, have maintained that warmth is the most crucial and pervasive factor affecting the child.

Major Parent-Child Dimensions

Investigators		*Psychological Dimensions*
Symonds (1939)	Dimensions	Acceptance-rejection Dominance-submission
Baldwin, Kalhorn, and Breese (1945)	Syndromes.	Democracy in the home acceptance of child Indulgence
Baldwin, Kalhorn, and Breese (1949)	Clusters	Warmth Adjustment Restrictiveness Clarity Interference
Roff (1949)	Factors	Concern for child Democratic guidance Permissiveness Parent-child harmony Sociability-adjustment of parents Activeness of home Nonreadiness of suggestion
Jenkins (1953)	Factors	Dependence-encouraging Democracy of child training Organization and effectiveness of control
Milton (1958)	Factors	Strictness of non-permissiveness of parent behaviour General family interaction or adjustment Warmth of the mother-child relationship Responsible child-training orientation Parents' attitude toward aggressiveness and punitiveness
(1959)	Dimensions	Autonomy-control Love-hostility

Symonds' Studies. After a careful review of the literature, Symonds (1939) concluded that the matter of acceptance or rejection was one of the two most significant considerations in the home, the other being autonomy as opposed to control. Although it left much to be desired methodologically, since its findings were based on case histories compiled by Symonds' former students, the study was fruitful enough to warrant examination. These were some of the parent behaviours that served as evidence for acceptance or rejection according to the study:

Evidence for Acceptance	*Evidence for Rejection*
Participates with child in games, sports, hobbies, takes trips together, special vacations together, pals. with siblings	No interest in child. No time for child—neglect Unfavourable comparison
	Verbal punishment—nagging, scolding
Parents make rearing child their main job-devoted.	Failure to support child. Criticism or blame of child.
Interested in child's plans and ambitions. Gives child loving care and protection.	Physical punishment or cruelty Turned out of home or threaten to place in an institution.
Interested in school progress.	Does not speak well of child.
Demonstrative in affection.	Ridicule.
Speaks well of child.	Child unwanted at birth.
Wanted at birth.	Suspicious of child's behaviour.
Child encouraged to bring friends home.	Too much supervision.
	Neglect health, clothes, training etc.
Parents worry when child is ill Accepted as individual rather than as child.	
Child trusted.	
Parents talk over plans with child.	
Parents do not expect too much of child.	
Parents give wise counseling and encouragement.	

Symonds sought to find differences in behaviour between accepted and rejected children in order to discover the causes of such differences in the marital relations of the parents and in the parents' own childhood. In general, he noted that accepted children engaged predominantly and socially and acceptable behaviour, whereas rejected children manifested the number of unacceptable behaviours. Specifically, the behaviours characteristic of accepted children included good-naturedness, consideration of others, cheerfulness, interest in work, friendliness, cooperativeness, and emotional stability. Among rejected children, on the other hand, attention-getting behaviour, tendency toward delinquency, and problems in school were evident. More important, however, than descriptions of behavioural differences between accepted and rejected children is the need to understand how parental acceptance and rejection produce them.

Symonds (1949) observed that an individual's attitudes toward himself grew out of the attitudes displayed toward him by his parents during childhood. A child who was rejected developed feelings of insecurity and inferiority because it seemed to him that if he were unworthy of parental love, he was evidently worthless. A low conception of the self resulted from a low view of the child by his parents.

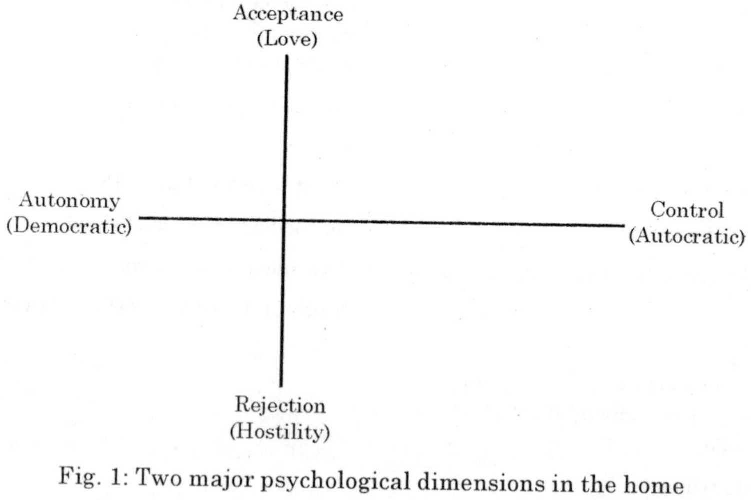

Fig. 1: Two major psychological dimensions in the home

Such rejection brings on attempts by the child to win parental affection. These efforts may take the form of various attention-getting behaviour: refusal to eat, refusal to talk, temper tantrums, bed wetting, and whining. If these tactics prove futile, two general types of behaviour often result: the child becomes hostile and aggressive or withdrawn and submissive. Symonds pointed out that whereas rejection might led to good social adjustment outside the home and to close identification with and attachment to one's peers, it more frequently resulted in more negative consequences—feelings of insecurity, inferiority, inadequacy, worthlessness isolation, humiliation, and anxiety. Even though a number of childhood experiences might not exert long-range influences on the child, a pattern of rejection might very well prove pervasive in its effect on the child's adult personality and adjustment.

In a later study Symonds (1949) examined a number of factors, conscious as well as unconscious, contributing to the parent's rejection of the child. Among the more obvious were the economic burden imposed to the youngster, the invasion of the parents' privacy and activities, the strain of childbirth and child care on the mother, the child's failure to meet parental expectations, and parental disappointment in the sex of the child. Symonds maintained that some children are easier to accept than others; the child who is easiest to accept is the one most likely to be accepted by his parents. In this respect, the characteristics of the child definitely figure in the degree to which he receives parental acceptance.

Six elements, in particular, play an unconscious part in parental rejection, Symonds believed. First, the pattern of rejection adopted by a parent might be similar to the one experienced in his own childhood. Second, the parent might kindle in the child the hostility he felt toward his own parents. Third, one parent might show hostility towards the child as a means of injuring the other parent. Fourth, the parent might transfuse into the child the hostility he felt towards one of his own siblings. Fifth, he might implant in the child some of the feelings of hostility and rejection that he feels toward himself. Sixth, a mother—or a father, for that matter—might be so immature and narcissistic as to be unable to lover another person wholeheartedly, and the resultant guilt might cause her to reject the child.

Fels Studies. Let us now explore parental acceptance as seen in the Fels studies (Baldwin, Kalhorn, and Breese, 1945). The Fels Research Institute has dealt largely with the scientific collection of data on the environment. Too quantify these data obtained from direct observations and interviews with mothers, the Institute devised a series of rating scales. The theory underlying the choice of areas for study and the rationale behind the assessment procedure have been described in detail by Champney (1941a, b). The Institute's directors assumed that the parent behaved consistently in certain ways toward the child from situation to situation, thus providing the child with an environment for leading from which he could develop social habits and form his personality.

Generally, the studies found the receptant home warm, granting unconditional acceptance of the child and characterized by a relatively non-coercive policy of child rearing. Rejecting homes, on the other hand, fell into two types: non-chalant and actively rejecting. In the non-chalant home, the child was largely ignored but punished severely for infractions or disturbances. In the actively rejecting home, autocratic control required the child's constant compliance, thus reducing the chance of disturbance. Aggressiveness typified the parent's relationship with his child in both types of rejection; he was expressing his hostility toward the child.

In these studies the investigators sought to establish a link between the atmosphere in the home and the child's behaviour in nursery school and later in grade school. Children were observed both in preschool and school settings, and were rated on a variety of child behaviours. In emotional traits, the actively rejected preschool children were characterized by high emotionality and low emotional control (Baldwin, 1949). They showed a certain amount of resistance to adults, but were more active physically than accepted children. Indulged children were high in both friendliness and quarrelsomeness with other children. At school age indulged children seemed shyer and less sociable than during preschool years, whereas rejected children showed a marked increase in quarrelsomeness and a great deal of sibling hostility. Although much of the difference between the two types had disappeared by the time all of them had reached school age the rejected children still showed themselves to be more energetic.

The Pattern Study. One of the scales used in the Pattern Study for rating extensive interviews with mothers was labeled "Mother's Rejection of the Child." From the mother's report, the investigators endeavoured also to evaluate the father on his degree of acceptance or rejection of the child. Acceptance was defined as the giving of love without reservation, where rejection meant a withholding of love. Of the interviews assessed in this area, 220 mothers showed no rejection of the child and 101 were thought to indicate some rejection. The majority of these 101 instances however, were closer to the receptance end of the scale than the rejection end. As to the fathers only 47 were judged to evince some rejection.

Acceptance or rejection was seen to influence several child behaviour. First of all, children experiencing some rejection tended to show more dependent behaviour than accepted youngsters. Acceptance, it would seem, promotes the wholesome development of independent behaviour and of independence. The rejected child, far less secure in his relationship with his parents, needs their constant reassurance of willingness to nurture him. Thus a continuing need for dependency in a child might very well reflect a lack of dependability on the part of his parents. Second, rejected children were slightly retarded in the development of conscience. Third, how much or how little a child adopted his parents' standards and values depended in part on the warmth and acceptance they accorded him.

Because indulgence and overprotection would seem to contain elements of both acceptance and rejection, they are pertinent to this discussion. Certainly these parental behaviours cannot be thought of as representing the extreme of acceptance. Yet their influence on the child suggests otherwise. In a classic study of maternal overprotection, in which he dwelt on 20 cases of "pure" overprotection of 19 boys and one girls, Levy (1943) pointed to four aspects of excessive maternal care in their mothers One was excessive contact; "the mother is always there." Another was infantilization; "she still treats him like a baby." A third was preventing independent behaviour; "she won't let him grow up" or "she won't take any risks." The fourth was lack or excess of maternal control; the mother may either dominate or be dominated by the child.

A number of factors in the personalities and backgrounds of the parents of these overprotected children seemed related to the overprotection. For some of the mothers there was a prolonged period of anticipation of childbearing. In other cases there were spontaneous abortions, still-births, and long periods of sterility. Still others experienced marital dissatisfaction and sexual incompatibility. Apparently many mothers sought to compensate for an unhappy marital relationship by establishing intimate bond with their sons.

Incompatibility seemed to extend to social activities. The parents engaged little social life in common. Many of the mothers withdrew from nearly all outside social contact. Throughout the backgrounds of these overprotecting mothers ran a common thread of a lack of maternal love. The term used by Levy to describe the need in an individual that stemmed from lack of parental love involving affection, security, sympathy, and recognition was "affect hunger." It was as though these women attempted to satisfy their strong need for affection by maneuvering the child into an intimate affectional relationship in which he was somewhat isolated from other contacts. Yet these overprotecting mothers were, in general, responsible, stable, aggressive women who possessed strong maternal tendencies. Frequently their ambitions for education or for a career had been thwarted. The fathers of the children were seen as good providers, stable, but submissive, playing little or no authoritative role in relation to the child. They were ineffectual in counteracting the overprotective influence of the mother.

What about the children? How did they fare from overprotection? Those who, due to lack of maternal control, dominated their mothers were ill adapted to classroom discipline and reacted poorly to the authority of the teacher. However, the classroom behaviour of overprotected children generally contrasted markedly with behaviour at home. In achievement, they demonstrated relatively high success in language and showed special interesting in reading, although they often fared poorly in arithmetic. Moreover, these children were restricted in contacts with agemates. Evidently because of the great impact of the overprotective relationship on their social life, they experienced difficulty in making friends or in having friendly relationships with peers.

Some overprotected children behaved rebelliously, aggressively, defiantly, and tyrannically toward mothers who were submissive toward them. They were disobedient, impudent, excessively demanding, and prone to temper tantrums. They were selfish and undisciplined. Others who were dominated by their mothers were, on the other hand, submissive and dependent.

Later, however, the behaviour of both groups of overprotected children was better on the whole than might have been expected from their deviant early relationship with their mother. Attributable as this may be in part to the countering effect of peers and school, it may also indicate that overprotection is far less deleterious than rejection in the long run. At least the child develops a sense of self-worth when overprotected.

In the Schaefer and Bayley (1963) study, also discussed, the love-hostility dimension included the following variables: Positive mother-child relationship, Equalitarianism, Expression of affection, positive evaluation of the child, and Emotional involvement, as opposed to Ignoring, Punitiveness, Irritability, and Use of fear to control. The following scale for ignoring illustrates the manner in which the maternal behaviour data were rated.

Symonds' Studies. Returning to Symonds' (1939) early study, these were some of the characteristics that described the behaviour of dominant parents. They insisted on complete obedience. They supervised the child closely in the youngster's choice of activities. They provided too much supervision. They trained the child carefully. The expressed concern over trifles and criticized the child. Submissive parents, on the other hand, let the child have his own way. They could not control the child. They employed lax, inconsistent discipline and allowed the child to upset the home routine.

Although fathers satisfied many of their personality needs outside of the family, mothers were especially likely to fulfill their needs for dominance or submission by controlling or letting themselves be controlled by their children, Symonds noted. This finding supports the widespread notion that mothers exert a greater influence on the child than the father. The primary obligation of the mother's role is rearing the children, whereas occupational success and economic support of the family are important aspects of the father's role. Small wonder, therefore, that the mother may be more emotionally involved than the father in the end result of the child-rearing techniques used. Failure may cast a dark shadow over the mother's feelings of competence and adequacy. The father, however, can compensate for any deficiency as a parent with success in his job and the recognition it achieves. Whereas several recent investigations (Becker et al., 1959; Peterson et al., 1959) suggested that the father's attitudes and behaviours were as intimately connected as those of the mother to the development of problem behaviour in the child, this finding might reflect an increased paternal participation and involvement in child rearing. It further signifies that the father's role is an important one in contemporary, urban, somewhat isolated psychologically, small-sized, child-oriented families.

Symonds found differentiation in a number of behaviours between children of dominating parents and those of submissive parents. The former were better socialized as a rule; their behaviour was more acceptable, more conforming to the group. They seemed to be more interested in school work. Yet they tended to be sensitive, shy, self-conscious, seclusive, retiring, and submissive as compared with children who were given more freedom by their parents. The children of submissive parents inclined toward disobedience, irresponsibility, lack of interest in school, stubbornness, and defiance of authority. They were able, however, to express themselves effectively.

As to personality, the dominated children were more likely to be courteous, loyal, honest, polite, and dependable, albeit submissive and docile. The children of submissive parents were aggressive, disrespectful, and antagonistic, although independent and self-confident.

Fels Studies. In the Fels projects the scales fitting the syndrome "Democracy in the Home" included justification of policy, democracy of policy, non-coerciveness of suggestion, readiness of explanation, direction of criticism (approval), clarity of policy, understanding of the child, and non-restrictiveness of regulation. From the scale's descriptive phrases it is apparent that the principal criterion of democracy is the practice of consulting the child in family decisions, giving him a voice in the policy of the home. In the autocratic or dictatorial home all decisions are made by the parents, with the child accorded little participation or choice.

Rejection often shows itself in an autocratic home, but this is not invariably the case. Some parents adopt an autocratic method because they feel this is the most desirable manner of training and rearing children. Undoubtedly the parent's personality and his conception of child nature both influence the choice of a non-democratic approach. This choice may be a matter of expediency or of policy. Similarly, a democratic approach to child rearing may reflect an intellectual policy of the parent, who may, be trying to follow the latest "expert" advice, or it may flow from a warm, accepting, understanding relation between parent and child. Thus, there is the scientific, intellectual democratic home and the warm democratic home. To the Fels researchers the latter types was the ideal home for the development of a healthy personality in the child.

The Fels group concluded that democratic parents were more likely to be better educated and more intelligent than autocratic ones. However, education was not the only element involved in producing democracy. Objectivity and emotional maturity in the parent were also involved. The parent unable to separate himself psychologically from his child not, by the very nature of the relationship, be truly democratic.

Many child characteristics were found in the Fels studies to be linked to the presence of democracy in the home. First, as compared with other types of home atmosphere, the democratic seemed most conducive to intellectual growth. The children from such homes showed increases in IQ over a period of time (Baldwin, Kalhorn, and Breese, 1945). A democratic environment not only permitted greater freedom but also often encouraged exploration and experimentation. Restriction was at a minimum.

On such intellectual variables as planfulness, curiosity, and originality the democratically raised children rated high. At the nursery school these youngsters were active, aggressive, fearless, likely to be leaders, somewhat cruel, non-conformist, and disobedient (Baldwin, 1948). Although strict control in the home tended to reduce disobedience, quarrelsomeness, and negativism; it also decreased fearlessness, planfulness, tenacity, and aggressiveness. Taken together, these qualities seemed to described a well-behaved child but one subject to constricted personality.

Perhaps autonomy is not too different from acceptance in influencing child behaviour. Both recognize the individuality of the child. Democracy, of course, the environmental condition for autonomy, takes special note of children's need for activity and exploration.

It is apparent from both the Fels data and the Symonds findings that a certain type of home atmosphere may produce both "good" and "bad"—that is, desirable and undesirable—behaviour in the child. Should child psychology ever reach the point at which it could accurately predict the exact behaviours to be expected from any single type of home environment, the kind of child produced would still depend on personal preference and individual value judgment. Some parents prefer a well-behaved child at the price of originality and curiosity. Others would be willing to have a child who is somewhat rebellious and non-conformist but who shows inquisitiveness and inventiveness. Child psychology cannot make these decisions. Individuals must make them on the basis of the kind of society they want.

Finally, there is the question of permissiveness. Perhaps no other word is so misunderstood, so badly abused, and so maligned. Thus becomes difficult to formulate a clear definition of the term. Perhaps permissiveness might be considered as deriving from permit; if so, it implies that permissive parents allow their children to engage in a certain range of behaviours and make certain decisions appropriate in their capabilities. Permissiveness should not be understood to mean that a parent allows a child to do anything the child pleases; this is not permissiveness but license, a laissez-faire approach to child rearing. Once this distinction has been made, the situation becomes more understandable. Complete abdication of parental control and responsibility suggests indifference, neglect, and rejection of the parent role. This is not permissiveness.

The Pattern Study. This study considered permissiveness versus strictness and used the following scales to describe maternal child-rearing practices in this area:

1. High restrictions on play in the house and with furniture.
2. High demands for good table manners.
3. High restrictions on making noise.
4. High demands for being neat and orderly.
5. Severe toilet training.
6. High standards for strict obedience.
7. Strong emphasis on doing well in school.
8. Strict and rejective response to dependency.
9. High use of physical punishment.
10. Severe punishment for aggression toward parents.
11. Low permissiveness for aggression toward parents.
12. Low permissiveness for aggression among siblings.
13. Low permissiveness for aggression to other children.
14. Low permissiveness for nudity or immodesty.
15. Low permissiveness for masturbation.
16. Low permissiveness for sex play with other children.

The moderate interrelation of these scales suggests a consistency in a mother's behaviour with respect to strictness or permissiveness. The authors of the Pattern Study spoke of a particular trait underlying a mother's use of permissive practices. One mother seemed to be fairly consistent in her tolerance of her child's child behaviour—that is, his aggressiveness, his noisiness, his sex impulses—whereas another tended through punitive means to try to put an end to such behaviour.

The autonomy-control dimension in the Schaefer and Bayley (1963) analysis was defined in terms of the following scales: Autonomy, Strictness, Social isolation of the child, Wish to control the child, Instructiveness, Excessive contact, and Fostering dependency.

Although the correlations between this maternal behaviour dimension and child behaviour were neither as significant nor as numerous as with the love-hostility dimension, some interesting relations were identified. At the 9 to 12 year level, autonomy is negatively related to a boy's ratings to friendly, cooperative, interested and exerts effort, suggesting that a closed relation with the mother contributes to certain positive behaviours in boys. An excessive amount of autonomy may well limit the degree of parental influence on the child.

At adolescence high maternal control combined with hostility related to maladjustment in daughters, as defined by a cluster of trait including defiant, hostile, sulky, discontented, and gloomy.

In general, in the Schaefer and Bayley study the autonomy-control dimension showed less consistency over time than the love-hostility one. Several explanations appear plausible. First, the growing in dependence of the child requires that he be granted an increasing amount of autonomy. Second, this dimension may be less a reflection of the basic personality structure of the parent and more a product of his intellectual view of the parent role. And this view undoubtedly is modified in a variety of ways, including the individual's experience as a parent, the changing needs of the child, and changing expert opinion, as well as discussion with friends regarding problems involved in child rearing.

Present Status of Autonomy-Control Dimension. Traditionally couched in democratic-autocratic terms, this dimension has received far more attention than the love-hostility dimension. In part this is because this aspect of child rearing is easier for parents to discuss on an intellectual level, whereas parental acceptance or rejection of a child is a deeply emotional area. Another reason for study of authoritarian approaches to child rearing may be that such approaches are thought to reflect more general authoritarian attitudes, which have broad political overtones. The disproportionate attention given the autonomy-control dimension is particularly interesting in view of the Schaefer and Bayley data described above, which show much greater effect on the child of maternal acceptance or rejection. Shifting trends in child rearing advice by experts have been discussed.

Summary of Parent Behaviour Dimensions. Research attempting to identify the effects on children of various parent characteristics has conceived increasing attention in the last decade. Because of the complex of this area, much remains to be done before we will be able to make precise statements, based on research evidence, regarding the nature of the interrelations. Research has become increasingly sophisticated in terms of methodology, with numerous attempts to conduct carefully controlled investigations in which parents and children are observed in the laboratory in standard situations (Bell, 1964). Several points emerge from an examination of current research in this general area.

1. No longer it is possible to speak of the effect of parents on their children. The sex of the parent and the sex of the child must be specified. For example, a complicated study of mother-child interaction (Hatfield, Ferguson, and Alpert, 1967) found that mothers reward aggressiveness in their sons but not in their daughters, while the reverse is true for dependency. In an interesting study (Rothbart and Maccoby, 1966) in which parents gave their immediate reactions to taped statements made by a four-year old, fathers showed greater permissiveness toward girls than boys for both dependency and aggression while mothers showed greater permissiveness toward boys. Bronfenbrenner (1961) has argued that there is a risk of oversocialization in girls because they receive a combination of high affection and love-oriented discipline. Boys receiving less affection and more physical punishment (which is less effective than love-oriented discipline in inhibiting behaviour) may be undersocialized. Bronfenbrenner maintains that an optimal balance between affection and control is different for boys and girls.

2. The effect of certain parent behaviours and attitudes may depend soon the age of the child. Encouragement or acceptance of dependency, for example, may be less harmful at one age (preschool) than at another (adolescence). Schaefer and Bayley (1963) found the maternal dimension of love-hostility to be significantly correlated with sons' behaviour up to the age of 12 years, but not thereafter, whereas the reverse was true of the autonomy-control dimension. In their report of longitudinal data from the Fels research, Kagan and Moss (1962) found that early maternal restrictiveness has a long-term effect in inhibiting behaviour. Restrictiveness later, when the child is better able to judge the inappropriateness of this restrictiveness, is likely to generate hostility.

3. It has become apparent that it is not fruitful to attempt to establish relation between specific parent characteristics and specific child characteristics. Parent variables do not operate in isolation but in combination, so that effects upon the child can be predicted only by considering the patterning the interaction among the parent dimensions. In a study of child care antecedents of several patterns of preschool children's behaviour, Baumrind (1967) found parents of competent and mature boys and girls to be firm, loving, demanding, and understanding. Parents of children showing disaffiliative behaviour were firm, punitive, and unaffectionate. Further, parent variables that we have thought to be related may not be. Baumrind and Black (1967) found firm, demanding behaviour on the part of the parent not to be associated with punitiveness or lack of warmth. Undoubtedly there are a great many combinations and permutations of parent behaviour.
4. Any particular type of home atmosphere gives rise to both desirable and undesirable child characteristics. Fearless, curious, and planful as children may be from homes in which a psychological climate of democracy and autonomy prevails, they are also inclined toward cruelty, rebellion, and non-conformity. On the other hand, the well-behaved child of a home characterized by strict control may show signs of a constricted personality.
5. In the past much of parent-child research has been concerned with the development of social-emotional behaviours in the child. Increased attention is being paid currently to parental antecedents of cognitive development and cognitive abilities in children. Although some of the parent dimensions examined in this area deal with the emotional relations between parent and child, most are directly related to intellectual stimulation of the child, such as amount of time spent reading to the child (Bing, 1963), the level (quality) of the mother's communication with the child (Hess and Shipman, 1965), and parental expectations of the child (Wolf, 1964). Freeberg and Payne (1967) have constructed a questionnaire to assess parental practices that previous research has shown to influence the child's cognitive development. Six factors emerged from a factor

analysis of the responses to the questionnaire of a large group of parents of preschool children: Willingness to devote time to the child, Parental guidance, Parental aspiration for achievement, Rejection versus Acceptance of the child's behaviour, Provisions for the child's intellectual needs, Dependence upon external resources (toys, nursery school at-tendance).

6. The role of the father in affecting the child is receiving increased recognition (Nash, 1965). Although American society is considered a matricentric one, it is apparent that the father influences the children directly, and indirectly through the mother. The concept of identification, to be discussed shortly, has drawn attention to the importance of the father in affecting a boy's development. For example, the delinquent boy has been shown to hold strong feelings of parental rejection and neglect (Medinnus, 1965b). Since in our culture the role of the father in the family structure is less clearly defined than the maternal role, one might speculate that there are wider differences among fathers than among mothers in their parent behaviour, and that the way in which the father assumes the role more clearly reflects his personality needs than the mother's behaviour reflects her personality needs.

Patterns of Parental Behaviour. Although each pair of parents has its won individuality, the behaviour of parents in general towards their offspring may be classified roughly into eight types, based upon different combinations of three main variables. The first of these is the degree to which the parents accept the child. They may reject him, accept him, or be causal or indifferent toward him. The second variable concerns the extent of their indulgence and varies from subservience to his every whim to a non-chalant indifference to his needs. The third is the pattern of authority within the family, which may vary from an autocratic issuing of commands by the parents to a family democracy in which everyone's vote is of equal value in theory there could be many possible combinations of these three variables, but actually there are only eight frequent configurations. These will be described briefly.

1. Actively rejectant parents are consistently hostile, unaffectionate, disapproving critical, and distant. They seek actively to dominate the child by means of autocratic

commands. Warm, social, trusting relations are missing. The home is full of tension and conflict, and there is a feeling of resentment on both sides. These parents dislike children, have no understanding of them, and rule them in a dictatorial manner. They are not intentionally cruel and they do not physically mistreat their offspring. They are cold, unsympathetic, and irritable toward those who are to them mainly a nuisance.

2. Non-chalent, rejectant parents have the same basic dislike for and indifference toward the child, but instead of continually nagging at him, they are merely indifferent to what he does, as long as he does not bother them. They ignore him as completely as possible and maintain only the slightest-contact with him. When, however, the child does get in their way, they become autocratic and hostile, so as to get the point at issue, settled quickly and with as little inconvenience to themselves as possible.

3. Casually autocratic parents neither accept the children with understanding nor reject them with resentment. Some are more consistently autocratic than others. All of them believe that a parent's authority is definitely above the desires of a child, but some of them are autocratic on principle, all day and every day, on matters large or small, whereas others try to maintain a friendly atmosphere, but resort to commands on the important matters, merely from expediency. These autocratic—by expedience parent's have no theories about child training, so they react to each situation as it arises. They are likely to have no fixed policy about anything, and their home is usually on the change side, with the children having a good deal of freedom and a moderate degree of attention, but meeting an autocratic handling if an issue is important enough.

4. Casually indulgent parents are mildly indulgent and in general tolerant, but rather haphazard. They maintain a fairly pleasant atmosphere in the home and they often let the child do as he pleases, provided he does not bother them too much. They do not go out of their way to be indulgent, but they find that giving in is easier than resisting. They take their children easily, have no rigid standards for them, have no fixed policy about handling them, are often diverted

from punishing them, and are inclined to baby them at times, although not consistently.

5. Acceptant-indulgent parents show a deep emotional attachment to the child, they are unduly anxious about him, they protect and baby him, they identify them-selves so completely with him that they try to live their own lives over in his. They almost smother him with demonstrations of affection, and they put themselves to endless inconvenience in order to keep him happy. They do not, however, admit him as an equal who helps them make decisions. Their attachment to him is definitely neurotic and is so close that they cannot be objective about him or his problems. These parents have, however, definite standards for their child's behaviour, although their method of procedure consists in leading him gently through their love for him rather than in coercing him.

6. Acceptant-casual-indulgent parents are sometimes just as indulgent as those in the above groups—although usually they are less extreme—but their indulgence is based on impulse, and they do not identify themselves with their child. They let junior have almost unrestrained freedom, and they submit to a good deal of disobedience and bad manners on his part. They admit their child's shortcomings, but they think freedom is the best way to let him develop his capacities, even though it may be trying at times. Because they are basically casual in their relationship, they do not mother their child with affection, or seek to overprotect him, or try to make him conform to an ideal. They just let him run wild most of the time and give into him when conflict arises, because it seems to them easier than opposition.

7. Acceptant-indulgent-democratic parents are basically indulgent and believe in treating children as their own equals in a family democracy. The children are allowed to criticize their parents, to express their own views, and to make decisions on most minor and some major issues. They are treated on the surface as if they were adults, but they are also subject to a good deal of parental pressure that is applied indirectly via the close bond between parent and child. The parents use democratic practices as a means of

making their child into the ideal companion they want him to be. The home is child-centred and rests upon a neurotic degree of contact between parent and child, and a neurotic identification of the former with the latter.

8. Acceptant-democratic parents are emotionally mature people who believe in the participation of children in family decisions and the independence of the child as an individual. Some parents of this type purposely repress expressions of affection and try to be objectively scientific in their treatment of their children. They are so afraid of influencing him too much that they often do not help him, even when he needs their aid to resolve a conflict. They make little or no effort to protect him from dangers of any kind. The more "scientific" parents do not act impulsively, but think matters over in view of basic educational principles and try to be rational. The child is respected as an individual, is encouraged to voice his opinions, is often consulted, and his decisions are allowed to stand without adult coercion. Children in such families often call their parents by their first names, an outward evidence of complete democracy. Parents and children meet on a companionable intellectual ground, but there is little overt affection between them. The child has his own place in the family council, and his desires are given whatever weight seems just in relation to the needs and wishes of the remaining members of the group.

Effects of Parental Attitudes upon Children. A careful and experienced observer can make a shrewd guess about a child's parents from noticing his behaviour when he is away from them, because the child reflects to some extent at least the environment in which he has lived and the treatment he has received. It should be understood, however, that there are individual variations in the reaction of children and adolescents to their homes and that the following remarks apply only in general when one summarizes results from a large number of cases.

Thus the child who has been actively rejected by his parents is passive toward authority, docile, outwardly decorous--since, only by such behaviour can he escape their nagging and punishment--but he is also hostile, withdrawn, fearful, frustrated, insecure, stubborn, and passively resistant. He is hostile in response to his parents hostility, withdrawn because his contacts have been reduced to a minimum, fearful with good reason, but stubborn and resistive, since only thus can he achieve a small assertion of his ego, a slight retaliation of hostility, and an inactive expression of resentment. In one interesting study of twenty-six children who had dominating parents, fifteen of the children were passive, submissive and dependent, six were rebellious and resentful, and five were passively resistant.

The child of non-chalant, rejectant parents shows a different picture. He does not have to fight against hostility but against indifference. He is a type of neglected child. There is so little interaction between him and his parents that he can get their attention only by misbehaving. He has a moderate degree of independence, thrust upon him by parental refusal to help him. He makes desperate attempts to get attention, to arouse affection, and to achieve status. He soon discovers that he can obtain from age-mates the satisfactions that his parents deny him, and from then on he is likely to be in open conflict with his home.

Children whose parents maintain a neutral attitude but are at the same time autocratic in discipline are likely either to be nervous, timid and compliant in their efforts to win recognition, or else to be aggressive and rebellious in order to assert their independence and individually. If, in addition, the autocratic handling alternates with indifference--as is the case if treatment is based upon expediency and impulse--the children learn to be sly, to wriggle out of difficulties, to test the limits to which they can go, to bend temporarily before the storm, to delay requests until mother is in an amiable mood, and generally to circumvent a discipline that is of an uncertain and varying nature. If the casual parent is indulgent rather than autocratic, the less assertive child reacts by feeling insecure and anxious, by showing a tendency to be withdrawn when among other children, and by clinging silently to the fringe of groups without trying to take an active role. The aggressive child reacts to the same situation by running wild, by being destructive, and by thrusting himself into groups. Children of indifferent parents thus tend either to resign themselves to receiving little attention or else to become determined attention-getters.

The children of indulgent parents are likely to feel secure, protected, and comfortable. They soon learn to give an outer conformance to parental desires, at the same time getting their own way by being loving, cute, wheedling, disappointed, hurt, or amusing, as the occasion demands. Behind the façade of compliance and close attachment, however, they are domineering, self-centred, selfish, and determined to do as they please. Because they feel absolutely secure, they become smug, self-confident, somewhat self-righteous, and certain of their power over others. When they go to school, however, they discover that their age-mates are not so easily handled, and these overprotected children are usually unpopular. If they are smug enough to resist the shock, they become more aloof from others than before and more firmly entrenched in their own superiority. Success in meeting parental pressure intensifies the complacency of the accepted child into a precocity of mind, a maturity of outlook, a cocksureness of attitude, and an absolute belief in his own powers that makes him thoroughly obnoxious to everyone but his parents. Since, however, "democratic" parents tend to withhold open demonstrations of affection towards a child–lest they overprotect him–he is inevitably caught in a conflict: those who approve of him give him little warmth, and those from whom he might get affection either dislike or despise him. A vigorous child makes violent attempts to break out of his isolation. Since his democratic home treatment has taught him that he need fear no one, he is uninhibited, aggressive, and confident. As he grows older and develops understanding, his desire to be popular may led him to try a more friendly means of approach. An extreme of democratic treatment may thus set up undesirable reactions.

Parents who are acceptant, moderately indulgent, democratic and warmly affectionate have a home that is as near to satisfaction as can be expected and their children are generally well balanced, secure, and happy. They may, however, be a little too comfortable within the family circle and reluctant to leave it, either actually or emotionally. They are sometimes too much exposed to pressure from siblings because their parents will not step in and protect them from aggression. Those who can come up to expectations, protect themselves, and adjust their desires to those of other people emerge as successes from this type of home.

In another investigation children of demanding parents were found to score high in intelligence, reading, and general achievement in school. Children of overanxious parents were equally high in intelligence, but their school achievements were far lower. Children of unconcerned and indifferent parents scored low on all tests. It would seem that even scores on objective tests taken in school may also reflect parental pressures–presumably through the amount of stimulation and orientation towards success in school.

Teachers in general tend to prefer as pupils those youngsters who come from homes in which the parents are dominant to those who come from homes in which the parents are submissive to their children's demands. Since teachers have twenty-five to forty children in a class, one can see the reason for this preference. The child with dominating parents is usually courteous, obedient, interested in school, modest, generous, responsible, docile, attentive, loyal, and careful. He accepts authority, keeps his desk in order, is careful of his clothes, has good manners, does not talk back when reproved, puts things back where he found them. Children from homes with submissive parents are rated by their teachers as being disobedient, irresponsible, disorderly, lazy, selfish, stubborn, sulky, aggressive, self-confident, talkative, independent, and antagonistic. They defy authority, are fussy about their food, lack interest in school, have bad manners, are often tardy, express themselves well and fluently, get on with their age-mates, and are general classroom nuisances. It should be noted that the two groups of children show both virtues and faults. One child is pleasant for a teacher to have around, but lacks initiative; he depends upon authority, he is hesitant in speech, and he has a better adjustment to older people than to his age-mates. The other child has the faults of irresponsibility, selfishness, and disobedience, but the virtues of independence, initiative, and fluent self-expression.

Individual differences such as these can be of considerable importance in the earliest mother-child relationships. It is well-known, for example, that mothers react quite differently to the varying characteristics of their different children. Most babies seems of and easy to cuddle, but some seem stiff when they are held, from the very beginning. Others feel like a long of bares. These congenital differences are by no means trivial. Mothers themselves comment spontaneously on the pleasure they get from holding a "cuddly baby," and their disappointment that a stiff baby gives them. Perhaps we need to add to the old concepts of accepting and rejecting mothers the newer ones of accepting and rejecting babies.

While an active and sensitive mother may be continually disappointed by a slow-moving, uncreative baby, a phlegmatic mother may find an active, energetic baby disturbing to her, and a sensitive baby quite unintelligible. Greedy energetic rooters and feeders actually frighten some mothers; they seem to be attacking, devouring little monsters. To other mothers a greedy, rooting infant seems only an amusing, eager little trencherman. Indifferent, apathetic little feeders seem to frustrate and annoy some mothers, while in other mothers they arouse tender concern.

6

Factors in Parent-Child Relationship

For an understanding of the psychology of parent-child relationships, three topics are significant. These are the child's perception of his parents, the matter of identification, and the question of discipline. We conclude this chapter with a consideration of each of these.

Perception of Parents

As we saw earlier, attempts to link parent attitudes to various child behaviours have not proved fruitful. Sufficient research is now accumulating to indicate that a more profitable approach is to elicit the child's report of his relations with his parents. Perhaps more crucial than the parent's attitudes and behaviours is the child's perception and interpretation of them. This approach is not without problems, however. First, attempts to identify cause-and-effect relations are especially tenuous. Let us say that a poorly adjusted 15 year old perceives his parents in a very unfavourable light. It is just as likely that his present poor adjustment causes him to view all of his interpersonal relations negatively, including his relationship with his parents, as it is that his negative perception of this parents has produced his poor adjustment. Second, the young child is not a very reliable informant, not through any desire to deceive, but through inability to express himself adequately in his early years.

For example, in line with Piaget's notion (1932) that the young child felt that the harsher the punishment the "better" and more efficacious it was, one study (Radke, 1946) found that 74 per cent of preschool children interviewed mentioned spanking as the type of punishment they received, although parents said they used it rarely. In addition, 83 per cent said that spanking was the best punishment when they were naughty. Quite clearly the young child's response to the questions was not related to the actual quality or quantity of the punishment he received, but to his conception of what the most appropriate punishment was. Yet although the young child is not a very reliable informant. There is some evident for relating a child's perception of his parents. The sickly one: appears to enjoy illness and the family attention that sickness demands. Role taken by any child in the family.

The spoiled one: expects and secures much attention, highly dependent and accustomed to extra privileges. Role is frequently assumed by the youngest child in the family.

Children's Perceptions of and Attitudes Toward their Parents

Children's attitudes toward their parents are an interesting and highly significant consequence of child-rearing antecedents. These attitudes tend to generalize across the social spectrum. The boy who develops resentment and hostility toward his father tends to resent during later life any male who symbolizes authority: the "boss" the policeman, the judge, and so on. Positive emotional attachment to parents seems a necessary antecedent of the acceptance and interiorization of parental attitudes and values. People tend to see their own behaviour tendencies and personality traits in people whom they like (Lundy, Lundy, et. al.). Boys who perceive themselves as being highly similar to their fathers tend to show the most favourable personal and social adjustment (Gray), and less anxiety (Lazowick).

Using a sentence-completion approach ("My father...." "My mother...."), Harris and Tseng found that boys and girls hold generally favourable attitudes toward their parents in this culture. Mothers are regarded somewhat more positively than fathers, however, girls display a pronounced increase in positive attitudes towards fathers as they grow older. Positive types of parental discipline appear to be associated with favourable attitudes toward parents (Nakamura). Children who receive the most warmth and affection from their parents develop the strongest needs for warm personal relations in adult life (Schutz). Boys who perceive their parents as low in love and authority on the Parental Authority-Love Statement test (PALS) are more likely to have delinquency records than boys with high evaluations of their parents in these areas (Williams), Children who perceive their parents as placing reasonable and non-threatening controls on their range of activities (as measured by the Hawkes-Lewis scale of parental control) tend to indicate fewer adjustment difficulties within the home environment (Howkes, Burchinal, and Gardner). All of these research findings seem to support the generalization that socialization and wholesome psychological growth are positively correlated with children's attitudes that their parents are affectionately concerned in a sympathetic manner and are trying to guide them toward fairly specific goals of acceptable behaviour.

Harris and associates have shown in a very definitive fashion that responsibility in children is fostered when they perceive their parents as being constructively oriented toward them. Responsibility in children is definitely not associated with the assignment of home duties. It would appear that responsibility in children is a by-product of favourable personal and emotional relationships between parents and children.

Parent-Child Interactions

It would be most native to conclude that parental variables are always the antecedent conditions in the parent-child relationship. Parents are themselves influenced by the developing behaviour characteristics of their children. The mother who responded warmly and affectionately toward her dependent infant may, or may not, have the same acceptant attitudes toward her offspring during the assertive preschoold years. Methods of punitive control may produce child hostility and aggression which may in turn eventuate in sterner attempts at control–and so on for an ever widening circle of mutual frustration. The mother or father who attempts to curb independence in the preschool child may be disappointed with the dependent attributes of the same child in preadolescence. Parents influence their children, children influence their parents, and these influences may change substantially with the passage of time. It is the interaction effect that makes it so very difficult to identify the variable of child training that are associated with given patterns of child behaviour.

Something of the complexity of the interaction process is illustrated in an experimental study by Isch. Preschool children's responses in a doll-play situation were observed after they had been exposed to aggressive maternal actions, maternal direction, or maternal non-intervention in a prior experimental session. The children whose mothers had been aggressive tended in their doll-play fantasies to depict the child doll or the mother doll as being the recipient of a great deal of aggression.

Rejection of Parent by Child. No one would be surprised if the boy just described rejected his mother; indeed, it is obvious that he has done so. Probably the typical outcome of rejection by the parent is rejection by the child, and this too can have important significance for rebellious, aggressive, delinquent behaviour. In a study bearing directly on this issue, Nye comments that "through intimate and continuous contacts parents become the most crucial agents in the internationalization of the mores. If the child rejected the agent it appears unlikely that the internalization process would be effective". Conditions which may lead to rejection of the parent by the child, he suggests, may include: children of immigrant parents who with to assert their identification with the majority culture; upward-mobile yoursters who are "ashamed" of their parents, having adopted middle class-standards; and parents who deviate in any substantial way from the norms of other parents in the community.

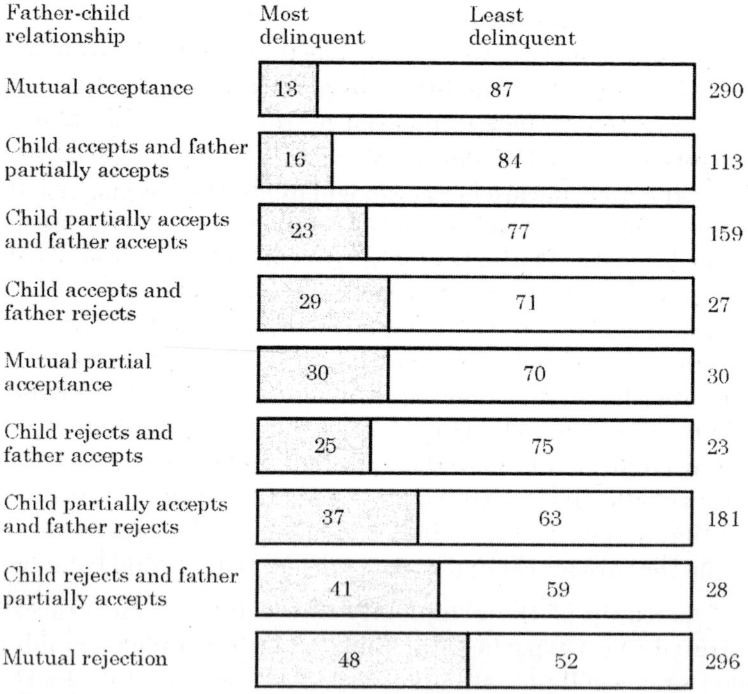

Fig. 1: Father-child rejection and delinquency. Degrees of mutual acceptance and rejection are shown on the left; percentages reporting delinquent behaviour within the bars.

We have indicated above that rejection by the parents is not only a desperate threat to the child, but also a source of frustration and aggression. Such aggression may to some extent be controlled by inhibitory responses, by awareness of social norms. But if the child has also rejected the parents, then he probably rejects the norms which are symbolized by the parent.

Nye's data indicate that, in a group of high school students, rejection by the parent goes with more delinquent acts; and rejection of the parent by the child also goes with such behaviour. Combined, they give a sharply increased frequency of delinquent acts. The proportion of youngsters falling into Nye's "most delinquent" category increases rapidly with degrees of mutual rejection.

Control of Aggression by Punishment. The control of aggression through punishment is especially tricky because of the dual role played by punishment. As has been stressed several times, we conceive of aggressive behaviour as being set off by frustration. When the child acts aggressively, he frequently encounters parental punishment; but this punishment is also a frustration, and hence a stimulus to further aggression. It is easy to recognize here the possibility of a vicious circle. The environment triggers aggression, the parents punish the aggression, and this sets off more aggression. The so-called "incorrigible" delinquent is often if not always an example of such a cycle.

To support this analysis Sears (1950) conducted a careful study of 42 preschool children on whom observational data of home treatment were available. Sears predicted that home punishment would relate differently to overt aggression (attacks on other children in the preschool) and to fantasy aggression (attacks on dolls in a play situation). Severely punished children, would be more frustrated and hence would be tempted to behave aggressively; but the beginning of such an act would set off anxiety, and so overt aggression would be inhibited. In the doll-play situation, no anxiety would be aroused, and hence this group should show maximum aggression. The results nicely confirmed Sears's reasoning. When the children were classified into three groups by severity of home punishment, the most punished group was at maximum in the doll-play aggression, but the middle group was at maximum in the overt aggression measures. The least-punished group was lowest in both respects.

Identification A child learns to be like his parents, a son learn his father's heavy walk, his slow speech, his dislike for drinking, his love of hunting, his attitude toward women, and his moral principles. Some of these things he learns by trial and error; that is, of the many things he does in a day, only a few are like things that his parents do, and when these few things are rewarded by his parents, the child learns them. Something he learns by being taught; for example, a father may carefully explain to his son why he should hunt and should not drink.

But probably most of what the child learns is neither a matter of chance nor a matter of instruction. It is a matter of identification, the process by which a person practices acting like another person without he sees his parent playing?

When a boy accept his father or a girl accept her mother as a model, a favourable condition for personality development is established. When a child rejects the parents of the same sex as a model, some disturbance is almost certain children of immigrant parent, for example, often face difficulties because their parent fail to present them with suitable model.

How closely a child identifies with his parents is depend upon many factors. In the first place a child's inherited drives and temperament may make it difficult for him to identify with either parents. In second place, parents are not the only persons with whom a child identify. He may identify with other relatives, friends, teachers, current heroes, historical or fictional characters etc. The more persons with whom a child identifies the less similar be becomes to any one of them.

Most important of all, however, are the attitudes of the parents toward their child and the method they use in rearing him. Their acceptance or rejection of him, the punishment and reward they use, and their strictness or permissiveness largely determine the degree of his identification with them.

There is a powerful striving on the part of a child to incorporate certain of the parental characteristics into his won personality. Mannerisms, posture, ways of moving, inflections in speech as well as kinds of words used, attitudes toward things, people, and institutions; all these and many more become parts of the child through the central process of identification. One can add to the list and almost infinite variety of types of thing that can be accounted for through this process and provide countless examples of the way in which it operates. But first, our task is to understand the nature of the process itself. What is mean by identification, and how does it operate in the child's life?

Identification is the process by which an individual incorporates certain aspect of someone else's behaviour, attitudes, and characteristics. The terms copying, modeling, and imitating are sometimes used synonymously with identification. However, these connote a conscious process, whereas identification may encompass even more. The discussion of identification in the young child primarily concerns his identification with sex role, that is, the process whereby he develops characteristics similar those of the parent of the same sex. However, numerous other behavioural traits seem to emerge from this process. Aggressive behaviour, behaviour and attitudes towards others, leisure-time pursuits and a host of other characteristics may sprout from the child's identification with another person–usually, in early years, the parents.

Why the need for such a notion as identification? Are not the principles of learning sufficient to explain the reason for the child developing characteristics similar to those of the parent of the same sex. Parental approval should be reward enough for behaviours valued by the parent, and thus encourage their repetition. However, child behaviour seems to go beyond what would be predictable from learning theory. A tremendous amount of learning occurs without any direct teaching as such.

Two types of identification have been described in psychoanalytic literature. Analytic or developmental identification is based on the young child's anxiety concerning the loss of love, usually from the mother, with whom a nurturant, affectionate relationship has been established. The child gains some measure of security by introjecting or incorporating the qualities of the mother. From this point of view one would predict that the warmer and more nurturant the adult figure the stronger the identification.

The second psychoanalytically based type of identification is defensive or aggressive identification. According to the theory, this occurs in the boy at the time of the resolution of the Oedipal conflict. Fearful punishment from the father because of incestuous wishes toward the mother, the boy identifies with the father, adopting his characteristic. While it is apparent that aggressive parents frequently have aggressive children.

'Whiting' has proposed a status envy theory of identification. The degree of identification with another person depends on the extent to which that individual controls desired resources. The parent, for example, may give reward, either social or material; he may withhold it, or he may deprive the child of such reward as he already has. "The more a child envies the status of another with respect to the control of a given resource, the more he will covertly practice that role". In an experiment designed by Bandura, Ross and Ross, children more frequently imitated a model who possessed rewarding power, not with the competitor for the rewards, as a theory of defensive identification might suggest.

At what age does identification begun? No specific age seems identifiable, although it would appear that it could not occur until the child was able to put himself in the place of someone else, as in taking the role of the parent in play, to pretend, to "assume the role of another". Certainly by ages two to three there is evidence for the beginning of such behaviour in the child.

Turning to the literature on sex role, identification Lynn (1961) has hypothesized that marked differences exist between boys and girls in several aspects of the identification process. As he saw it, both sexes in the very early years identify with mother. Later, however, the boy has to shift his identification to the father and to a masculine role. No such shift is required of the girl.

For the girl, of course, although she continues in her identification with her mother, she discovers that the female role is devaluated by society. She thus experiences some difficulty in identifying with the role appropriate to her sex. Moreover, her mother may feel some ambivalence about the female role because of society's downgrading of it. And there is less pressure on her to be girl like in all behaviours than there is far boys to be manly. No punishment attaches to her wearing certain items of male apparel. Nor does tom boyishness in girls incur the stigma of sissified behaviour in boys. Girls may play with boys without censure, but boys are ridiculed for playing with girls.

For these reasons Lynn believed that with increasing age girls became less firmly tied to the female role, whereas boys who successfully make the transition from identifying with their mother to identifying with their father become more fully associated with the male role.

There are types of parent child relationships that encourage an appropriate sex identification. Sears (1953) noted that sons of fathers who were warm, permissive and easygoing tended to behave in a manner appropriate to their sex. In the doll play situation, boys who choose the maternal role came from homes in which the mother, but not the father was high in warmth. In an earlier study, Sears (1951) observed that boys whose father served as the son's model for aggression, it might also indicate that a boy whose father was absent experienced fewer frustrations.

In conclusion, identification clearly serves an important function in the child's life. Gratification (increased security and sense of mastry) derives from behaviour that emulates that of a significant adult, and in practicing the behaviour of an adult, as in doll play, a child learns something of his future adult role and acquires some understanding of it. Although initially children identify with their parents, other adults serve as model later. Moreover, there is never a one-to-one relation between the child's behaviour to imitates. The child is selective and innovative, modifying the imitated behaviour in various ways to produce a novel and individualistic pattern.

Although specific behaviour can be imitated, it seems unlikely that more general and pervasive (and therefore more important) personality characteristics of the adult can be discerned and imitated.

In small and large ways, for better or worse, children are molded by the personality of their parents. Psychoanalysts in particular, guided by their clinical observations of patients in therapy, have emphasized the powerful influence of parental personality.

Discipline. In current thinking, discipline is often equated with guidance. However, discipline might be more appropriately described as the methods used by parents to ensure their child's compliance with that guidance. The socialization process of getting the child to conform to what society expects of him creates conflicts between these social demands and the child's wishes and desires. Thus discipline becomes an inevitable aspect of the parent-child relationship. That discipline may take a vast number of forms and vary widely in the frequency of its use from parent to parent is also true.

What is the functions of discipline? Most obviously, parents use disciplinary methods to obtain conformity to their demands. Discipline also provides the child with cues to behaviour. For maximum effectiveness these cues should apprise the child of what constitutes approved or acceptable behaviour. However, when it takes the form of punishment discipline supplies only the cues to unacceptable behaviour. This leads to a distinction between the short-term and long-term goals of discipline. Whereas the former is conformity to parental demands, the latter is the development of self-control or inner discipline. Some types of discipline are more conducive to accomplishment of the short-term objective, other better suited to achieving the long range goals. Which disciplinary techniques receive the more frequent use? According to Clifford's (1959) study based on records kept by mother over three week period, it was found that there are number of techniques that are used most often by mothers for their 3-9 years old children. These are reason, scold, coax, spank, divert, threaten, ignore, remove child forcibly, isolate, social disapproval. This study also reflect that generally those mothers who were above average in the group in the use of positive sanctions were also above average in ratings on warmth and affection shown to children, on satisfaction with their roles of wife and mother, and on esteem felt for their husband. This would suggest that the use of praise and rewards reflected a mother's satisfactory adjustment to her life situation. Perhaps, then, there may be some relation between a women's adjustment to the mother role and the reasonables of her behaviour in it.

Why is discipline used and when is it most frequent throughout the day? Clearly the most important single reason for discipline is disobedience the child's non-compliance with parental demands. The Clifford study identified the following categories as areas requiring discipline: sibling relationship—that is, quarreling, aggression, interference, eating-refusal to eat, making a mess, having the table during the meal, sleep-refusal to eat, making a mess, leaving the table during the meal, sleep-refusal to go to bed, noise in bed; dressing refusal to get dressed, soiling clothing, changing clothes, activities—

conflict over television, Sunday school, school-preparing to go to school, refusal to go to school, health-medication, general health protection, inappropriate behaviour—irritability, boisterousness, destructiveness, forbidden behaviour, adult interaction—refusing an adult request, interference with adult activity persistent demand of adult attention, home neatness of home, refusal to put things away, social—inappropriate social behaviour, insistence on own rights, interference with activities of others.

Punishment versus Reward. All parent try to control their children. In trying to do so, they may punish him, that is create an unpleasant situation for him after he has done something they do not want him to do, or they may reward him that is, create a pleasant situation after he has done something, they want him to do. These punishment and reward may be *object-oriented*, that is concerned with such tangible matters as the giving or depriving of money, present and privileges and the use of physical punishment.

On the other hand it may be *love-oriented*. That is concerned with such relatively intangible matters as giving or depriving of attention, love and praise.

No discussion of discipline can ignore the effects of discipline on the child. Although discipline may achieve a behavioural goal, it accomplishment may be nullified by the emotional and attitudinal side effects it produces in the child. Several studies have shown a positive correlation between aggressive behaviour in children and severity of discipline in the home. There is little doubt that harsh, arbitrary and inconsistent discipline arouse resentment, hostility and anxiety in the child. From strong discipline a child builds up a store of hostility that he directs towards others. This is borne out by a study conducted by Hoffman (1960). Mothers were rated according to how they coerced the child to change his entire current pattern of behaviour immediately. A significant positive relation was found between a mother's use of what Hoffman called "unqualified power assertion" and the child's hostility towards others, his power assertiveness, and his resistance to the attempts of others to influence him. Thus the conforming, docile child at home may be tiger on the outside.

Strict discipline by parents often leads to prejudiced antidemocratic attitude in the child. Severe and punitive parental treatment awaken hostile and aggressive impulse in the child. Since these impulses can't be directed toward in parent, they are leveled against others who are made into scapegoats and innocent victim. It is true that frequent use of parental discipline sensitizes the child to power relations along a strong-weak or superior-inferior dimensions.

Child Rearing Practices and its Effects on Child's Personality

Child rearing practices is an area of divergent and confusing evidence. There are opinion that, similar child rearing practices lead invariably to similar adult personality. But similar adult character types may be found in societies having different child rearing techniques and that similar child rearing method may lead to different types of adult personality.

Child rearing is not a technical term with precise significance. It refers generally to all the interactions between parents and their children. These interactions include the parents' expression of attitudes, values, interests and beliefs as well as their care taking and training behaviour. Child rearing is a continuous process. Each moment of a child's life that he spends in contact with his parents has some effect on both of his present behaviour and his potentialities for future action.

Child rearing practices can be defined as idea, beliefs and attitudes widely held in a community on how to bring up children. These practices are likely to change as the time advances. Thus the idea prevalent on this subject a hundred years ago, may appear remote and alien to us. However the attitudes of the post generation may retain more of a hold on us than we realise. Ideas we are not conscious of may continue to exert influence on the levels of conceives feelings, which are transmitted from one generation to the other through the process of child rearing itself. This process of child rearing is generally influenced by the characteristic ways of thinking, feeling and acting, prevalent in the cultural group to which the family belongs.

SECTION C
MOTHER AND CHILD RELATIONSHIP

7

Role of Mother in Socialization

What of the mother? Society dictates that she provide physical care for the children-feed them, keep them healthy and, if possible, clean. She must comfort and console them when necessary and in general nurture them and provide emotional support. Long extolled by novelist and bard, the role of mother has been made almost impossible of fulfillment by the ordinary woman.

The young child depends totally on these parents who must be capable of meeting his needs. As the child grows older, the dependency on the parent lessens, so that father and mother must be able to relinquish some of the earlier control. Different behaviours and attitudes are required at different times; this is the price of parenthood. To say that some adults find the parental role more satisfying than others is to belabour the obvious. But how acceptable a woman finds the maternal role may indeed influence how adequately she performs it.

The Nature of Parent-Child Relations

Although all human relationships are unique, those existing between parents and child possess certain characteristics that explain the tremendous and permanent impact of one upon the other. The intimacy and intensity of contact and the everyday interaction and interchange exist in an emotionally charged atmosphere. A child serves a mirror to the parent, who sees reflected there his own childhood, his own unresolved and frequently long-term conflicts, and his own needs and aspirations.

Several studies have looked into the similarity between parent and offspring in their handling of the parental role and into the influence of a person's own childhood and early attitudes toward parents on her own performance as a parent. In a study of four groups of parents—accepting, rejecting, dominating, and submissive–Symonds (1939) of served that the accepting type grew up in homes marked by good adjustment and acceptance. Dominating parents were dominated by their parents, whereas submissive parents enjoyed much freedom in their own childhood. A parent behaved just like his own parents and established a similar relation with his children; he repeated his early experiences in the home. More specifically, Symonds held, parents adopted an attitude toward their children that resembled the attitude taken toward them by the parent of the same sex.

Radke (1946) noted a tendency for parents to use disciplinary techniques similar to those remembered from their own childhood. And in Bronson, Kalten, and Livson's study (1959), mothers were inclined to exercise strong authority in their homes if they remembered their own mothers as having done so. An individual's perception and memory of parental treatment in childhood may have significance for his own behaviour as a parent, it would be useful to have actual information of what happened years go.

Attempting to trace the transmission of authority in the home from one generation to the next, Ingersoll (1948) defined the patterns in terms of leading or controlling the *family activities*. Four main patterns were discerned: *matricentric*–a pattern of authority in which the mother had the greater control; *patricentric*--the father exercised the greater control; *balanced*—fairly equal husband-wife control and *intermediate*—lying midway between balance and control by either husband or wife. The parental backgrounds of second-generation couples were homogramous or heterogamous. In the former, husband and wife were reared in homes having the same prevailing pattern of authority, whether matricentric, patricentric, or balanced. In the heterogamous situation, husband and wife came from homes of opposing authority patterns. Among homogamous marriages, the patterns of parental authority tended to be reproduced. In heterogamous marriages, the patterns were modified to form a balanced compromise. Nevertheless, in all cases, the Ingersoll study found that there were exceptions to the dominant trends.

In a study of the backgrounds of a group of normal children, Harris (1959) noted that what had happened to the mothers "as children was happening to their own children; what happened to their parents was happening to them as parents".

Mother and Child

The kinds of continuity experienced by a mother with her own children affected the adjustment she made to the maternal role. Too rigid an adherence to the past or too much conflict with it created problems of dependability and understanding between mother and her children. Three types of mothers were discerned: traditional mothers, rebellious mother and dependent mother. The *traditional mother* was satisfied with her own mother child tactics and attitude and used them as a reference point in raising her own family. The *rebellious mother* sought to be less controlling than her own mother, with whom she was dissatisfied because of excessive control, strictness and interferences. The children of such mothers tended to rebel against any role interfering with their quest for pleasure Indeed there were some evidence that these mother, was endeavouring to work out their rebellious feelings against their own parent through their children. The third type *dependent mother* was dissatisfied with her own mother because she thought she had not been accorded proper attention, love or interest. Children of such mothers seemed to search for interpersonal warmth.

Not all factors of continuity may operate at the conscious level nor do they necessarily work directly on the child. Moreover, how a woman regards her husband may in subtle way, affect her children's attitude towards him. Thus although parental behaviour may not be inherited in a biological sense through the genes, it may be transmitted through the mechanism of personality.

In typical circumstances, a child's mother is with him throughout at least the early years of his development. She is who make decisions regarding his upbringing and who is more and more responsible for the enforcement of standards of conduct. Sometime, indeed, the mother's role in the upbringing of children can become so intense, that she even resents what she sees as 'interference' by her husband in matter of discipline. Strecker has described what he regards as the ill-effects of the feminization of child-rearing upon boys. Bossard and Boll have drawn attention to the possibility that the behaviour and attitudes of girls may also develop less healthily if their fathers cease to play a considerable role in their upbringing.

Although it is nowadays generally agreed that a child's mother is the most important person in his environment, the precise effects of particular features of maternal care upon a child's social development are imperfectly understood. Far more is known about the results which follow from a loss of maternal care-maternal deprivation. There have, indeed, been few successful attempts even to define the types of maternal behaviour which exist, through the use of the statistical technique known as 'factor analysis' has enabled such writers as Sears, Maccoby and Lavin to identify some of the Seadings under which maternal behaviour might usefully and realistically be studied. The factors which they identified relate to a mother's permissiveness or restrictiveness, the general family adjustment, the warmth of her relationship with her child, the child training orientation, her views regarding aggressiveness and punishment, her perception of her husband, her attitude towards the child's physical well-being and the pattern of control she exercises over her child. The statistical identification of each of these eight factors enables us the better to understand the inter-relatedness of particular types of maternal behaviour.

One must take care not to assume, just because such investigations as that of Sears, Maccoby and Levin, reveal a statistical relationship between certain types of maternal behaviour, that any given mother will be consistently permissive or restrictive, consistently warm or cool towards her child and so on. Nor does it necessarily follow that certain types of maternal behaviour, even if reasonably consistent, will always result in the anticipated behaviour or attitudes on the part of the child. The importance of this caution is indicated by a study carried out by Sewell, Musser and Harris (1955) who failed to find any consistency from one area of child rearing to another. Some parents, for example, claimed on the one hand to encourage early independence in their children and on the other to engage in much activity with them. Nevertheless, it is useful to be offered some 'categories' of maternal behaviour and not to have to regard each facet of a mother's interaction with her children in isolation from every other.

Patterns of Authority

Since there are two parents, there can be only three general patterns, although subdivisions within each are possible. Authority may be in the hands of the father or of the mother, or it may be equally divided between them. In the investigation, by Ingerso 11, an intensive analysis of 37 homes, five main types were recognized: the mother-controlled, the mother led, the father control, the father led and equal control, of which there were four subtype. These are :

A.	Mother-controlled, autocratic	4
B.	Mother-led, democratic	5
C.	Balanced	
	1. Equalitarian, democratic	7
	2. Equalitarian indulgent	2
	3. Equalitarian neglectful	2
	4. Equalitarian inconsistent	2
D .	Father led	
	1. Autocratic	2
	2. Democratic	7
E.	Father-controlled, autocratic	3
	1. Pseudo father-controlled	3

Brief descriptions are:

1. The mother-controlled family contains the passive husband so frequently referred to in discussions of the (supposedly) increasing number of matriarchal families. Characteristically, this husband is indifferent to his wife, he looks upon child-rearing as a women's responsibility and he prefers men's companionship and masculine activities to the company of his wife and children. His wife controls the home and family, first because he apparently delegate that responsibility to her while he earns the living or not, as the case may be and second, because she apparently feels some compulsions, or need to assume the dominant role in family control.

2. In the mother-led family the decisions regarding family policy are jointly made but with the wife assuming the lead she is apparently recognized as the stronger, more capable person of the partnership and her leadership appears to be accepted without resentment on the husband part. There is warmth and affection in the family. The husband tends to be secure emotionally and thus to need more affection than his wife.

3. The partners in a democratic marriage have worked out a complex but unified system of authority based on a common philosophy of family life. This philosophy becomes so much a part of their thinking about the family that one partner

often knows without asking what the other's reaction will be to a proposal. Therefore, authority over the various sphere of home and family life in the equalitarian family, for the most part, becomes a joint activity except in areas when one partner is felt more capable of judgment than the other.

4. In the father led-family the father is definitely the head of the family. Although family is apparently unified and arrived at through agreement of both husband and wife, the husband's leadership is more often followed in family planning and decision making than is his wife, although she manages the home and family, including the rearing of the children, to conform with joint family policy and with his expectations. His authority supports her discipline consistently and firmly. Occasionally he may lay down the law or become autocratic in his control but for the most part he is the respected and loved democratic husband and father.

5. In the father controlled family the husband expects to be absolute master of the house. He sets the family policy and makes the major plans and decisions. His unpredictable temper is his keenest and most feared weapon in maintaining control over his wife and children. He is likely to set standards of behaviour for his children that are beyond their abilities to achieve. He expects his wife to see that his children are bought up to suit him. He criticizes her when they are not a credit to him. He takes the attitude that he is a superior being and wife is inferior. He prefers men's company and masculine sport and activities. Wife and children are almost compelled to share his interests. Conflicts between him and his wife are often unresolved. There is little or no affection expressed toward each other by either of the partners.

The reaction of the children could be prophesied from the family situation. In the mother-controlled homes they are erratic in maturing, some showing parental "fixations," some rebelling against or withdrawing from parental authority and others escaping from the family group as rapidly as possible. Generally speaking, these children show symptoms of disturbance in personality adjustment.

When the mother is a leader but not a despot the children appear to be more attached to her than to their father. They respect, admire and love her, but like their father also. The children confide in their parents. The general family atmosphere is warm and acceptant. The husband and wife who are equalitarian in their relationship to each other tend to guide their children from early dependency to a place of responsibility and individuality in the family group. These children learn how to cooperate, how to share in the family crises, how to contribute to family planning and how to use so-called democratic techniques in group living. They are encouraged to become self-reliant and independent of parents as they approach adulthood children in a father-led home often feel that their punishment is unfair and unnecessarily strict. The authoritarian father loses the confidence of his children, especially during middle childhood and early adolescent. They may rebel, withdraw or become overdependent. They may tie them to himself by his overprotection or force them to premature independence in order to escape his domination. Since the father in the father-controlled home is autocratic, erractic and unpredictable, he is not loved. He sets up adult standard for his children that suit his ends and represses them into docile submission. He discourages adolescent independence and is disapproving of his children's association with the opposite sex. He apparently hopes to run their lives as long as he can.

Importance of Mother's Personality

Psychologists and anthropologists have shown the relationship between various patterns of behaviour in children and child rearing practices of mothers. The child constantly comes in contact with mother from its birth. Nothing nourishes the child's mind more than the mother's love and acceptance. In dealing with the child, mother weaves a pattern of child rearing which is marked by the wrap and weft of cultural setting. Therefore, mother's role is very important in upbringing of her child.

Child rearing philosophies, like fashions, seem to go in cycles (Kephart, 1972). No one method can be considered "Best" for all children. Children are individuals. What works for one child may not work for another. One child may need very firm guidance, another may be devastated by mild reprimand. It is necessary, therefore, for parents to learn to be flexible, to adjust their philosophies and methods to the individual child. What is important is the quality of the parent-child relationship, total climate of the family setting rather than the particular philosophy of child rearing that is followed. A consistent research finding is that children of most ages choose the mother as the preferred parent. Mother is generally considered to be friendlier more accepting and more nurturing. Radian also concluded that maternal wramth may have far reaching effects on children.

Coleman Kris and Provence (In Jersild, 1969) pointed out that regardless of a mother's personality or character structure, she is likely to deal differently with a rugged baby than with a fragile and sensitive baby. This study gives greater importance to children's characteristic than mother's personality or characteristic.

Mother's Role in Child Rearing

In terms of time spent with the child, the mother has more opportunities than the father to the influence her offspring's psychological growth and behaviour. Tradition also favours the mother's influence, since child rearing in our culture is generally recognized as primarily the mother's privilege and responsibility.

What are the effect of this predominantly matriarchal control of children's behaviour? How do modern mothers typically approach their child guidance responsibilities. How do children respond to maternal guidance? One of the effect of this extreme degree of maternal attention is that both boys and girls prefer their mother's presence when they are in personal social difficulties. Although there are many individual differences among children, most boys and girls would like to resemble the parent of the same sex but rate the parents of the opposite sex somewhat higher in genial disposition and character. The need for mother's presence during psychological conflicts appear to raise no special problem in the rearing of girls. However, this response in boys has been viewed by some psychologists and psychiatrists with increasing alarm. Are we rearing generation of 'Mama's boys? What does it do to boys to be reared principally by their mothers, and then experience some eight years of instruction under a majority of female teachers? Are these guidance practices consistent with the social roles that boys are supposed to assume during adult life in our culture? There are no unambiguous answers to these questions, since maternal practices in childrearing are extremely varied.

Maternal Practices and the Child's Behaviour

The acquisition and continued practice of a given response are determined by a variety of familial and extra-familial experiences. The attempt to master intellectual skills, for example is number doubt influenced by a no. of factors, including success experience in school, peer and teacher recognition for intellectual competence, character of the role models available to the child, and parented encouragement and reward.

Theory and research have acknowledged the profound importance of the mother as a determinant of the child's behaviour. She inculcates goals and values and, by so doing, act as a mediator of her culture. She influences the child's development through the relationship she establishes with him. For example, be cold and detached or so lavish with affection that the child is infantilized; she may allow him autonomy or control his every activity. Finally, she acts as a model, and the ways in which she is perceived by the child determine many of the behavioural choices he will make.

The mother has been the family member must scrutinized in studies of child development. This choice has been jointly determined by the theoretical importance ascribed to her role and her availability and cooperative attitude toward research. This is not to deny the relevance of the father, more recently, investigators have included assessment of him in children of developmental processes. However, our date was gathered at the turn when mother was focus of inquiry. Four type of maternal practices are evaluated (1) maternal protection (2) maternal restrictiveness (3) maternal hostility and criticism and (4) maternal acceleration of the child's developmental progress.

Maternal Protection. This variable assessed the degree to which the mother rewarded dependent overtures and prevented independent development. Major sources of data included. (a) unsolicited and unnecessary nurturance of child (b) consistent reward of the child's requests for help and assistance (c) encouraging the child to become dependent on her (d) over concern when the child was ill or in danger.

Maternal Restrictiveness

This variable assessed the mother's attempts to force the child, through punishment or threat, to adhere to her standards, the degree to which she punished deviations (which were not necessarily a social) from her standards. In essence, this variable measured the mother's rigidity with respect to the child's development of idiosyncratic interests. Major source of data included punishment for any deviation from maternal standard and channeling the child into activities the mother valued, without regard for his abilities or interests.

Maternai Hostility

This variable assessed maternal criticism of the child and hostile statements expressed directly to the child or to other adult. It reflected both expression of dissatisfaction with the child as well as active rejection. Major sources of data included (a) criticism of the child's behaviour and derogation of his skill and personality (b) statements of preference for another sibling and (c) active rejection or neglect.

Maternal Acceleration

This variable assess the degree to which mother showed excessive concern for her child's cognitive and motor development and her tendency to place excessive expectation on his level of achievement. It reflected the degree to which the mother pushed the child's developmental level beyond his abilities and her concern with his achievement level.

The development of dependent tendencies is generally assumed to be a function of parental reward for his behaviour as well as severe restrictions on the child's independent, problem-solving activity. Further support for the relevance of these variables comes from another study of Schaefer (1959), using Guttman's circomplex model, where he analyzed rating of maternal behaviours made by a variety of investigators. Schaefer concluded that the same two orthogonal continua emerged from his many analyses. He labeled them as love versus hostility and autonomy versus control. Maternal protection, restriction, and hostility are intimately related to the variables defining Schaefer's two dimensions.

Baldwin, Kalhorn and Breese as well as Crandall and Preston (1955), identified similar clusters of maternal variables from an analysis of the Fels Parent Behaviour Rating Scales.

However, there is some evidence that the overprotective mother has an unusually deleterious effect on her son's social and emotional growth. The situation could be partially corrected by fathers' assuming a more active role in the rearing of their sons.

Bearing of Mother's Personality on Child's Behaviour

We may briefly consider here some studies which have tried to demonstrate how mother's personality affect the development of the child and his personality. Roff (1950) suggested that the direct measurement of a personality traits in the parents may be the most effective single predictor of that trait in the offspring.

Inghan and other and Nicholas (in Hurlock, 1956) have shown that children with psychopathic personalities are generally found to have parents with similar personality patterns.

Rosenzwing and Ishaw focussed their attention on interpersonal situation between mother and son by using T.A.T. protocols. These writer have mentioned that exploring the mother's personality structure as a source of trend in the son's personality trend is a desirable and feasible type of analysis. They further suggested the need of new research design which call demonstration definite sequence of casuality.

According to the Daw-at-alr the attitude of parents towards their children is markedly influenced by their own personality pattern and their attitudes toward children as individuals, even when a general culture attitude towards children exists. This study stress the need for studying mother personality. Hart carried out a study of authoritarianism in mothers and their pre-school children. The study is in agreement with other study which show similarity between the authoritarianism of mothers and that of their children.

A number of studies have stressed that importance of adjustment in life of parents in the problematic behaviour in children. Phillips observes that a child who gets poor parental model for imitation is likely to develop problematic behaviour similar to that of his parents. According to Field unhappy adjustment in marriages gives rise to the problem behaviour in children.

The role of parents, family society and culture in the development of child's personality is emphasized by sears et al. Within the home the mother plays the Central role in the molding process because she has a more and closer contacts with the child than any other family member. Schocfer and Bayley pointed out that warmth and affection towards the offspring are Central to the maternal role. It is not surprising to find just these maternal characteristic to be stable from infacy through the preadolescence of the child. Much of child's earliest development reflects the mother's personality. Thus scars places a focal emphasis on mother and her personality in the personality development of her child. Child is visible product of parental child-rearing effort.

The present study has included all important child rearing practices and personality characteristics of child in relation to its marital adjustment. Attempt at linking child's and parents characteristics are too numerous to be included in this brief introduction. However result of some of them indicate that mothers, probably have greater psychological involvement than father in child rearing. Some investigators have maintained that mothers are better informed by virtue of their relatively longer association with their children and are more available for furnishing information and above all, they are better reporters as some investigations have shown. This view has helped the present investigator to focus attention on child rearing practices and personality traits of children in relation to mother's marital life.

Pattern of Mothering

It will be more instructive if we turn an attention from general theoretical questions to studies of specific behaviour of parents toward their children. Implicit in our treatment of personality development has been the notion that the child acquires percepts, positive and negative valences, habits and a self-image from his interactions with his environment. This view can be validated only if we can show consistent relations between parental treatment and child personality.

The best procedure for such investigations would be to observe the parent child interaction, then wait a year or so and gather data on the child's personality. Longitudinal studies of this kind are being conducted, but the returns are not yet clear enough to interpret. A second method is to gather dependently data on the parent's behaviour and the child's personality. This technique encounters the difficulty that some of the parental behaviour may be determined by the child, nor the other way round. A third method, used in early researches and still useful within limits, involves asking the child or adolescent to describe how his parents treated him, and correlate these reports with personality data. The obvious weakness here is that one do not get 'real' parent behaviour, but only the child's view of it, which may be quite misleading.

A first task, in this frame of reference, is to find the dimensions along which parental behaviour differs. A good beginning in this respect is the work of Brody on Pattern of Mothering. She studied very intensively 32 young mothers with their babies, paying particular attention to methods of feeding, cleaning, handling, offering objects to and speaking to the baby. She found that she could divide the mothers into 'type' one was composed of the mothers who were most sensitive to the infant's needs, most consistent in their treatment and most attentive. The other group deviated from this ideal in being insensitive to the child, inconsistent in behaviour, overactive overattentive, or excessively sensitive (Brody objects to classifying her mothers as 'accepting' or 'rejecting' because such terms imply more than the behaviour she observed). There were also important differences among the groups in their attitude toward motherhood, toward methods of child care, and so on.

Brody notes that we cannot identify the affectionate relationship with the mothering relationship. Several mothers were obviously very fond of the babies, yet succeeded in disrupting the normal rhythm of the child's activity by failing to observe or perhaps by lack of understanding. Brody's data do not give us much information about specific effects on the children. To the extent that ratings are available, they seem to indicate that mothers could deviate from an optimal way of treating the child in the direction of doing either too much or too little and either was likely to be somewhat detrimental.

The Sears study less intensive, but covering much more behaviour and more cases in the study by Sears, Maccoby and Levin (1957), which deals with child rearing practices of over three hundred young mothers in the Boston area. Their interview schedule included questions about child care, sex and modesty training, restrictions on aggression by the child, handling the child's dependency attitudes, use of physical punishment and threats to withdraw love. At this list shows, the mother is constantly interacting with the child during his first few years, providing sensory stimuli and also meanings, as he grow older, which will become merged in his perception of her.

A factor analysis of the ratings made by interviewers in the homes led to the conclusion that specific situations (considered in the tool) had less significance than the mother's personality and attitudes toward the child. Mothers who demanded neat table manners were severe in toilet training and were restrictive with regard to active play in the house. Thus, one concludes the molding of the child's personality is not limited to one particular biological function (or even stages, as Freud suggested), but depends on the mother's attitudes in general, and upon other concepts of family life. The significant dimensions along which mothers differed one from another were as follows.

1. **Permissiveness-Strictness.** Mothers varied from highly permissive to quite restrictive, and this attitude came out in a wide variety of behaviours. It played a substantial role in determining certain aspects of the child's personality. Obviously it determined the frequency of frustrations, and conversely, of gratifications, in a number of areas.

2. **General Family Adjustment.** Mothers who perceived themselves as worthwhile, who gave high evaluations of their husbands, and who were satisfied with the current life situations could be said to process high morale in their another role. Such a home situation obviously gives the child a chance to develop generalized images of adult human being as happy, secure and friendly home with low mother morale presents images quite different from these. Another studies show, many of the child's traits can be related quite directly to this aspect of home life.

3. **Warmth of Mother-Child Relationship.** A mother may care for her child with statistical precision, but without communicating affection and warmth. The warm-cold dimension was revealed in time spent playing with the child, affectionate interactions with him, use of praise, etc. This factor seems to have particular importance in determining how the child will perceive other actions of the mother; e.g., use of physical punishment by a "warm" mother have desirable social effects, whereas, such punishment by "a cold" mother leads to antisocial aggression.

Effect of these Variations. What are the effects of variations in these aspects of parental treatment of the child? We do not as yet have follow-up studies which will give satisfactory answers. In the Sears data a member of relationship are reported of which few are mention below:

1. **Strictness and Warmth.** A cross-comparison with the dimension of warmth of affection, however, revealed that severity is upsetting primarily where the mother is relatively cold toward the child. Thus it is not single aspect, but a complex of aspects, which determines how the child will respond.

2. **Rejection and Dependency.** Dependency as a trait in small children is an important facet of personality. The Sears data indicate that if the mother seems to reject the child, he is more dependent than if he feels accepted. Punishment for aggression toward the parents produces more dependency, although punishment in general is not related. The Sears data seem to point toward an anxiety about helplessness, which is intensified by continued

separation from or rebuff by the mother, and reduced when the mother gives affection and encouragement.

3. **Rejection and Aggression.** Sears found that the effect of permissive or severe attitudes toward aggressive behaviour differed depending on the warmth of the mother's affection. Generally, severe attitude and punishment increased the level of the child's aggressive behaviour, and this effect was exaggerated if the mother was relatively cold toward the child.

Parent-Child Interaction and Birth Order

For both birth order and sibling position the literature and findings are as contradictory as they are voluminous. This results, of course, from the importance of a child "psychological position" in the family, which may bear no relation whatsoever to his order of birth.

While parents play the major role in influencing the child in a variety of areas (sex-role learning, attitudes, interests) but perceived parental favouritism toward a sibling and the general interaction and relationship among siblings are important factors to be considered in understanding and interpreting an individual's behaviour.

Three studies in particular have probed the crucial area of maternal attitude. In the first of these Dean (1947) asked 20 mothers of pairs of children of the same sex to compare their youngsters with regard to a number of traits. The mothers reported their older child to be more fearful, dependent, worrisome and anxious whereas they described their younger one as more physically aggressive, negativistic, stubborn, affectionate, happy and good-natured. Whether these children actually possessed the characteristics is less important than the fact that the differences in how the mothers perceived their first as compared with their second child were consistent. If expectations as to behaviour of first and children are uniform, they could well exert an influence on the outcome.

In the second study, Lasko (1954) compared the behaviour of mother toward first and second children. Mothers of 46 pairs of children were rated on Fels Parent Behaviour Rating Scales, based on interviews with the women and observations of mother and child interaction in the home. In general the mothers were less warm emotionally and were more restrictive and coercive toward their first child than toward their second. Moreover, they tended to baby and protect the second child more than the first. Analyzing the shifts in parent behaviours as the two children grew older, Lasko concluded that the most important trend for the first child was a lessening of parent-child interaction. There seemed to be no parallel change for the second child. The first child was subjected to much verbal stimulation and attempts to speed up its development during the first two years of life, whereas no such regimen was imposed on the second child. There was also a tendency for disciplinary frictions to be exacerbated in dealing with the oldest child. As women had more children, they seemed to develop warmth combined with a sense of strictness.

In an interesting experiment study Hilton (1967) attempted to identify differences in maternal behaviour toward first and later born children in such aspects as interferences and inconsisting. Each child was given a series of puzzles to complete, with the mother instructed to remain unobtrusive while observing him. After five minutes the testing was interrupted and the mother was given either a success or failure induction, the child's performance was either complimented and praised or it was noted he did not measure up to his age level. Subsequently the mother was observed interacting with her child for a five-minute period. First with regard to child behaviour, first-borns as compared with later-born, were significantly more dependent. They were more likely to run to their mothers during the intermission period and to ask help and reassurance. The mothers of the first-born were more likely to interfere with and direct the child's behaviour. They were more extreme and more inconsistent in their emotional responsiveness to the child. These mothers showed a significant decrease in their supportiveness following the "failure" comments by the examiner, whereas the mothers of the later-borns showed little change. It is clear from the result of this study that there is a higher level of interaction, and greater emotional involvement between a mother and her first-born as compared with later-born children. The inconsistency and intemperateness of the mother's behaviour may well serve to produce dependency in the first-born child.

That the differences in maternal attitude and behaviour pointed out by Lasko and Hilton could produce differences in the personalities of children is indeed plausible. The reduction is babying and protectiveness, the decreased contact with the mother, less parental solicitude and the less child centred home experienced by the first could well influence his perception of the extent to which he is accepted by his parents. The first child, upon the birth of a sibling, must adjust to a change in the quality of his interaction and relationship with parents. The second child, on the other hand, enjoys a greater stability of parental policies. From all these considerations, we can see how position in the family may very well explain differences in personality and behaviour among children. In cases where differences related to birth order have been revealed, they are usually attributed to variations in interaction with parents and siblings associated with the unique life experiences found in children with that position in the family.

This is particularly true in the unusual role of the first born child. Eldest children are the only ones who, until they are dethroned by the birth of a siblings. How distressing the dethroning of the first-born child will be depends to a large extent on the responses of the parents. The birth of a new baby usually decreases the amount of interaction between spouses and between mothers and older children (Dunn, 1983; Taylor and Kogan, 1973). Following the birth of a sibling many firstborn children, especially boys, show emotional and behavioural problems (Nadelman and Begun, 1982). These problems are related to the temperament of the child and to the emotional state of the mother, with children of depressed mothers and children with difficult temperaments having more difficulty adjusting to changes in the family situation (Brody, Storeman and Burke, 1987; Stocker, Dunn, and Plomin, 1989). These outcomes seem to be mediated to a large extent by changes in mother-child interaction. Mother become more negative, coercive and restraining and engage in less playful interactions with the firstborn following the birth of a second child (Dunn and Kendrick, 1980,1982). If mothers continue to be responsive to the needs of the elder child and discuss the feelings of the younger child with the older child. Intense sibling rivalry is unlikely to occur (Bryart and Crockenberg, 1980; Howe and Ross, 1990). However, increased involvement of the father with the firstborn child also can counter to some extent the child's feelings of displacement and jealousy of the younger sibling (Legg-Sherick and Wadland, 1974). In fact, since the demands of parents are increased by the birth of second or subsequent children, it has been found that a positive effect of the second birth may be that it requires greater participation in child care by fathers (Lamb, 1979; Steward, Mobley, Van Tuy' and Salvador, 1987).

In spite of the fact that a new infant or younger child necessitates more attention and care from parents than does an older child, there seems to be an especially intense and concerned involvement of parents and firstborn children that is maintained throughout life. Parents interfere more with the activities of firstborn than secondborn children. They have higher expectations of firstborns and exert greater pressures on them for achievement and the acceptance of responsibility (Baskett, 1985; Caushna, 1965; Hilton, 1967; Lasko, 1954; Rothbart, 1971). Firstborn children also have greater disciplinary friction with their parents. At any age, more physical punishment is likely to be administered to a firstborn than to a later-born child. In contrast, parents are more consistent and relaxed in disciplinary functions with later-born children, perhaps as a result of self-confidence gained from practice in child-rearing. In a sense, the firstborn is the 'practice baby' on which the parent through that and error, learns parenting skill.

Mother-Child Relationships and the Child's Self Concept

A favourable self-concept (self esteem) is essential to personal happiness and effective functioning both in the child and in the adult. Persons who seek psychological and psychatric help frequently acknowledge that they suffer from feelings of inadequacy and unworthiness. They tend to perceive themselves as helpless and inferior have difficulty in either giving or receiving love and tend to feel isolated and to derogate their own potential and accomplishment. Not surprisingly, a high anxiety level and a negative conception of the self tend to be correlated. Furthermore, the anxious child's tendency to derogate himself tends to generalize and affect his image of his bodily integrity and adequacy as well. A negative self-concept appears to promote defensiveness in the child's reactions to himself and others. Finally a negative self-concept appears to imparental school adjustment and subsequent academic progress.

As child's self-concept is affected by the way in which his peer and teachers respond to him, it appears likely that for most children the way in which they are treated by parents is of overriding importance in determining their perceptions of themselves.

What is self-esteem? For the purpose of this discussion, self esteem is a personal judgment of worthiness that is expressed in the attitudes the individual holds towards himself. It is subjective experience which the individual conveys to others by verbal reports and other overt expressive behaviour.

What pattern of parental characteristics and behaviours distinguished between children high and low self-esteem? In general, children with high self-esteem tended to have parents who were also high in self-esteem. These parents, in contrast to parents of children low in self-esteem, also tended to be more emotionally stable and more self-reliant, resilient and effective in their attitude and actions regarding child care.

Mothers of children high in self-esteem were more accepting of their children and even more importantly tended to express their acceptance through specific everyday manifestations of concern, affection and close rapport. Low self-esteem mothers were likely to depreciate their children and to treat them as a burden. Their emotional responses to their children tended to range from hospitality to indifference.

Interestingly, mothers of high self-esteem children were more likely to enforce established roles carefully and consistently. They used reward as the preferred mode of affecting behaviour, but used straightforward and appropriate punishment rather than harsh treatment a loss of love when some sort of punishment was required.

While parents of high self-esteem children were more likely to provide carefully defined standards and limits on behaviour for their children, within these limits parental treatment was non-coercive and emphasize the right and opinions respected and concessions were often granted to him, if differences existed. The freedom that prevailed within broad limits permitted the child to enter into discussions as a true participant and to gain confidence from the assertion of his own views. While most parents of low self-esteem children, tended to stress "discussion and reasoning" as methods of obtaining the child's cooperation and compliance, most parents of low self-esteem children tended to stress "force and autocratic" measures.

Finally, in their encouragement of independence, parents of high self-esteem, children tended to fall between the parents of children with low self-esteem and parents of those with moderate self-esteem of children with high self-esteem seemed to be trying to establish a reasonable balance between protectiveness and encouragement of autonomy.

In summary, it appears that the kinds of parental practice to promote desirable social behaviours are also those that promote a confident self-image in the child.

Mother-Child Relationship: An Interactional Process

Individual differences: the child Coleman Kris and Provence (1969) pointed out that regardless of mother's personality or character structure, she is likely to deal differently with a rugged baby than with a fragile and sensitive baby. This study gives greater importance to children's characteristic than mother's personality or characteristics.

Everyone who deals with newborn infant is impressed with the individual differences with they show in their various sensitivities and behaviours. At one end of the scale are the extremely sensitive neonates at the other end are those who require strong stimulation before they react. Likewise, the tempo of some children is consistently fast in everything, while the tempo of others is consistently slow.

It is clear that each newborn enters into the formation of the early mother-child relationship with unique persistent qualities. He has his own individual patterns of sensory equipment and mural organization. He quickly develops has own distinct set of rhythms, tempo and co-ordinations—internal as well as external perceptual as well as motor. He has his own peculiar combination of sensitivities, his own levels of readiness to discharge tension and to achieve satisfaction.

Individual differences such as these can be of considerable importance in the earliest mother-child relationship. It is well-known that mother react quite differently to the varying characteristics of their different children. Most children seem soft and easy to handle but some seem stiff when they are held from very beginning. Mothers themselves comment spontaneously on the pleasure they get from handling a cuddly child and their disappointment that a stiff child give them. Perhaps we need to add to the old concept of accepting and rejecting mothers the newer ones of accepting and rejecting children.

While an active and sensitive mother may be continually disappointed by a slow moving unreactive baby, a phlegmatic mother may find an active energetic baby disturbing to her, a sensitive baby quite unintelligible.

Individual Differences: The Mother

The newborn's mothers, is also a unique individual. Unlike her baby, she enters the relationship already equipped with highly complex personality the product of many years of social living and of private thinking and feeling. Thus personality she has built upon the biological foundation with which she herself was born, and her biological foundations may have been different in more than one respect from those of her newborn child. Besides this, she has been reared in a particular kind of family with its own special values, ideals, prejudices and expectations, its own emotional qualities and its own variety of sub-culture. The mother was once herself a baby who entered into a mother-child symbiotic unit with her mothers.

To the mothering situation, the mother brings the background of her own childhood experiences of having been mothered she brings also the background of her lifelong fantasies, her daydreams and genius of being a mother.

8

Marital Happiness and Children

Marriage is a universal institution. In one form or the other, it is found in all groups and societies. It is looked upon as the backbone of the healthy society. Marital adjustment has been the concern of the individual as well as society. It is pointed out that the quality of marriage determines the emotional climate of the home in which the offspring will live and grow. A happy marriage provides a setting for the wholesome development of the children. The dynamics within the family affect the way the parents react towards the children. If the parents are happy within their relationship, they tend to be satisfied with their infants and enjoy them more.

Traditional vs. Modern or New Marriage

Traditionally in the East, marriage was a religious obligation, a holy union for performing religious rites and bearing a son for continuing the family life. The roles of husband, and.wife were clearly demarcated. The man was the provider and woman's duty was to look after the house and children. Bearing many children was her means of fulfilling the feminine role. She was expected to be of service to her in-laws as well as to her husband and children, all of whom usually lived in a joint family. So the concept of Hindu marriage is widely different from the one which is followed in European countries.

While discussing the concept of traditional Indian marriage and family life, Kapadia, wrote, "Marriage was a social duty towards the family and the community and there was little idea of individual interest. The social background provided by the authoritarian joint family and caste. With its domination in all spheres of life afforded no scope for the recognition of any personal factor, individual interests and aspirations in the relations between husband and wife."

But with the change in the approach and outlook in thinking, now the marriage is no longer considered only as a religious sanctity. Values of social life which the old generation had were definitely different than what those are today. New marriage is more intrinsic that is, its value is not a means to an end but an end in itself and this end is love companionship, and the satisfaction of emotional needs. New marriage is closet to what other refer to as companionship marriage.

Traditionally, people were married for economic security, physical protection, to provide goods and services for one another, to raise children, or to gain status and prestige. This type of marriage was utilitarian, a means to an end.

In new marriage, "The husband and wife are much more nearly equal, with both enjoying similar rights, so that decision making procedures are more likely to be democratic. In traditional marriage, the wife is subservient to the husband and decision making is more likely to be autocratic."

New marriage places a great deal of emphasis on the worth and value of the individual. The marriage is considered important only because of what it will and can do for the individuals involved. The individual's well being and happiness are of primary importance. New marriage facilitates self-fulfilment and self-actualization. It enables persons to continue to grow as individuals, it fosters the development of personhood and the clarification of identity. It allows persons the opportunity to find emotional fulfilment and love through voluntary commitment and involvement. This means that new marriage involves a close, loving supportive relationship in which each person accepts and loves the other person as he is.

The emphasis in new marriage is on intimacy personal contact, and emotional fulfilment, open communication is a necessity to release tension and avoid misunderstanding. Success in this marriage is measured by the extent of marital integration which is defined by Eshleman as "The extent of which each marital partner receives from the other partner the attitudes, services and goods needed". It is also measured by the degree of satisfaction, happiness and the extent to which the couple feels fulfilled.

Today, however, the conditions seem to be changing. Industrialization and urbanization have brought about modifications in family life. First of all the joint family is becoming less prevalent and conjugal family is gaining preference. Living in joint family is becoming less feasible and acceptable to young couples.

Secondly, the status of women has undergone considerable change. In every group and section it is being realised that the women should be given higher regard and respect, be that Hindu, Muslim or Christian society in India. They have innumerable opportunities for fulfillment of intellectual and professional potentialities. They are seeking education in every area of professional training. They also work in factories, offices and various professional fields such as teaching, medicine, government administration etc. Their employment bring social contacts, a change to use skill and capabilities and a sense of work satisfaction. She feels that it is wrong to consider that she is either a burden on the parents or on the society. Many societies all over the country have come up to champion her cause. She now feels that she is partner and co-sharer in social and national progress.

It also brings status and independence. In view of the changes in her position the modern educated woman tends to seek marriage as a source of emotional fulfillment, companionship and lower rather than financial support. In such marriage it is the quality of relationship that matters. As Landis puts it, "Today marriage has come to be viewed as a means of personal happiness and companionship and not primarily as a means for status, subsistence and blood line continuity." He pointed out that marriage is a union of two different personalities in which they interact to complement each other for mutual satisfaction. It is a progressive evermoving relationship in which husband and wife depend increasingly on the judgement, the inspiration, co-operation and understanding of the other.

Marital Satisfaction and Marital Adjustment

According to "Ricepl marital satisfaction may be defined as each person's evaluation of the extent to which each marital partner feels he or she receives from the other partner the feelings, attitudes, services and goods needed."

Marital satisfaction depend on the intimacy between couple. Calderone found that the development of intimacy involves several distinct components choice, maturity, reciprocity and delight. Two people choose each other because of a mutual attraction. They exchange reciprocal confidence and accept each other's vulnerabilities in a sharing, predictable way, developing a solid trust. In such a atmosphere, intimacy can be achieved by acceptance of self and of each other in safety and delight. According to a Researcher, McCary Intimacy is destroyed by denial of feeling, particularly anger. Fear of rejection also block intimacy, especially when it leads to false identities designed to cater to others rather than to fulfill important internal needs.

There are number of important factors which are related to marital satisfactional. Lewis (1975), Miller (1976), found that marital satisfaction is greatest among those spouses whose occupational status, income and educational levels are higher, spend greatest proportion of leisure time in joint activities, have good verbal and non-verbal communication and are mentally and physically healthy. These authors further stated that spouses, who express more affection, trust one another, confirm to the marital role expectations of one another, fulfil one another's emotional needs and have equalitarian relationship are more satisfied in their marital life. Studies done by Laws and Stukert on marital satisfaction show the general trend as somewhat curvilinear, i.e., to be high at the time of marriage, lowest during the child rearing years and higher again after the oldest child is beyond teenage. "Apparently bearing and rearing children interferes with marital satisfaction".

The research in the field of marital satisfaction indicates that equalitarian patterns result in high marital satisfaction. Laws, Landis and Landis, reported that 47 per cent of the couples they studied had a 50-60 pattern of dominance and these received the highest happiness ratings. Studies report that marital satisfaction is highest when power is exercised autonomically as when the husband is dominant. It is the fact that no couples are completely satisfied. There are always some gaps between expectations and fulfillment. Therefore, second concept is needed that is marital adjustment, which emphasises the dynamic nature of marriage the necessity to give and take in continuing evolution of the husband-wife relationship.

Communication in Marriage

Communication has also an important place in the marriage. It is the process of transmitting feelings, attitudes, facts, beliefs and ideas between them. Many authorities contend that good communication is the key to the family interaction and the life bond of the marital relationship. Power, Hutchinson and Klemer had given importance to the communication between husband and wife. These authorities pointed out that communication lead to understanding,

understanding to acceptance and acceptance to adjustment in marriage.

Living together in a marriage life creates the same problems that newlyweds face. Conflicts resolved through a complex process of "negotiation collective bargaining." Essential to this process is constant, effective communication. As in marriage, with its readymade roles and expectations, clear communication is a constant struggle, and it may be even more important and more difficult within the vague boundaries of living together. So the couple living together must deal with the issues of commitment, fidelity, and permanence.

Communication is most possible when couples really show they care about one another. Couples who frequently make positive statements about one another have much higher marital adjustments than do those who are very negative or disparaging in what they say.

When husband and wife have more common experience to talk about it may have a positive effect on marital satisfaction. Wife may feel secure emotionally when both do things together as a family. The wife is more likely to express satisfaction with her marriage. Blood and Udry pointed out that where joint decisions are taken, where couples consult each other on decisions are more likely satisfied with their marriages.

Marital Happiness and Children

It is popularly assumed that children and marital happiness go together. This assumption received no support from research in sixties. According to Rossi "Once the child arrives, there are new stresses, challenges and the role change is rather abrupt. Both parents experience new feelings of pride and excitement, coupled with a greater sense of responsibility that sometime is overwhelming". Some men are envious of their partner's ability to reproduce and of the close emotional bond established between mother and infant. Couples need to renegotiate time for each other and for other interests. Indeed, there appears to be less communication and sharing of personal interests, more sexual problems, and more marital conflicts in many marriage following the birth of a child.

Hurley and Polonen obtained evidence that the higher the ratio of children per year of marriage, the less was the marital satisfaction experienced. Blood and Wolfe found marital satisfaction to be enhanced by children as long as the number did not exceed three. Above this number marital satisfaction declined rapidly.

Research in seventies substantiates the fact that the birth of the child has negative impact upon most marriages especially for wives. Evidence also amassed during this decade which suggests that the number of children and their spacing may not have as strong an effect differences in the quality of parents' marriage as was previously supposed. Whereas studies in sixties suggested the opposite. Miller found no direct relationship between child density and marital satisfaction. Most of the current evidence is congruent with the notion that the presence of dependent children in the home puts a "Crunch" on the time, energy and economic resources of parents and results in decrease in marital satisfaction of parents.

A certain amount of conflict and discord may be considered as a normal part of every marriage. Husbands and wives often differ with one another on their basic philosophies of child rearing, a situation that can create marital conflict and confusion for the child. Hicks and Platt reported that one of the most surprising summaries of the marital research of the 1960's was the conclusion that children tended to detract rather than to contribute to the marital quality of their parents.

Berman pointed out that 'Parent-child' relationship is not static but it is in a constant flux and naturally requires adjustment on the part of both. As children grow, their demands changes while parents demand conformit to home and social group. He stressed the importance of psychological equilibrium in family adjustment which is frequently upset by variance between expectation and results. McCarthy found out that disturbed family relationships make children emotionally insecure and maladjusted. Banjamin's study shows that maladjustment in children results where mother fail to give the children sufficient time, where there are few siblings and the marital life of parents is unhappy. Erikson stressed the necessity of a child to develop a basic trust in his relationship with his parents as a requirement for the development of a healthy personality.

Marital Relations of Parents

Marriage is probably mankind's most widely distributed and successful social invention. It minimizes sexual conflicts provide for the next generation and its offer its participants not only sexual gratification but also economical security, a sense of belonging, status, opportunities for self expression, and a chance to escape from their limited selves by identifying with others.

Johsons and Terman (1935) matches 100 happily married couple with 100 unhappily married couples and with 100 divorced couple. All completed an extensive battery of personality test. Rating of marital happiness were obtained from marital partners and from their friends and associates. The happy married husband and wife had in common a relatively high degree of emotional stability, social adaptability and conservatism. The unhappily married people were non-socially withdraws, showed more neurotic tendencies and tended to have intolerant attitudes.

Mental Adjustment and the Child

The personality of the child is further open to this important influence viz., the mutual relation between husband and wife. If the husband misbehaves towards the wife then the child, particularly the male child, takes exception to it and this increases his hatred for the father. This can, under certain circumstances, lead to terrible consequences. Similarly if the wife misbehaves with husband, the female child is particular is likely to dislike it and hence she hates her mother constant conflict and quarreling between husband and wife leads to the creation of an atmosphere of security in the home which is not all conducive to the development of the child's personality. If the relations between husband and wife are good the children have a good and encouraging ideal is front of themselves which they can initiate to good effect. They then try to be good themselves. It is only natural for the child to develop some personality defects of the relation between his parents is not good.

Based on the conclusions of clinical status that marital conflict and divorce affect the adjustment of children, many writers have attributed a number of child behaviours to domestic discord. Delinquency, stealing, trauncy, lying, disciplinary difficulties, jealousy, hyperactivity, problems of speech, reading problems, poor social adjustment and homosexuality are all said to result from marital strife.

A number of studies have sought to identify the marital factors in the home that have contributed to the behaviour of the young child in school. Children from the "happy, calm" homes tends to be less negative than youngsters from the opposite type of home. The latter showed more signs of emotional disturbance, such as jealousy, fear, grumbling, nervousness and sulking and tenseness. Baruch and Wailcox (1944) named the following five main tensions in the home as influencing poor adjustment among preschool children-tension over sex satisfaction, tension over lack of consideration, tension over insufficient expression of affection, tension over inability to talk things through, and tension over ascendance submission relations. The first three were interpreted as indicating a lack of security in the marriage relationship. The fifth reflected on the child's feeling of adequacy no doubt both parent security and adequacy exert important psychological influences on the adjustment and personality growth of the young child. But the primary significance of marital adjustment seems to be its reflection of a more basic adaptation of the two people involved in the relationship.

The Impact of the Marital Relationship on Parents and Children

A satisfying marital relationship is after regarded as the cornerstone of good family functioning which directly or indirectly facilitates effective parenting, positive sibling relationships and the development of competent adaptive children.

It is important to remember that parent have a relationship with each other as well as with their children Parent serve as source of mutual emotional and physical support and comfort and such support is especially important in their roles as caretakers, Increased parent-child relationships have been found when spouses are mutually supportive (Cowan, Miller 1991; Cox et al., 1989, Crnic, Greenberg, Ragozin, Robinson and Basham, 1983; Feldman, Nash and Aschenbrenner, 1983). Dual participation in household chores and caretaking can free both parents for more playful and pleasurable interactions with their and relieve some of the burdens often experienced by parents, especially mothers with young children.

A home environment that is characterized by quarreling, nagging and disagreement has deleterious effects on both parent and children (Dix, 1991). High conflict between parents is associated with negative feelings and behaviour directed towards their children and in turn with disruptions in social and cognitive competence and increased antisocial behaviour in children (Emery, 1982; Hethinington Cox and Cox, 1982; Cowan et al., 1991; Hethinington and Clingempeel, 1992).

Boys are much more susceptible to the negative effects of family disharmony than are girls (Block, Block and Morrison, 1981; Hethinington et al., 1982; Rutter, 1977). Because boys are more likely to be directly exposed to parental bickening and physical abuse than are girls. Parents quarrel non-often and their quarrels are longer in the presence of their sons. Parents are non-protective of daughters and this protectiveness extends to protection from parental conflict.

The Impact of the Birth of a Child on the Marital Relationship

As is true in considering the role and functioning of any family subsystem we must view these marital relations in terms of the total family system. At the same time as the relationship between the parents is affecting how they respond to their children, the presence and the birth of a first child, in particular are associated with a shift toward a more traditional type division of family roles (Cowan et al., 1991). This shift toward more stereotyped masculine and femine roles occurs whether or not the initial role division in the family before having children was traditional or egalitarian. Inspite of rhetoric concerning equality of roles for men and women, even in relatively untraditional homes, there seems to be an implicit assumption that the role of the mother with young children is in the home and that of the father is to provide. Although in rare cases a father takes time from his work to be with his wife and new born, that time rarely exceeds two weeks, and then even in families when both parents have worked, it is the wife who is most likely to give up her occupation. It is thus not surprising to find that the most marked immediate decline in marital satisfaction following the birth of the first child is found in mothers (Belsky, Long and Rovine, 1985; Cowan et al., 1991). Decline in marital satisfaction also occur in fathers but emerge more slowly as men become increasingly aware of the restrictions imposed on their lives by a baby and no longer being the focus of their wives attentions and sometimes because the mother and child form a close relationship from which the father is excluded. Mothers not only get more of the responsibilities but often also more of the pleasure in raising a child.

Children have an impact on the relationship between their parents in other ways. Temperamentally difficult, deviant, or handicapped children impose additional stresses on parents that may be reflected in marital conflict. The presence of a demanding, recalcitrant child may be enough to fragment a fragile marriage. However, couple who were satisfied with their relationship than those who were previously distressed. Thus the birth of a child usually neither salvages a bad marriage, nor destroys a good marriage.

Since the transition to parenthood is a time of heightened risk to the mental relationship and subsequent parent-child relationship, preventative interventions are being designed that are aimed at strenghening couple relationship and reducing the adverse consequences of the transition to parenthood.

Divorce (Effect of the Broken Family)

when relations between the husband and wife deteriorate the family is reduced to a broken family. This is because the relations between the two members retain their original charm and goodness. A broken family is one in which the family relations have been severed. Family does not mean the living together of some individuals but rather the ultimate and profound relations that exist between them. In the absence of this intimacy the family is disbanded and in the broken family problem and disturbed children are reared and brought up. In the broken family the children are not looked after or cared for. According to some specialists, the broken family tends to create the criminal tendency in the female children more than it does in the male child. In the broken family the relation between the husband-wife, parent-child and brother-sister do not remain healthy. Hence, it is natural for boys and girls to tread the path of mistakes, crime and degradation.

That divorce hampers child adjustment can't be denied. However its precise effect are not easy to determine because most of the data come from clinical case studies. How much of a child's maladjustment may be charged to the divorce as such, or how much result from the long period of conflict, tension and discord leading to divorce is hard to say. Then, too, how much may be attributed to the poor personality adjustments of the partners in the particular marriage. Whatever the case, many child behaviours stem from parental divorce, as several research studies have indicated.

Many researches indicated the children from broken home showed less psychosomatic illness, less delinquent behaviour and better adjustment to parents than those from unhappy, unbroken homes. It can be conclude that in some cases separation and disruption of the home is desirable. Perhaps this might follow from the additional finding that the adjustments of parents individually and to their spouses were superior in broken homes than in unhappy homes that remained intact.

In our culture parents feel a responsibility to the child, not only for his physical welfare but also for his emotional welfare since divorce threatens the child's emotional stability, the parent contemplating such action often experiences strong feeling of guilt. These feelings may also arise from resenting the child who renders the divorce situation more difficult. To compensate for them, the parent may attempt to be overprotective of the child and to show excessive concern for its welfare. Yet, just as divorce may foster feelings of guilt in the parent, it may arouse similar sentiments in the child. To the youngster's mind, the separation may seem punishment for his own past "naughtiness" or for unconscious, hostile feelings towards his parents.

Parents themselves in a predivorce situation are not sure of the course to be followed; their uncertainty and auxiety are communicated readily to the children. The tension and vague threat of change are hard for the child to cope with psychologically. It is quiet evident that an unstable home environment, for whatever cause may have harmful implications for the child's psychological adjustment.

Following divorce, moving often becomes necessary. This add to the adjustment problems facing the child, especially if he is of school age. Furthermore, arrangements for substitute care for him may be required if the mother returns to employment outside the home.

Process of identification whereby the child patterns his behaviour after that of the parent of his own sex get impaired in many ways when there is only one parent present in home. In most of the cases the mother receives custody of the child. This certainly affects a boy's identification with a father figure, and a gap in learning certain aspects of future adult roles may well occur when there is one parent lacking in the home.

Many literature indicates clearly that paternal absence during childhood has the effect of feminizing the young boy, creating difficulties in his peer relationships, and producing initially aggressiveness and greater maternal dependency. A boy who lack a male identification figure in his growing years, evidences problems in several areas. He found difficulty in adjusting to the masculine sex role and in accepting authority and deficient in the internalization of standards. The exaggerated masculinity of adolescent boys from divorced home shows insecurity in this area. This insecurity is reflected also in their inability to accept and identify with any adult models. Exaggerated independence in these boys very likely involves a denial mechanism.

It can be concluded from many researches that, girls from divorced homes did not show the strength of identification with their mothers as those from intact homes. There was a psychological distance between these girls and their mothers; the girls developed strong and mature peer friendships and they sought other adult models. In general, boy suffer far more than girls from the effect of divorce. This is probably because of girls' greater resiliency and adaptability and the harmful effect of loss and devaluation of the like-sex model for the boy.

In the family, in general, the parents tend to serve as buffers or neutralizers in their mutual influences on the child. This is familiar in fiction and folk literature where the mother often is pictured as the intercessor between father and son, attempting to temper the severity of the fathers punishment. When there is but a single parents in the home, the child's relation with that parents is unmitigated by the presence of another. Any conflicts and antagonism already in existence may become accentuated.

Thus, even though research has yet to separate the effects of divorce from those of the marital strife that might have proceeded it, factors present in the divorce situation are known to exert harmful influences on the child's psychological adjustment. Tension, instabilities, lock of proper figures for identification, hostilities, guild feelings—all these come to the fore when divorce occurs. To understand and identify the precise impact of divorce on any child one needs to know-how much love and understanding will continue after the action and how much real concern and affection exists for the youngster. In other words, does the child perceive the divorce as punishment and rejection or has the situation been approached with maturity and insight so that the child's love for and confidence in the parent not get shaken.

9

Effects of Maternal Employment, Culture, Family Size and Family Composition on Children

Maternal Employment and Child Rearing Practices

Rapid socio-economic changes that are characterising contemporary Indian society induce certain adaptive changes in the family which in turn lead to modification in socialisation and child rearing practices, changes in family experience that work as proximal antecedent factors to the psychological and behavioural dispositions and characteristics of children and parents (Sinha, 1988). In today's nuclear family system parent-child relationships are very intimate and interactions are intense in nature. In recent past, mothers were expected to remain at home to take care of their children, particularly during their early years of development. Today the scene is changing because an increasing number of women are opting to work outside the home which has changed the traditional style of housekeeping, mothering and child care. Hoffman (1989) suggested that a woman handle the diverse roles and responsibility of a working woman and mother simultaneously. Many feel that in the midst of busy work schedules, conscientious working mothers skillfully do manage to give their children love, care and nurturance needed for their growth and development of their personality and realisation of potentials.

Maternal employment has a greater impact on family structure than an specific aspects of the children's psychological adjustment; perhaps it is for this reason that so much attention dimension of reward punishment. Agarwal and Singh (1977) concluded that working mothers from upper middle class families showed greater approval of comradeship and sharing with their children than did non-working mother. Many studies suggested that the mothers attitude toward employment affected her relation with her children. Mothers holding positive attitude toward work employ less severe discipline and less power assertive technique. They feel more sympathy, more affection, and less hostility in their interaction with their children.

Discussion of the research concerning the effects of maternal employment is divided into three main areas husband-wife relations, adjustment of mother, effect on the children.

Husband-Wife Relationship. It seems clear that the mother's employment outside the home alters the traditional structure of the family including such aspects of husband-wife relationship as participation in household tasks, decision-making and power and dominance roles. Indeed, when the responses of children of working mothers were compared with those of non-working mothers regarding parental performance of various household tasks, the former group reported that the mothers participate less and father participate more in all areas. Related to this is the fact that working mothers makes fewer decisions about routine household matter while the father have more. However, with regard to general family decisions especially the economic area, the working wife play a more powerful role than the working one

Although most studies show more quarreling and more marital conflict in families where the wife is employed, a number of other variable such as social class, reason for the employment, and the husband's attitude toward his wife employment, are important here.

Adjustment of the Mother. A number of aspects of maternal adjustment in relation to employment have been examined. These include emotional adjustment, satisfaction or dissatisfaction with employment and with the maternal role, physical health and community and recreational participation.

As compared with non-employed mothers, employed ones express more satisfaction with their daily work and with the community in general. In addition employed mothers express more positive self-attitude, including higher self-esteem. Moreover they reported fewer physical symptoms suggesting that their health is not impaired by the demands of home and employment.

In summary, maternal employment has not been found to exert marked effect on the behaviour and adjustment of the children involved. It is the quality not quantity, of interaction between mother and child that is of psychological significance. There is some evidence that the childrearing practices of working mothers may differ from those of non-employed mothers, particularly in the area of independence training. Except in cases where mothers feel guilty about leaving their children in order to work, employed mother encourage their children to become self-sufficient and independent and to assume responsibility for house-hold tasks at an earlier age. This early independence training may be beneficial in leading to high achievement motivation, achievement behaviour and competence. However, maternal employment in some families is also associated with less supervision and monitoring of school-aged children. Lack of monitoring is associated with especially adverse consequences for boys—lower school performance, more behaviour problems, and an increase in mother-child conflict. For both boys and girls, lack of supervision is associated with earlier dating behaviour, precocious sexuality and greater peer involvement.

Effect on the Children

Whose mother frequently choose employment for achievement reasons, working class adolescent girls spend less time with their families and yet exhibit greater emotional dependency on them.

The variables of age and sex of the child may interest in determining the effects of maternal employment. In early childhood a boy may be adversely affected, showing dependency, withdrawal and maladjustment. These finding may reflect an inadequate male model in families in which the mother is employed, or in our discussion of divorce, they may suggest that a young boy is more negatively affected than a girl by any deviation in the family structure that reduces his feelings of security.

In Indian context some studies have been conducted to study the relationship between maternal employment and child rearing practices. Suseela Devi and Devdas (1970) found that disciplinary techniques adopted by mothers differed according to their educational status and not according to employment of mothers. Singh and Sharma (1975) obtained significant difference between working and non-working mothers on maternal employment, provisions for substitute care, the consistency between mother and substitute in attitude and behaviour, the personality and personality needs of the particular child, the motivations for maternal employment, and the mother's attitude toward working and toward child care while Douvan and Adelson (1966) found little relation between maternal employment and adolescent boy's activities and psychological characteristics, several effects were noted for the adolescent girl. Daughters of working women are more likely to share in home responsibilities, they participate in fewer leisure activities. As compared with daughters at non-working women, these whose mothers work admire and respect their mothers more. They enjoy close relationship with their mothers and identify with them. In addition maternal employment affects the daughter's conception of the female role. In Hartley's study more daughter's of non-working mothers said 'housewife' when asked what they expected to do when they grew up, whereas more daughters of working mothers mentioned various professional aspirations. Also more daughter of working mothers said they would continue to work after marriage.

Maternal employment (part or full time) affected adolescent girls in a positive fashion in several areas, the social class variable was an important consideration. As compared with upper-class girls has focused on this variable. By tradition, "the mother's place is in the home", and she seeks outside work only if the family's economic situation demand it. The position taken by a particular group of psychologists, that the child's eventual personality adjustment depends upon a close relationship with his mother during his early years, has lent support to this point of view. The position stresses that unless there is a continuous mother figure, present, harmful consequences are likely to ensure. While it is difficult to say whether maternal employment has led a more equalitarian conception of the family structue, or whether this conception has made maternal employment more acceptable, the fact remains that family organization has altered considerably in the past three decades. Limitation of family size and labour saving devices resulting from technological advance have contributed to this change.

Early research investigations that compared children of working mothers with those of non-working mothers ignored important variables that cut across this division. Some of these variable include age and sex of child, social class, full-time versus part time surprising that maternal employment is associated with more egalitarian views of sex roles by their children particularly by daughters. In middle-class families, maternal employment is related to higher educational and occupational goals in children. Maternal employment also is associated with fewer traditional faminine interests and characteristics in daughters. Daughters of working, as compared to non-working, mothers more often perceive of woman's roles as involving freedom of choice, satisfaction and competence, and they themselves are career and achievement oriented, independent and assertive and high in self-esteem. Sons of working mothers in contrast to sons of unemployed mothers, not only perceive female as more competent but also view men as warmer and more expressive.

Attitudes. The attitudes of both parents towards dual work status and the mother's satisfaction with the work with modify the effects of maternal employment on children. If the working mother obtain personal satisfaction from employment, if she does not experience excessive guilt about being away from her children and if she has adequate household arrangements to prevent her from being stressed by dual-role demands, she is likely to perform as well as, or better than, the non-working mothers as a parent.

Non-working mothers who have a sense of satisfaction and competence in their home-making role and working mothers who enjoy their employment both show more positive relations with their husbands and with their children than do unhappy, non-working mothers who would like to be employed. However, mothers and fathers both display more negative feelings and behaviour toward their children which their attitudes towards maternal employment and the wife's work status are not congruent.

Maternal Employment and the Use of Disciplinary Techniques

Discipline is an important instrument in the process of socialisation through which maternal employment, provisions for substitute care, the consistency between mother and substitute in attitudes and behaviour, the personality and personality needs of the particular child, the motivations for maternal employment and the mothers attitude towards working and towards child care. Only if the fact of maternal employment were more pertinent to the well-being of the children than these other factors would one expect to find significant distinctions between the children of working and non-working mothers.

Over the past decade there has been a steady increase in the number of mothers who are employed. This increase has been most marked in the mothers of pre-school children. Mother no longer feel compelled to remain in the home when their children are infants or toddlers. It seems likely that as mothers spend more time in their places of employment and less time in the home, family roles and patterns of family functioning will change. What are some of these changes in the family roles and interaction that have already occurred and how do they influence children's behaviour?

Role Models. When both parents work outside of the home, the role of the mother may be perceived as similar to the role of the father, not only because the mother works but also because the father participated more actively in family and child rearing tasks, often regarded as part of the maternal role. Children with employed mothers therefore are exposed to less stereotypical models of the father as breadwinner and the mother a housekeeper and caregiver. It should be noted that in dual-career families although father participation increases the mothers report that time is their scarcest and most valued resource. Both working mothers and their school-age children complain that the employed mothers have too little time to spend with their children. It is not parents guide children in the direction of what is socially acceptable in his/her culture. In this context, maternal employment constitute a major factor in determining the mode of disciplining children. Maternal employment to some extent, influences the family environment, parental interaction and also treatment with the child. It is generally contemplated that due to dual-role responsibility, employed mothers as compared to their counterparts, might use more punitive methods while disciplining their children.

In a study conducted by Kiran Mathur on working women and non-working women, it was observed that when the child disobeys, employed mothers used 'spanking' relatively more frequently, whereas unemployed mothers usually deprived that child from something desired.

Employed mothers usually demanded very high level of discipline in their children as compared to their counterparts.

Concept of Culture

The concept of a 'culture' is imprecise necessarily so. Children are born into a society whose predominant social patterns, institutions, beliefs and attitude are identifiable as forming a singlex complex : yet within this complex, or 'culture' are many sub-culture. These subculture may be based on obvious differences in religion, occupation, racial origin, wealth, geographical location, etc., or they may be more subtly related to such factors as social class. The easy dissemination of knowledge and ideas through television and radio may even permit the apprearance and ideas through television and radio may even permit the appearance of subculture, related to an understood affinity between otherwise unrelated members of a statistically—meaningful section of the practices.

The term culture embraces a great deal. It designates man made artifacts activities people perform and ideas and feeling. (John Honningman, 1962). Honningman further says, "when I speak of a culture I mean a way of life belonging to a designated aggregate of people. Cultural traits are natural yet they are not a part of nature." These traits are specific influences and pattern of responding for similar situations and they characterise different families and groups. These in turn get transmitted to the offsprings. Their transmission takes place to a substantial degree through the informal interaction between parents and children which occurs in the course of child rearing.

A search for studies in child rearing practices indicates that practices and ideas on bringing up children vary extensively in different culture in different geographical and socio-economic groups. In a broader sense, child rearing methods are prescribed to the cultural group to which the family belongs. Cross-cultural studies of Benedict (1935), Erikson (1954). Whiting Child (1953), Barry (1952) and Wright (1952) bring out the influence of different types of cultural on the personality of the child.

One of the earliest contribution to the field of child rearing practice was by Freud. He emphasised the importance of the early years, especially the effect on later personality and behaviour of the child's relationship with the parents during early years. Later Freudian mechanism of fixation displacement, projection and development of guilt were found to be related to early oral and anal indulgences by whiting and Child (1953). Karen Horney (1937) has pointed out that inconsistence and confusion in the value system of modern culture produces basic anxiety in the child, which gives rise to a neurotic personality, while Kardiner (1939), believes that culture provides the basic personality structure.

Child rearing is usually directed towards comfort for the child with avoidance of pain, discomfort and frustration. The goal of child rearing is to mould the child, so that he will be able to adjust to the traditional roles prescribed by the cultural group. However, culture is consistently changing and there is no single pattern and there is no overall philosophy of child rearing. As a result the methods used depend upon the values and attitudes of the parents. This means there are wide variations in the specific training methods, even though all have the same aim to produce well adjusted person.

Allport explained the concept of basic personality assumes—

(a) Cultural traditions determines the lesson the parent will teach to child, the way in which lessons are taught.

(b) Different cultures have different ways of training the child and different lessons to teach.

(c) The child's early experience exerts a lasting effect on his personality.

(d) Similar experiences tend to produce similar personalities within the culture.

Since the turn of the century dogmatic authoritarian methods of child rearing have in large measures given way to more democratic and permissive methods. There has likewise been a shift from the use of punishment to enforce an approved pattern of behaviour to the use of education, discussions, explanations to teach the young one to want to do what the social group expects of him.

Some Central Questions of the Effects of Culture on the Child

Just how does culture influence the child's development? This general question can be answered, in part, if we can provide answer to certain more specific questions. Consider, the question, *who is responsible for the care of the child*. If the answer seems obvious to us it is probably because we take for granted the responsibility of the child's mother to provide for routine child care. We assume that the mother will therefore be the primary influence in the life of the baby and young child. There are societies, however, in which this is not the case. In some there are servants or nurses not biologically related to the child, retained for the special purpose of child care. In some the mother's primary responsibility is for food production or for work in the field, and the care of the baby and young child is in the hands of older women of the tribe, who may or may not be related biologically. The role of male relatives in child care is also variable from one group to another.

Another question might have to do with the *place or position a child holds* in relation to his family, and to adult in the community. In some, a child is not really viewed as a person, or even as being essentially human, until he reaches an age beyond the preschool years. This is in marked contrast, obviously, to our society, which places great emphasis on the individual needs of children and admonishes parents to regard their children with love, respect and dignity we not only regard the period of childhood with great importance as a foundation and forerunner of adult personality, but we cherish childhood and respect it for its own sake, as a period of life having validity of itself, apart from what it may portend for the future. Similarly, one society may value children as economic or cultural assets, while another may tend to view children as liabilities. And one group may place special significance on certain features of individual children—their sex, their position in the family at the expense of other features we could certainly conclude that children are not viewed in the same way by adults in all societies.

Another central question about cultural effects on the child has to do with *what is allowed and what is forbidden.* Child behaviour which is accepted and even encouraged in one group is sharply curtailed and perhaps severely punished by another group. In our own—while enlightened parents are aware of the natural curiosity of their children toward sex—sex play and experimentation is severely controlled. In some societies, however, it is ignored; in others it is a matter of humour and joking on the part of adults.

Still another central question has to do with the nature of discipline the *amount, kind, quality of disciplinary measures* used in the group. In our societies there is a great deal of hard-slapping threatening, scolding and deprivation of privileges. In some societies there are purposeful efforts to frighten children into being good, in others, while fear is not purposely used, there may be threats of great bodily harm, or of dire consequences in the form of magical or supernatural events, which are designed to keep the child in line.

Other questions would have to do with the kind of *learning experiences provided for children in order to induct them properly into the adult society.* What are the experiences that teach the child what he must do, what he must not do, and what he must value, if he is to be an acceptable member of his group? Are these experiences ritualized and attended with great ceremony and attention? or are they almost unnoticed incidents along the way experiences that bleed into a total pattern of living, which gradually provides the child with a definition of acceptable and unacceptable behaviour? Are they retained exclusively as the province of a family, or of particular members of a family. These are part of the larger question of how a society organizes those of its experiences designed to socialise its children. These and perhaps many other fundamental question underlie the concept cultural effect of the child. Scientists who study culture are extremely cautions about attributing the personality characteristics of a child or adult to any one particular child-rearing practice or cultural characteristic. There was a time in the study of cultural when authropologists tended to see a special peculiarity of the adult members of a society as being the direct outcome of a special or peculiar child-rearing practice prevalent in the society. Current thinking, instead, emphasizes the total cultural context in which the child is living and growing and learning and tends to view cultural effects as an unbroken network of experiences with no single experience in the child's life especially meaningful apart from the total network. It is the cultural pattern then, not isolated practices or experiences, which seems to bring about personality qualities of the members of a society. Nevertheless, a keener insight into the nature of the child, and into the complex task of growing into a useful member of his society, with which he is confronted, may be achieved through study of the cultural practices of different groups. It is to this objective, the achievement of keener insight into the nature and tasks of the child engaged in the socialization process.

A number of cultural influences upon behaviour have already been discussed. Changes in family structure and in child-rearing practices, for example, are 'cultural' changes which have had a profound impact upon the development of patterns of social behaviour. There, in addition, several other cultural features influencing the social development of children.

In industrial societies generally, the age of marriage has tended to fall. It appears that these earlier marriages are far more likely to end in divorce than alliance contracted by couples some years older. Children born of these young parents (many of whom married young anyway because of a premarital pregnancy) thus suffer the disadvantage of parents who are less mature, and therefore less able to guide them in their social development; also the satistically greater probability that their parents will be divorced. It will thus be seen that the trend to early marriage is likely to affected individual development adversely.

Partly as an economic consequence of early marriage, partly because of changed social attitudes, far more mothers now go out to work than hitherto. The 'working mother' has become the butt of many a self-righteous (and perhaps jealous) attack, but as the practice becomes more common, its effects upon her child's development seem far less serious than was at first thought. Undoubtedly, children below the age of 3 years need a loving mother-substitute (an aunt, perhaps, or a nanny), and may suffer insofar as they become alienated from their real mother on account of her tiredness after a day's work or her late arrival home. Again, children of school age may develop the habit of soliciting food and favours from neighbours if they habitually arrive home to find a cold, empty house. Where a mother is forced to work at an uncongenial job in order to help out with the family finances, she may find herself transferring her frustration to the children, who suffer in consequence. However, in cases where the mother had considered the problems, where she works because of the stimulation and enjoyment it brings her, and has made suitable arrangements, it is easy to exaggerate the ill-effects upon her children. Indeed, the additional interest and monetary reward which a working mother brings into the home may actually be beneficial to her family. Her widened horizons may make her a more interesting person, better able to guide the intellectual and social development of her children.

Vaughan (1961) has suggested that children may be exposed to cultural inconsistencies before they have the maturity to understand them; and it certainly does appear to be the case that external social and cultural forces may undermine the standards which many parents seek to impose upon their children.

Even within the confines of the family's four walls, parental standards may be challenged by the invading mass-media of communication. Dybwad (1959) has pointed out that magazines, radio, television, and so on, may suggest to children the patterns of behaviours they should expect of their parents: if this is so, one can envisage conflict between the generations developing, particularly since suggestions derived from such sources bear a stamp of impersonal authority.

Where it is needed, a secure base from which child excursions may begin, and a refuge to which their offspring may return.

Culture referes to the learned behaviour of a people. It includes such diverse elements of one's social world as technology, finance, politics, religion, values, art, ethics, music and patterns of family living and child-rearing. Even the manner in which individual children are taught to category their experiences is a reflection of cultural conditioning.

Family as an Agent of Socialization

Socialization is the process whereby an individual's standards, skills, motives, attitudes, and behaviours are influenced to conform to those regarded as desirable and appropriate for his or her present or future role in society.

Certain groups and organizations within society play key roles in socialization. Parents, siblings, peers, and teachers spend a great deal of their time communicating values and directing and modifying children's behaviour.

Although many social factors and groups affect the process of socialization, the family is frequently regarded as the most influential agency in the socialization of the child. Socialization has frequently been viewed as a process by which parents modify the behaviour of children. However, it would be more accurate to think of it as a process of mutual shaping. The family is best conceived of as a complex system involving interdependent functioning among members.

Families are not static; they change over time. Although most people recognize that alterations in the age and capacities of the child influence family functioning, few consider that every member of the family is changing and that these changes will be reflected in family relationships. Alterations in the marital relationship, the economic security of the family as parents gain more work experience, are promoted, or move in and out of the marketplace, and the changes in parents' relationships with friends and relatives all have an impact on the family.

Among the many social influences that contribute to the socialization of child, the family is clearly of central importance.

Although rearrangements in family ties are becoming increasingly common, family relationships remain the most intense and enduring bonds. Families have histories of shared experiences and expectations of future relationships over time. It is, in part, the continuity of this history that makes the family qualitatively different from shorter-lived relationships with friends, teachers, neighbours, or coworkers. The memories of past interactions are carried forward in standards, expectations, perceptions, and feelings about other family members.

It is only recently that socialization has been thought of as a complex process of family members influencing each other rather than as a process whereby parents shape the behaviour of children. Children play an active role in their own socialization (Bell and Harper, 1977). They elicit, interpret, and respond to the behaviour of others in a unique fashion on the basis of their abilities, temperament, personality, and past experience. The frequently reported finding of a correlation between physical punishment, rejection, and inconsistent discipline in parents and aggression or delinquency in children does not necessarily mean that these discipline practices led to the deviant behaviour in the child. Temperamentally difficult, non-compliant, antisocial behaviours in children also tend to evoke these punitive responses in parents. It is an interaction involving a feedback loop of mutual coercion. Parental punishment leads to antisocial behaviour in children and antisocial behaviour in children leads to rejecting, punitive responses from parents.

In this way, a person is socialised in the family. Defining family, Merrill writes, "Family is an enduring association of parent and offspring whose primary functions are the socialisation of the child and the satisfaction of the members. "According to Dewey and Tufts the family is social agency for the education and protection of the race. It is in the family that, the child acquires such important qualities as sincerity, sympathy, self-submission and realising responsibility etc. It is the character developed in the family which helps the child in becoming an important and responsible member of society. Wright was quite correct in stating that in every family, the child gets on opportunity for free expression of thoughts and developing his entire personality. Psychologists have incontestably proved that the proper development of the child is impossible, without a good environment in the family. The tendencies and habits which he acquires in the family, he finds impossible to shed later on. According to Freud, the viewpoint of a child towards the senior in the family determines his attitude and viewpoint towards the elders in society. The child's first is his home and family. According to Prof. Collingwood, the child's, education should be in the hands of the parents in family. The parents should participate in all the child's activities. A child, learns much by imitating his superiors. Mahatma Gandhi and such thinkers paid personal attention to the development of their children. It is the family which imparts practical education to the child concerning the customs in society, conduct, other important elements of culture, preservation of health, love, sympathy, cooperation etc.

Studies of Maternal Behaviour. Three studies in particular have probed the crucial area of maternal attitude. In the first of these Dean (1947) asked 20 mothers of pairs of children of the same sex to compare their youngsters with regard to a number of traits. The mothers reported their older child to be more fearful, dependent, worrisome, and anxious, whereas they described their younger one as more physical aggressive negativistic, stubborn, affectionate happy, and good-natured. Whether these children actually possessed the characteristics is less important than the fact that the differences in how the mothers perceived their first as compared with their second child were consistent. If expectations as to the behaviour of first and second children are uniform, they could well exert an influence on the outcome.

In the second study, Lasko (1954) compared the behaviour of mothers towards first and second children. Mothers of 46 pairs of children were rated on the Fels Parent Behaviour Rating Scales, based on interviews with the women and observations of mother and child interaction in the home. Because the families considered in this project had been participants in a longitudinal investigation lasting a number of years, ratings of the mother's behaviour toward her two children at the same chronological age could be matched. In general, the mothers were less warm emotionally and were more restrictive and coercive toward their first child than toward their second. Moreover, they tended to baby and protect the second child more than the first. Analyzing the shifts in parent behaviour as the two children grew older, Lasko concluded that the most important trend for the first child was a lessening of parent-child interaction. There seemed to be no parallel change for the second child. The first child was subjected to much verbal stimulation and attempts to speed up its development during the first two years of life, whereas no such regimen was imposed on the second child. There was also a tendency for disciplinary frictions to be exacerbated in dealing with the oldest child. As women had more children, they seemed to develop warmth combined with a sense of strictness.

That the differences in maternal attitudes and behaviour pointed out by Lasko and Hilton could produce differences in the personalities of children is indeed plausible. The reduction in babying and protectiveness, the decreased contact with the mother, less parental solicitude, and the less child-centered home experienced by the first child could well influence his perception of the extent to which he is accepted by his parents. The first child, upon the birth of a sibling, must adjust to a change in the quality of his interaction and relationship with parents. The second child, on the other hand, enjoys a greater stability of parental policies. From all these considerations, we can see how position in the family may very well explain differences in personality and behaviour among children.

Based on the conclusions of clinical studies that marital conflict and divorce affect the adjustment of children, many writers have attributed a number of child behaviours to domestic discord. Delinquency, stealing truancy, lying disciplinary difficulties jealousy, hyperactivity, problems of speech reading problems, poor social adjustment and homosexuality are all said to result from marital strife. This list is far from inclusive. Yet not much adequately designed research is at hand to help in sorting out the effects of a variety of factors and in identifying true cause-and-effect relationships. It may seem "obvious," for example, that divorce in an adolescent's background is the cause of current poor social adjustment.

Social Class. The class structure of a society may be regarded as an aspect of its culture. From another viewpoint, however, one must recognize that each class has its own culture. Each social class has characteristics which are so distinctive and powerful as to impress themselves on its members' standards. In particular, the social behaviour of each class differs from that of the others; and the social development of a child reared in a particular class is likely to differ from that of a child reared in another.

The patterns of family life differ markedly from class to class. Kaplan (1965) has suggested, for example, that the children of middle-class parents are sheltered and closely supervised; that they are required to be in the house earlier at night, and to work hard on school lessons; and that stress is placed on individual achievement, cleanliness, emotional restraint, responsibility, and self-control. Despite these limits on their physical freedom, however middle-class children appear to Maccoby (1954) to enjoy considerable psychological freedom at home, and as a result to be both less submissive and less bullying when organized in play-groups.

Because lower-class children are usually reared in crowded conditions, they are forced to live intimately with their parents, brothers and sisters. Since their parents are often acutely aware of them 'under their feet', physical punishment may be freely used to secure prompt obedience to orders; yet in other respects lower-class parents may be extremely permissive. Their children may be allowed out later at night, for example, without questions being asked as to their whereabouts. As a result, there may be an earlier identification with peer-groups about which the parents know nothing, a greater tendency to violence and overt aggressiveness as the child learns to defend himself, and greater sexual experimentation.

Reissman (1963) considers that lower-class children often find in school an environment unrelated to the realities of their home life, and that antipathy to school develops as a result. McCandless (1967) and Himmelweit (1955) suggest that this antipathy may be a two-way affair, in that the predominantly middle-class teacher either rejects the lower-class child, or at least gives evidence of preferring children of his own class. It is dangerous, however, to assume that the solution to the difficult problem of overcoming these class biases in teacher-pupil relationships lies simply in the recruitment of more working-class students to train as teachers. In the first place, such students may not have acquired from their parents the sense of responsibility which membership of a profession entails. Although there has been a shift in this direction of late, many such students find great difficulty in avoiding a regression to the ways of their own early upbringing when faced, for example, with disciplinary troubles. At the same time, working-class children seem actually to prefer a teacher who gives evidence of a cultivated background, in much the same way as the British Labour Party prefers a university don to a trade-union official as its leader.

The measure of rejection experienced by lower-class children at school, is a factor which tends to make them associate with peers of their own social status. This association is unlikely to be in a youth-club, which all too often is seen, like school, as a middle-class institution. Despite their efforts to find acceptance in their own groups, lower-class children give evidence, described by Keller (1963), of greater than average emotional instability, a fact which suggests that the pressures upon them may adversely affect their ability to adjust to the social demands of adult life.

The social development of children, then, is greatly affected by their class background. Several studies (for example Neugarten, 1946) have described the tendency whereby many individual children prefer as friends children of their own or of a higher social status. Their parents reinforce this preference by encouraging such friendships, and discouraging friendships with children from a lower social stratum. It follows that social interaction and the achievement of recognition is less easy for lower-class children, whatever their personal qualities, than for children fortunate enough to have been born into middle- or upper-class families.

The Koch Study. The extensive study by Helen Koch (1956a, b, c, d, and e; 1960) deserves special mention. It is one of the few relatively recent investigations of sibling influence on a child's psychological development. It rarity and extensiveness both stress the great complexity of this zone of research, especially if a study is to be designed adequately, employing most of the necessary controls. This study covered 360 five- and six-year-old children from two-child, urban, native-born, white, intact families (Koch, 1956e, 1960). Investigated as independent variables were the sex of the child under study, the sex of the sibling ordinal position, and three spacings between siblings—less than two years, two to four years, and four to six years. Each of 24 subgroups contained 15 children. Through analysis of the ratings assigned by teachers for a variety of traits, the impact of these variables on the characteristics of child behaviour was discerned. The following are samples of Koch's findings.

1. In language development (Koch, 1956a), first-born children consistently spoke more articulately than second-born. The greater the gap in age between siblings, the better the articulation tended to be. In addition, there were indications that stuttering might be related to the sex of the sibling and the difference in age between the two children; the amount of stuttering was thought to stem from how much jealousy and conflict there was as a result of the sibling's sex and difference in age. Similarly, the degree to which the child was frustrated by its sibling as well as the extent to which the child was allowed to express these frustration was felt to have some bearing on the amount of stuttering.

2. Identification with a sex role was studied through ratings of sissiness in boys and tomboyishness in girls (Koch, 1956b). Boys with a slightly older sister were rated as relatively sissified. This characteristic tended to decrease as the age differential between siblings widened. In parallel manner, girls with older brothers were considered more tomboyish than girls with sisters. Such findings provided evidence for the psychological impact of having a sibling.

3. In intellectual development, children with male siblings scored higher than those with female siblings on both verbal subtests and total scores of the Primary Mental Abilities Test (Koch, 1954). Possibly the broader experience of boys, a result of a higher level of activity, might have had some relevance. The greater competitiveness and aggressiveness associated with boys may create a more stimulating environment for the sibling.

4. Both ordinal position and spacing of siblings influenced range of interest. The wider the spacing, or age difference, the greater was the number of interests held by the child under study. Indeed, second-borns were noted to have more numerous interests than first-borns.

Again familiarity with an older sibling's preoccupations and association with his companions proved important influences on the later-born child.

5. Even when the gap in age was minimal, first-born children seemed better planners than second-born. To Koch this implied a greater responsibility as the lot of the first-born as well as a necessity to plan carefully in order to maintain his superior position.

In her findings, Koch proceeded beyond mere description to offer valuable clued and insights concerning the motivations for various traits and behaviours of children (Koch, 1956c). Her analysis of ratings of several emotional factors pointed to the existence of greater stimulation or strain when siblings belonged to opposite sexes than when they were of the same sex (Koch, 1956d). Perhaps this may be explained by sex rivalry, parental preference for one sex over the other, or other subtle factors in the family and sibling relationship.

Largely the data indicated that as spacing between siblings increased the tendency grew for each to go his own way. It might be said that the narrower the spacing, the more easily various emotional characteristics of the child could be imputed to sibling interaction, whereas the wider the gap, the greater were the influences of the child's interaction with his parents (Koch, 1956d).

Several studies have modified some of Koch's findings. While Koch's results indicate that male siblings enhance the IQ scores of their siblings, Cicirelli (1967) found that children in three-child families who have brothers only score lower on IQ and reading achievement measures. This suggests that in such families boys turn the sibling's attention to non-intellectual types of activity, including sports. Cicirelli also found that children with a like-sex sibling close in age scored higher on measures of creativity and reading and arithmetic achievement than children with like-sex-sibling separated in age or with an opposite-sex sibling. In a difficult-to-interpret finding Brittain (1966) showed that adolescent girls with an older sister were more peer oriented while girls with a younger brother were higher in parent conformity.

In a further analysis of the Koch data, Brim (1956) advanced several hypotheses from role interaction theory. Through interaction wih other an individual learns something of the characteristics of other roles. Thus a boy learns a great deal about a girl s role (her behaviour, attitudes) through daily contact with a female sibling. Moreover, this interaction results in a certain amount of assimilation of roles, the incorporation of aspects of another's behaviour into one's own behaviour repertoire. Related of this is the fact that an individual is more likely to adopt characteristics of a more powerful person than a less powerful one. The Koch findings reported above substantiated these hypotheses. Thus a girl with a male sibling was rated higher in masculine traits than a girl was a female sibling, thus showing the result of cross-sex interaction. Similarly, boys with sisters were rated as more feminine than boys with brothers. These findings were especially marked for the younger child, supporting the prediction that the more powerful figure (in this case, more powerful because of age) is more influential. An interesting secondary finding of the Brim analysis indicated that girls were rated more feminine than boys were masculine. This may be interpreted in the light of our discussion of sex-role identification. In the process of learning the sex-appropriate role, the girls continues to identify with the mother while the boy must shift from an early identification with mother to an identification with father somewhere around the age of five or six years.

The Koch findings illustrate the enormous complexity of both the research on sibling influence and the influence itself. While parents play the major role in influencing the child in a variety of areas (sex-role learning, attitudes, interests), the part played by siblings cannot be ignored. Sex and age of siblings, perceived parental favouritism toward a sibling, and the general interaction and relationship among siblings are important factors to be considered in understanding and interpreting an individual's behaviour.

SECTION D
ANALYSIS AND CONCLUSION

10

Overview Literature

Mothers who love and accept their children and who use love oriented techniques of discipline rather than material or physical techniques, produce relatively more, children with high conscience. Garrison emphasized that the developments of healthy personality pattern is not too much and too little love displayed in a developmentally appropriate form.

Personality is a multidimensional concept. It means in part the unique and distinctive characteristics of an individual. It is a consistent behaviour characteristic, that is the most characteristics integration of an individual's mode of behaviour, interests, abilities, attitudes, habits and aptitude and values of one's own groups through social interaction, social learning and socialization process.

According to Alexander (1951) three major factors are responsible in determining the development of the personality pattern (1) The individual's heredity endowment (2) Early experiences with the family and (3) Important events in later life outside the home environment.

The richest source of information about children's personalities comes from careful observation of how they actually behave. In every day life when we speak of a child's personality, we usually refer to his characteristic ways of behaving. He may be cheerful or moody impulsive or deliberate quick tempered or slow to take offense, dependent or independent, extrovert or introvert, shy or brash, characteristics such as these and the child's manner of expression them, become established through his interactions with his environment.

The child's primary social experiences take place in home. These social experiences are mainly with his parents, it is they who play the dominant role in molding his personality pattern when a child identifies with a parent, he develops a personality pattern similar to that of the parent. High attitudes towards self and others will lead to good or poor personal and social adjustments depending on whether the parent is well or poorly adjusted person. Behrans stated that the impact that mother's behaviour has on child development is more related to the total maternal behaviour than to any specific practices.

Analytically, personality of a child is consequences of acquisition, assimilation and adaptation of cultural norms and values of one's own groups, through social interaction, social learning and socialization process. Personal experiences are unique to each individual child and that is one of the factors of personality differences. The nature of personal experiences may be emotional, social or intellectual, it has, its marks on developing personality. Each child is born with potentialities for his own individual responses and for resistance to environmental influences. This is true not only with children of the different parents but with children of the same parents. Escalona from his studies noted that there may be differences among children in response to similar types of parental care.

Psychologists and anthropologists have shown the relationship between various patterns of behaviour in children and child rearing practices of mothers. Numerous studies regarding child rearing practices show its importance in the development of various traits in children. Bandura (1961) et. al. pointed out that aggression in children may arise because they look upon the parent as a model. Winder and Rau found that parents of aggressive boys scored higher in aggressiveness than parents of non-aggressive boys. Children respond readily to parents within the context of a loving, trusting, relationship of mutual esteem. Heise (1972) writes the degree of love and degree of control exercised in a parent child relationships are always seen to interact with each other.

Bell and Barper (1977) demonstrated that aggressive children have parents who use a lot of physical punishment. Lefkowitz et. al. (1963), indicated that aggression in children increases as parents increasingly rely on physical punishment for controlling child's behaviour. MaCord (1962) found that parental conflict and rejection of the child were prominent in the family backgrounds of extremely dependent boys. These findings support the view that dependent behaviour is the manifestation of feelings of insecurity in parent-child interaction.

Govalas and Briggs (1966) reported that depending persists when the parents reward dependent behaviour and fail to reward competent behaviour in the child. Heathers (1953) concluded that dependent behaviour in children resulted from maternal over protection. Peterson (1961) found that harsh parental attitudes are related to such personality problems as shyness, withdrawal and other conduct problems. Hatfield et. al. (1962) found that mothers reward aggressiveness in their sons but not in their daughters while reverse is true of dependency. Parents who mother their child with love generally have unrealistically high levels of aspirations for him and so he develops strong feelings of guilt, inadequacy and resentment when he falls below their expectations.

According to Dollard (1939) aggressive behaviour is a typical response to frustration. There is every possibility that children with maximum behavioural problems have mothers who use unhealthy child rearing practices and have marital discord. There are other factors such as age, socio-economic status, family background of mothers, which are related to child rearing practices. These factors indirectly influence the personality development of children. Out of these numerous factors marital adjustment is not given sufficient attention. Hence, there is a great need to investigate the relationship between the mother's marital adjustment and its effect on child rearing practices. It is important to note that mother's marital adjustment and child rearing practices have a great impact on child's personality development.

Studies in the field of child rearing practices are numerous but the results are often contradictory and inconclusive. Most of these studies are carried out in Western culture. India is a developing country and as compared to other developed countries mothers are less informed about the child rearing practices. It is necessary for mothers to know the factors of child rearing practices which have effect on child's personality development. They must have insight about their interactions and relationship with children, which are responsible for behavioural problems in their children.

A child who is developing needs a lot of love and guidance from his parents. A child who is deprived of basic needs of love-affection and security in early years of life cannot develop properly. Parental acceptance of children is believed to be one of the essential elements underlying the whole structure of the parent-child relationship. Parental acceptance is characterized by a keen interest in child but also does not find child care a difficult job. The accepting parents put the child in a position of important in home and develop a warm emotional relationship with him such a child is socialized, cooperative, friendly, loyal, emotionally stable and cheerful.

Such acceptance of children is possible only when mothers are aware of their roles as mothers and are properly adjusted to life in general and married life in particular. The present study has been designed with a view to study mother's marital adjustment and child scoring practices and its effect on child's personality.

Needs and Importance of the Present Study

Today due to many personal, social and economic conditions the traditional joint family system has given place to nuclear family pattern. Therefore responsibilities of the parents towards their children have increased to a great extent. The present study emphasises that family relationship play most important role in children's healthy personality development.

Number of studies conducted in the field are either on marital adjustment or on child rearing practices as revealed from the foregoing pages but no systematic and authoritative, study has investigated personality development of child in relation to their mother's marital adjustment and child rearing practices. Effort have been made in the present study to bring to light the sources of strength and difficulties in marriage relationship. It will give insight to mothers that poor marital relationship is responsible for poor personality development of the child. Mothers will recognize that wholesome happy family relationships leads to motivation to achieve, while unwholesome, happy relationship cause emotional tension which usually has a detrimental effect on child's abilities to concentrate and to learn new things. This study will also convey to the parents that poor family relationships not only affect the social and personal adjustment of the child but each and every area of his life.

The present investigation throw light on how husband-wife relationship, mother-child interaction and parents-child relationship are inter-related and interdependent on each other. If anyone of these relationship is unhappy, unhealthy or discouraging it may result in poor personality development in children. Thus, it will serve as a guideline for parents especially to mothers who play active and important role in the child's personality development.

Lastly, this study will be of great help to all those who are closely associated with the children, i.e., the child psychologists, pediatricians, teachers, psychiatrists, students of child-development.

The present study has been designed with a view to study mothers' marital adjustment and child rearing practices and its effect on child's personality.

Aims of the Study

The main aims of the present study is to study the personality traits of children in relation to their mother's marital adjustment and happiness and child rearing practices used by them.

In view of the main aim of the study the specific objectives are as follows :

1. To assess marital adjustment of mothers.
2. To study child rearing practices used by the mothers.
3. To study the various personality traits of children.
4. To find out the effect of marital adjustment on different measures of personality.
5. To study the effect of child rearing practices on various measures of personality.
6. To find out the relationship between child rearing practices and marital adjustment of mothers.

Delimitation

1. This study is limited to the investigation of marital adjustment of mothers only.
2. Further it is planned to study the effect of happiness, agreement and disagreement in marital life on personality development of the children.
3. The study also intended to find out the effect of child rearing practices on personality of children.
4. The effect of above mentioned variables will be studies in both the sexes and in the age group of ten to thirteen.
5. Effect of other relationships viz. father-child, teacher-child, peer and sibling relationships are not included in the study.

Studies carried out in America and other countries in the area of research are likely to have limited practical utility in our country because of the wide and varied difference in culture, socio-economic status and scientific and technological development. This justification for every study of relationship between child-rearing practices and their influence on the personality development in children, undertaken for different socio-economic and socio-cultural environment. The present study which aim at evolving the mother's marital adjustment and mother's personality with the personality of children may claim justification on similar ground.

The trend in the field of child rearing practices indicates that there is an inevitable causal relationship between child rearing methods and adult personality. There is an ample evidence in the western literature to prove the significance of a number of parental behaviour that are correlated with personality attributes in the children. In fact it is now well-established that childhood environment predetermines the behaviour tendencies of a child to a considerable extent.

For the normal development of child psychologists have recommended family relationship. The term normal is related to the development of socially accepted behavioural pattern and often regarded in almost all the societies and culture. There are several studies which demonstrate that pathogenic family relationship helps in developing socially disapproved or anti-social behavioural characteristics in the children.

In the present study while reviewing the studies in search of finding the influence of marital happiness and marital adjustment on the development of children's socially approved personality characteristics, unfortunately no direct studies were observed. The evidence in this respect come from the studies of anti-social personalities. Thus, there is a dearth of relevant studies demonstrating the influence of marital happiness and marital adjustment on the development of children's personality. There are large number of studies showing direct relationship between parents child rearing practices and the developed personality characteristic in children. The relationship between father and mother plays a crucial role which inevitably influence the rearing pattern of the child.

The personality dimensions measured in the present study are bipolar in nature. The one end represents socially approved behavioural characteristic, while the other refers to socially disapproved characteristics. Thinking in other way round, there is much scope to assert that pathogenic family patterns do develop socially disapproved behaviour. Barker and Adam, in their study found that about 65 per cent of the anti-social come from the pathogenic family background. In these families the relationship between the mother and father were not normal. In some cases the parents were on the verge of divorce. Morrist and his associates found that aggressive behaviour was more prominent among the children having multiple parental figures when the relationship between the parents is not satisfactory than either the father or the mother exhibit rejection towards the children which ultimately develops hostile, defiant and unsocial youth. Children coming from such family background lack formal inner control.

An important study was carried out by *Shainberg*. He studied 1500 young deliquents. The finding showed that 90 per cent of them had severe difficulties with their father. The father was perceived as vague lacking in warmth and difficult to communicate with when the relationship between the parents is unsatisfactory or there is a disagreement between the spouses, then the relationship are full of conflicts. The father is unable to communicate with or discipline their sons, while the mother either overprotect the children or discard them. This might lead again ink developing the socially unaccepted behavioural characteristics.

Bacon, Child and Berry in a study found that the family which typically a restrict opportunities for the children to identify with father or mother are likely to develop unaccepted behavioural patterns. The parents who were unsatisfied in their marital relationship and poor in their marital adjustment were labelled as socio-pathic father and mother. According to Scharfman and Clerk such parents contributed in developing the socially disapproved behavioural characteristic.

In the development of the child's personality the role of mother has been overemphasised while the role of the father has been a sorely neglected subject. The psychologists discovered long back that the effect of fathering are evident in the personality development of their sons and daughters. The most obvious feature of father-child relationship pertain to sex-role behaviour in a number of studies conducted over past 30 years. It has been clear that the boys who have been deprived of their father in early childhood, displayed feminine behaviour. According to Carlsmith Biller and Levin such boys are less aggressive and more dependent than other boys of their age.

Apparently there are no such studies which shows the effect of marital happiness and behavioural pattern when examine minutely. Several studies shows that the relationships of pathogenic family behaviour, ultimately suggest that marital happiness and marital adjustment of mothers do influence the development of behavioural pattern of the children. Here it can be pointed out that there is a research gap relevant to the investigation exploring the influence of degree of marital happiness and marital adjustment on the development of children's behavioural characteristics. The following review of literature presents a few relevant studies supporting as an evidence to the hypothesis framed and tested in the present study.

Marital Happiness and Adjustment

Marital life tends to be regarded as a private world not to be discussed with an outsider. Therefore research about marriage was almost unknown until the late thirties. Burgess and Cattrell, the pioneer in this field studied 526 subjects to assess their marital adjustment. The findings of their study supported the hypothesis that affectionate and intimate companionship mutual confiding were the basis of marital adjustment. The result also indicate a moderate positive relationship between marital unhappiness and number of complain about marriage and the spouse.

Locke's findings revealed that equality of interests and common friends were associated with good marital adjustment. Subjects were happy in their marriage mentioned 'love' as a motive for marriage.

King from his study indicate that adjustment in marriage was better where relationship was equalitarian rather than dominated by husband and wife. King also stressed the fact that demonstration of affection and confiding are conducive to marital adjustment. Results further revealed that women were better adjusted in marriage than men and were active in putting further efforts to make the relationship satisfactory.

Luckey studied the congruence of role perception as related to marital happiness. Analysis of her data revealed that satisfaction in marriage was related to the congruence of the husband's self-concept and that held to him by his wife. His findings concluded that marital satisfaction was associated with the wife accurates perception of her husband.

Roth and Peck studied the social class and social mobility factors related to marital adjustment. Result indicated the adjustment scores tended to be higher in the case of same class marriage.

Kotler found that congruence of perception was significantly related to husbands and couples' marital adjustment scores, but not wife's adjustment scores. Result from Tayler's study showed a greater similarity between self-perception and spouse's perception of self which was related to good marital adjustment.

Navran studied communication in marriage. The findings revealed that happy married coupled had both verbal and non-verbal communication than did unhappy couples. Good verbal communication was found to be more strongly associated with good marital adjustment.

Promilla Kapoor studied 300 educated working women. The result of her study indicated that where spouses agreed on the sharing of the household jobs adjustment was better than those who did not agree on this and resolved disagreement by mutual give and take. She also found that more serious complaint in marriage were positively related to marital maladjustment.

Gurin et. al. found that the quality of inter-personal relationship and personal involvement in marital life was positively related to marital happiness.

Murstein, Gladin found that a balance of good or reading characteristics was important for marital happiness. There was some relationship between negative types of personality characteristic and unhappiness in marriage. According to this authors emotional suitability, adaptability and flexibility correlated positively with marital happiness.

Smith stated that possession of higher self-esteem was significantly correlated with dyadic adjustment. Individuals who had social confidence tended to have better adjustment marriage.

Orden and Bradburn found in their study of marital happiness that satisfaction was reflected in the companionships and sociability that spouses enjoy and tension was reflected in the disagreement the spouses encounter. Thus, satisfaction was positively related to marital happiness while tension was negatively related.

Whitehurst from the result of his studies revealed that higher involvement in family activities and more conventional styles of life was associated with higher marital adjustment.

Blood and Udry pointed out that where joint decision was taken, where couples consulted each other on decisions were more likely satisfied with their marriage.

Devidson and Bernard studied the relationship between perception of equity/inequity in marriage and marital adjustment.

The results revealed that the greater the inequity in material dyad the lesser the marital adjustment. Relationship that both partners view as equitable would yield the greatest average marital adjustment.

Yelsma explored whether couples who had more effective marital adjustments had more congruent perceptions of each other's communication practices. Result revealed that happy subjects had significantly more congruency between their self-perception and their spouses perception of their communication practices.

Dean et. al. tested the hypothesis that pressures from outside the family social system tended to decrease marital adjustment while satisfactory relationship support it. Results showed that communication was the best predictor of marital adjustment for both males and females.

Marital Status and Child Rearing Practices

Yarrow et. al. investigated the relationship among marital status, child rearing practices and maternal satisfaction. Result showed that there was a relationship between maternal satisfaction and the mother child rearing practices. Mothers satisfaction correlated highly with a number of child rearing practices. Maternal dissatisfaction was related to more authoritarian disciplinary techniques and irritated responses to children's attention demands.

Since the child rearing practices are directly seen influencing the development of personality of the children. There is much space to assert that marital happiness is related to the development of personality of the child.

According to Nancy Colleclta, Mothers who were satisfied in their marital life was seen more likely to use withdrawal of love, reasoning, isolation or deprivation of privileges as preferred punishment techniques. Dissatisfactioned mothers on the other hand were more likely to use authoritarian discipline to expert more immediate obedience.

The result of Becker and Crug's study indicated, girls with highly anxious maladjustment mothers showed a pattern of introversion or withdrawal in school, while at home they showed primary hostile behaviour.

Korian observed changes in status of women and child rearing practices also, despite repeated attempts of maintaining basic traditions, changes are also democratic as against traditional dominance.

Jacobson studied the impact of marital separation/divorce on children, parental communication and child adjustment. It was found that there were significant differences in the adjustment of children. (a) The more the attention from parents in dealing with the separation, the better the adjustment. (b) The more the encouragement in discussion after the event the better the adjustment. (c) Those who bought problems to parents regarding separation after the event were better adjusted. The findings reflects well on the development of behavioural or personality characteristics, the influence of parental behavioural pattern.

Hodges et. al., examined parent-child relationships and adjustment in pre-school children in divorced and intact families. Results revealed that quality of contact with parents was unrelated to adjustment in children from intact families. Parental warmth and permissiveness predicted adjustment in both types of families.

According to Hetherington et al divorced parents when compared to the parents of intact families it was found that divorced parents were less affectionate, less consistent in discipline, poorer at communication and less inclined to make maturity demands. Other observational studies done by Santrock, Meadows and Lindbergh have shown that single mothers often have difficult setting limits and controlling their sons' behaviour.

According to Biller children with single parents were differ than the children living with both parents. Boys in father-absent families are often less interested in masculine toys and activities than boys in two parents home.

The effects of parents' death or divorce, abandonment and other stressful events experienced in early childhood on personality traits in later childhood were examined by Cioata. Results showed statistically significant differences between two groups on all personality traits. The stressed subjects were more rigid, distant, emotionally unstable, excitable, anxious and suspicious, had a lower ego strength and less group attachment. This emphasizes that early childhood stresses lead to profound personality changes.

Hoffman said that the child in a home where the mother is employed experience a more egalitarian parents relationship, more care by people outside the family, and more responsibility for household chores than children in other families.

According to Huston, children of employed mother often have better social and personality adjustment in school more egalitarian concepts about sex roles and less traditional stereotypes of male and female activities than children with mothers who are full time homemakers.

Westbrook studied the reactions to child rearing and early maternal experiences of women with differing marital relationships. Positive marital relationships were linked with calmer reactions. Self-oriented relationships were characterized by mutilation anxiety directly reflecting a personality trait.

El-Guebalay and Offord used behavioural questionnaires to determine some of the variables involved in the psychosocial adjustment of the child. Results revealed that group of emotionally disturbed children was related more to the presence of an unsetting situation and poor school performance.

Maternal behaviour towards the child on the love hostility dimension has been found to be the consistent over time. Hough pointed out that unhappy childhood of mother is an etiological factor immaternal overprotection. The overprotective group exceeds the control group in such traits as unhappy childhood, early development of a responsible role and extra hazards presented by children. Figge has also pointed out that the difference between rejecting and non-rejecting group of mothers are greatest in respect of unhappiness of their childhood and in their social frustration through marriage although social and sexual incompatibility are also important.

According to Meradin, mothers makes their relationship with their children more difficult when they react toward their children in a way that is determined by their own unhappy experience their feeling of professional insecurity or their intolerance to social variation.

These studies show that there is a relationship between the parental background condition and child personality mediated by the attitudes and behaviour of parents. The relationship is not directed but their is some linkage between parental background variable and child variable.

Bossard and Bell showed that young parents takes the responsibility of children lightly while overage parents are over-protective, exacting and demanding. Merill found that mother who are conscious of their status use severe methods of control in child rearing. A belief that maternal employment was associated with juvenile delinquency was contradicted by Glueck and Glueck. Cyrus pointed out that working class mothers are less frustrated and capable of more warm interactions with their children. The opposite view is that mother may feel guilty that she devoted less time towards her children and she may overprotective them or she may be so overburdened by duties in his home and at the place of employment that she might completely neglect her children. The overall pattern of such findings suggest that the mother who like her work, will use mild discipline and the child will be relatively non-assertive while the mother who does not like her work, will use stricter disciplinary method and in response to this child will become more assertive and hostile.

According to Hoffman, "Maternal employment has a different effect on the mother-child relationship and on the childs behaviour depending on whether or not the mother enjoy working.

Mother-Child Relationship. While the role of parent-child relationship in personality development of a child implies relationship with both mother and father, the relationship with mother has the most vital effect on the child. The obvious reason for this is that the child is with his mother more than with his father, and as a result the mother's influence is far greater than the father's. In general, mothers are more acceptant, nuturants and democratic and less restrictive and authoritative than fathers in the parent-child relationship.

Sears, Maccoby and Levin (1957) opine that of all the human relations influencing a child, development, the personality of the mother is of central importance. Her attitudes towards the child and his need for understanding affection, acceptance, approval and control are vital.

Yarrow (1963) observed that 'there is extensive evidence of the importance to the child's psychological development of the close interrelationship between mother and child and birth and even before birth.'

Shainess (1963) suggests that 'the maternal attitude toward her forthcoming child is channelled into a direction predominantly accepting or rejecting. He also theorizes that the maternal attitude is a distillate of the woman's personality, philosophies, relationship with husband, security and motivation for pregnancy, conditions of pregnancy, delivery and early post-partum period make important contributions to this attitude'.

Heinstein (1963) confirmed this finding and concluded that 'the coldness or the warmth of the mother's attitude toward the child is related to the child's adjustment or maladjustment. Children nursed a long time by a warm mother were the best adjusted. Those breast fed by the cold mother were found to have a large number of behaviour problems.

Bayley and Shaefer (1960) reported that the early warmth and affection of mothers is associated with calm, happy and co-operative behaviour from children throughout the years prior to adolescence. Furthermore; if suddenly deprived of mother's love, children may feel unwanted and unloved.

Koppitz (1957) stressed the importance of the mother's personality and adjustment in relation to the adjustment of the child. A child will be inclined to feel anxious and guilty during his early years.

Chance (1961) suggested that 'an importance aspect of the child's adjustment to school is preparatory independence-training by the mother. It should be such that the child can leave his mother and can adjust to other adults and other children for the necessary time span for school attendance.

Clarke-Stewart (1973) working with children of 9 to 18 months, found that stimulating responsive maternal behaviour influenced the child's intellectual development ; in the area of social relations, through children influenced mothers.

Belsky, Rovine and Taylor (1984) working with infants at 1, 3 and 9 months of age discovered that maternal involvement was predictive of infant fusiness.

It may be concluded that the most important single factor influencing the survival and welfare of infants appears to be the interest and ability of the mother and the quality of care which she provides. Thus, getting off to a good start in life consistently requires adequate mothering which during infancy, generates those forces that lead toward later personality adjustment.

Mother Role in the Aquisition of Standards. Mothers are the most important socializing agents for the cognitive and effective development of the child. An implicit goal of virtually all family systems is to faster growth and development in non-academic dimensions such as personality, morals and social skills. Following parents, the primary responsibility for the positive development of mental and emotional health of the children is attributed to the mothers, for they are the chief architect of the child's personality. It is through the mother that the child acquires the dominant beliefs, values, motives and behaviours of his culture. Mother plays a role of teacher at the very early stage of child development. She teaches the child, what is right and what is wrong which is related to the moral standards. Because crystallization of major standards, motives, anxieties, expectancies and defenses occur during the early childhood, this period offers a dramatic individual differences among adult which can be discerned by the time the child is 10 years old. At this stage, motives for affiliation, mastery, hostility and sexuality as well as for dominance, affection, acceptance and recognition can be seen to exist in different hierarchies in a group of children and the standards for sex role behaviour, rational judgements and autonomy of action etc. are formed. Since children are not born with a concept of right or wrong or with an understanding of what behaviour is permissible and what is frowned upon. The acquisition of standards are shaped by how parents discipline their children and by the examples they set in their own behaviour. These include standards of morality common to their society as well as sub-cultural values related to the parents' race, religion, ethnic origin, social class etc. Moreover, children respond to their parents influence by forming two complementary sets of internalized standard—first, as they incorporate prohibitions and taboos imposed by their parents, they begin to develop conscience, an inner voice, second, as they incorporate the positive goals and values endorsed by their parents, they begin to develop an ego-ideal of what they ought to do. This process of acquisition of standards proceeds most effectively when parents discipline their children in ways that will help them from an adequate but not overly strict conscience and serve as models of social judgement and self-control with whom their children can identify. Discipline and identification are thus the two key factors in the acquisition of standards. Modeling theorists (i.e., Bandura, 1969 and Walters, 1963) posits that the direct observation and modeling of a particular behaviour is the essential process of acquiring that behaviour. For example, a daughter, will learn to drink alcohol because she sees her mother frequently drinking alcohol. Black, and Rollins (1982) observed that qualities of the mothers instruction and delivery of information such as a global teaching strategy is positively related to the child's successful performance.

Brook, Gordon and Brook (1980), Brook, Whiteman, Brook and Gordon (1983, 1984a, 1984b, 1985) etc. have demonstrated that parents traditionality, warmth and provision of structured environment are responsible for the personality characteristics of the adolescents. Garg (1983) study revealed that the practical behaviour of the parents significantly effect the class adjustment of pre-adolescent student.

Brook and Gordon (1986) found from their study that maternal personality attributes, maternal unconventionality (i.e., tolerance of deviance), poor control of impulses, poor interpersonal relatedness and poor psychological adjustment are highly related to higher stages of drug use in adolescents.

Kothari, Saroj (1987) made a study to know the relationship between the Mother's Academic Qualification and the development of the moral concept of her child. Her results showed that the mother's academic qualification has significant impact on the existing moral concept of her child.

Maternal Behaviour and Its Impact on Child's Behaviour

Mayer correlated ratings of maternal behaviour with child's domination cooperation index. Child's domination was seen positively related to disciplinary friction. Rapport with the child, understanding of the child's problems, readiness of explanations and intensity of contact were all negatively related to the child's dominant behaviour.

Merrill observed mother-child interaction and found that mother's use of directing, interfering, criticism as well directing and suggesting types of control were reflected in child's behaviour. Dependent behaviour resulted from maternal over concern.

Mohr showed that common attitudes of mothers may be responsible for their difficulties in child management. For example, over protection, attachment as a gratification of mothers own need for affection, rejection and ambivalence are unhealthy parental attitudes to which a child may have to adjust in the home. This type of adjustment made mother is carried over into general life situation and may be responsible for later anti-social behaviour.

Jenkins showed that youngsters who are characterized as 'over anxious' were likely to have an infantalizing over protective mother such mothers deny their children the needed opportunities for reality testing and development of competencies.

Miller and Swanson found love oriented techniques of child rearing appeared to contribute to guilt feelings in the child, while physical punishment, withdrawal of privileges and threats contributed to overt aggression.

In the examination of parental role perceptions of children, Ghosh and Sinha found that children perceived mother as more rewarding major source of affection and nurturance and had greater interaction with mother than father. They also perceived mother as more punitive than father.

Banner examined the relationship between child rearing attitudes of mothers and levels of academic achievement of their 11 years old children. Results showed that the mothers of under achieving sons were more dominant, rigid and restrictive in the sense of being possessive and intrusive, while the mothers of under-achieving daughters were more dominant, rigid and restrictive in terms of being protective.

Saraswati and Sundarsan perceived maternal disciplinary practices and their relation to the development of moral judgement. Results indicated a general pattern of negative correlation between maternal power assertion and children's moral maturity scores and positive correlations between maternal induction and moral maturity scores. These correlations were significant only in the case of upper-middle class girls.

Jones, Rickel and Smith examined the relation of nurturant and restrictive maternal child-rearing practices and maternal education to the types of social problem solving strategies. Restrictiveness was positively associated with the use of evasion and negatively with and negotiation strategies. Maternal nurturance was the discriminator for reliance on authority. Education of mothers was also positively related to maternal nurturance and negatively to maternal restrictiveness.

Block and his associates found that the mothers of neurotic children tended to be uncertain, tormented to worry and guilt and in constant need of reassurance.

Mash and Johnson in a study observed that the hyperactive children who had histories of physical activity and poor behavioural control, their mothers were more directive and negative than mothers of normal children. It was suggested these differences in the mothers' behaviour were probably due to their children's initial tendencies to be hyperactive and the children's behaviour was probably influenced in turn by the mother's responses.

Gupta and Agnihotri studied self-confidence as a function of perceived maternal child rearing behaviour. The analysis of the data revealed that boys with low self-confidence perceived their mothers to be controlling, inconsistent in the use of discipline, accepting and having an acceptance of individuation. Perceptions of maternal withdrawal of relations and non-enforcement were associated with high self-confidence in boys. The girls with low self-confidence perceived rejection, inconsistent discipline, lack of discipline, instilling persistent anxiety and nonenforcement in their mother's behaviour, while perceptions of withdrawal of relations and hostile detachment were associated with self-confidence in girls.

Shrivastava studied anxiety among primary school children in relation to employment of their mothers. It was found that girls were having significantly higher anxiety scores than boys and the wards of employed mothers were significantly lower in anxiety than the wards of non-employed mothers.

Law in a study of mothers of well adjusted happy children as contrasted with mothers of clinical children were more happy. Clinical children's mothers were discontented with themselves as individuals and their symptoms of deeper conflicts led to difficulties in child rearing.

Importance of Home Environment

Grant studied the effect of certain factors in the home environment upon child behaviour. Rating by three observers on eleven patterns of behaviour were obtained on 33 pre-school children. These pattern of behaviour were 'plays with groups' versus 'withdraws', 'self-reliance' verses 'dependent behaviour', 'ascendancy' verses 'submission', 'selfish' versus unselfish behaviour, 'Sadistic behaviour' versus its absence', 'nervous habits', versus their absence 'security' verses 'unsecurity', 'resourcefulness' versus lack of it' and 'responsibility' versus 'irresponsibility'. Parents practices rated over protectiveness versus rejection, logical versus illogical approach, encourage versus discourage, expression of idea fosters versus inhibition, social development and calm and tension. Afterwards training programme ten homes and the children were related. Outstanding change in personality were observed in all subjects.

Brounfenbrenner found that children from achievement oriented homes exile in planning and performance and they were more tense, domineering, aggressive and cruel. According to Moss and Kagon the democratic homes, maternal acceleration and a warm positive family atmosphere have been reported to increase childs intelligence especially verbal ability.

Social Behaviour of Child

Friedman while studying the inter-relationship between maternal and paternal child rearing attitudes and social behaviour of children, investigated that the father's understanding of child behaviour and the mother's attitude towards causation of child behaviour were significantly related to the child's social behaviour.

Results of Geismar's study indicated that across all ethnicities mothers and fathers appeared to share similar expectations of their children's behaviour and they indicated supportive and controlling dimensions of parenting.

Fe A Domingo investigated the socialization of nine behaviour patterns. Results yielded that although there was a close relationship between child rearing practices and actual behaviour the level of child's development and predominant cultural factors also affected the behaviour and personalities of these children.

In a series of investigation done by Santrock and Warshak, children from ages 6 to 11 who lived with their father were compared with children in mother custody and two parents families. Boys in father custody families were better adjusted than those who lived with mothers, but girls living with their father showed poorer adjustment than girl who lived with their mother.

Sanstrock and Warshak studied the effects of father custody on children's social development. Results indicated that subjects living with opposite sex parents were less well adjusted than subjects living with the same sex parents. In both mother and father custody families were positively linked with the subjects' competent social behaviour.

A cross-cultural comparison between Navajo and Anglo child rearing behaviours was studied by Abraham et. al. Results indicated that there was a comparatively higher supportive parenting style on the part of Anglos and protective and punishing parenting style on the part of Navios. Differences in parenting style were associated with cultural values.

Kagan et. al. examined maternal reinforcement style and cooperation, competition among Anglo-American and Mexican American 5 to 12 years old children. Results failed to support the theoretical formulations that postulated positive effects of a rewarding, non-punitive maternal reinforcement style for fostering prosocial development in children.

Aggression in Children

Major findings of Bekar et. al. were—

1. The degree of hostility of both parents and use of physical punishment was related to aggressive behaviour in children. Mother's child rearing anxiety strongly related to aggressive behaviour in child as was father's strictness, but not his restrictiveness.
2. If mother was hostile and punitive the child tended to be dominant than submissive. This relation was stronger for boys than for girls.

Leftowitz et. al. found that aggression in children increases as parents increasingly rely upon physical punishment for controlling child's behaviour.

A study done by Kafiluddin reveals that a person subjected to power-assertive discipline, reared in a nuclear family and being the only child or first born would be more aggressive than a person who has been disciplined by indirect methods such as love-withdrawal and induction, reared in a joint family, and being the middle or last born.

Kagan and Freeman found that what mother does is often a reaction to the child's behaviour. Maternal hostility may be a reaction to a very aggressive, hyperactive child. Just as mothers shape children's behaviour, so do children shape mother's behaviours.

Zecker and Wattenberg found if parents ignores their children and devote little time to them as they grow, their peer adjustment to environment frequently lead to delinquency.

Haimowitz in his article 'Criminals are made not Born, point out that delinquency frequency is a reaction to parental neglect.

Delaney found that parental restrictiveness than permissiveness was positively related to child aggression specially in boys. Parental aggression of mothers was more significantly related to aggression and perceived rejection in sons than mothers who assumed expressive roles.

Patterson viewed the role of the mother from the perspective of coercion theory. The results showed that mothers of aggressive children encountered higher rates of aversive events than mothers of normal children.

Punetha found that socialization play an important role on aggression tendency of children. Study conducted by him on tribal society to find out the presence of this traits relieves that Bhotia mothers used positive incentive technique to handle aggression so their children show degree of aggression as compare to DOM children whom mothers were more permissive and did not use positive incentive technique for motivating the children to give up aggression.

Robert and Deinty assessed consistency of assertive, aggressive and submissive interpersonal behaviour. Boys demonstrated remarkable consistency in their aggressive expression. The consistency of assertive behaviour for both boys and girls was unexpectedly high.

Dependency in Children

Maccord observed that parental conflict and rejection of the child were prominent in the family background of extremely dependent boys. These findings supported the view that dependent behaviour was a manifestation of feelings of insecurity in parent-child relationship. The high dependent children were the products of homes in which parents encouraged their children to rely on others for self care.

In an other study done by Stendler it was found that many parents encourage dependency on their children's part by expecting their children to take help and guidance from them. This makes their children over dependent. These studies point out proper and consistent handling of child's dependency demand to avoid over dependency in the child. Cummings pointed out that over protective children show more nervous symptoms. Kates showed that most children who are brought up by overprotective mothers are more sensitives to the father than to the mother.

Bender and Sears et al have pointed out that one of the most serious effects of over-protectiveness is overdependency on the child's parts Stendle has shown that if dependency needs of the body are not met satisfactory he is likely to feel insecure and afraid to be independence.

Grossman examined the relationship between parental warmth and children's dependency and responsiveness to social reinforcement. It was observed that more warmly treated children were not significantly less dependent.

Moore studied parental child rearing practices to the occurrence of dependency and autonomy in children's behaviour. Results indicated that the use of physical punishment by the mother was positively associated with dependency in boys but not in girls.

Restrictiveness was an important aspect of maternal behaviour which contributed to the dependency in girls low dependency in children and high maternal permissiveness were associated with high degree of autonomy in girls but not in boys.

Govalas and Briggs reported that dependency persisted when the parents rewarded dependent behaviour and failed to reward competent behaviour in the child.

Adjustment in Children

Shoemaker et al studied relationships between parental attitudes and child behaviour. Attitudes of both parents were seen intimately related to the occurrence and form of maladjustive tendencies among children.

Kagan and Lenkin examined children's perceptions of parents of 3 to 8 years. They found that fathers were perceived as more fear arousing, more confident and more punitive than were mothers. Mothers were perceived as nicer and more nurturant.

The perceptions of the parent-child relationship and its association to child adjustment was studied by Serot and Teevan. The well adjusted child perceived his parent-child relationship as relatively happy while maladjusted child's perception was far from ideal.

Characteristics of both parents in reference to certain behaviour tendencies among children were examined by Peterson. It was discovered that—(i) The attitudes of father were as intimately related as the attitudes of mothers to the occurrence and form of maladjustive tendencies among children. (ii) Personality problems such as shyness withdrawal among children were relatively independent of maternal attitudes, but were related to autocratic attitudes and lack of parental concern among fathers. (iii) Conduct problems were associated with general adjustment among mothers and with evident permissiveness and disciplinary ineffectuality on the part of the fathers.

Curiosity, Competence and Creativity in Children

Maw and Maw observed attitudes regarding child rearing practices and family relationships held by parents whose children differed in curiosity level. Results showed that neither mothers nor father of high and low curiosity girls differed significantly in their attitudes in these areas. However, boys differed significantly in some of these attitudes.

Relationship of parental treatment of children to dependence and competence were examined by Clapp. The parents of competent children were found significantly more permissive less restrictive, warmer and less hostile. The parents themselves were more competent and consistent in Philosophy and action than parents of dependent children. There were indications that parents especially mothers of competent children spent less, though, better time with their sons.

Krause examined relationship between mental health, socialization and creativity of 12 years old children. Mothers of highly creative subjects behaved more actively when engaged in problem solving with subjects. Mothers of low creative subjects interacted in a more guarded and cautious manner, yet with more visible demonstrations of positive effect. While on father's attitudes data seemed to oppose the belief that creative children has permissive, non-authoritarian fathers.

The relationship between children's activity level and parent-child interactions in 117 preschool children was examined by Buss. Parents of highly active children tended to intrude physically and described as getting into power struggles and competitions with their children. Impatience of hostility towards active children was observed in all parents. In contrast interactions involving less active children were generally peaceful and harmonious.

Martin studied relationship of parental strictness to competitive and cooperative attitudes of primary school children on competitive items, boys did not score significantly higher than girls but girls scored higher than boys on cooperative items. Girls perceived their parents as being correlation was more strict than boys. For boys significant correlation was found between parental strictness items and competitiveness and cooperativeness showed significant correlation with parental strictness. Results suggested that parental strictness may be significant in the development of sex differences in competitive and cooperative attitudes.

Sharma in her study aimed at identifying the high and low creatives and studying the parental behaviour which might play a significant role in determining the creative potentials of the child. The high creative group (verbal-non-verbal) had been observed to have much more emotional bonding with the parents as compared to their low counterparts. The creativity of an individual was affected by the sense of being rewarded by the parents. Punishment had different effect on verbal-non-verbal creative behaviour. The peaceful home environment promotes the growth of creative potentials.

Personality Development of Children

Hoffman analysed the effects of the use of power by the parents on the personality of the child. The findings suggested that the father appeared to function like a catalyst in affecting the mother's influential behaviour forward the child, this behaviour in turn affected the later's personality development.

According to Nicholas parents who are extrovert themselves will prefer extraversion is their children allowing to move freely with other children and secure for than advantages of play with the peer group.

Peterson found that harsh parental attitudes were related to personality problems such as shyness and withdrawal.

Siegelman examined relationship between personality of college students and their early parent child relationships. Children with extrovert personality inclinations had loving parents while introvert personality inclinations had rejecting parents and showed high degree of anxiety than children with loving parents.

Agrawal and Saxena organised discussion into studies of effects of parental child rearing practices, child rearing attitudes and personality on children. They inferred that the emotional development of the child is significantly affected by each of the three factors and was suggested that training programme and guidance clinics be opened to help parents to avoid victimizing their children.

A study conducted by Mathur on the children of both working and non-working women indicate that socio-economic status affects the I.Q. level of preschool children.

Sarker conducted his research on 400 healthy and unhealthy children and found that families today had mostly either autonomic or mother dominant family structure. The mentally unhealthy group of children had higher family tension than the healthy group. The children from families with syncretic division of functions had better mental health.

Current Family Setting and Children Personality

Scott studied some family life patterns and their relation to personality development in children with sample drawn from farm, small town and city. The question were with 16 selected items was used and factor analysis of the results was done. Two significant factors were selected and identified as confidence, affection and companionability, which, may be called as favourable pattern and parental misconduct or family discord were unfavourable pattern. Children from favourable pattern not only in personal and adjustment and appreciative attitude towards home life but also in their general personality development. Farm parents tended to have the least favourable attitudes and city parents the most favourable. The three group did not differ significantly in respect of attitudes towards self-reliance.

Erickson states the middle class parents are more exact in their expectation, train their children early, supervise closely and put greater emphasis on individual achievement than the parents from lower class.

Almost similar view was held by Davis and Havinghurst. They have reported that lower class mothers imposed fewer restrictions on the movement of their children outside of the home than did middle class mothers.

Levinger and Murphy pointed out that there are important differences in child rearing and training in rural and urban children and it is wrong to assume that findings from research on city children will also apply to farm city. The cultural ideology of parents and teacher is important with respect to their influence on child behaviour.

Francis studied the influence of socio-economic factors on the personality. Difficulties were associated more directly with parents attitude, discipline, allowance, recreation, child health and community activities, rather than to socio-economic status.

According to Crandall higher social class families employed less coercive pressure than families from lower class and the families from the lower class employed more severe penalties from misbehaviour than families from higher social class.

Child Rearing Practices and Attitudes of Parents

(1) *Sex Role Attitudes.* Singh examine the role of the personality of the parents in the development of sex role preference in their children. He found that when father were dominant and masculine and mother were submissive and feminine their boys preferred more masculine role and girl preferred greater feminine role. When father were submissive and feminine and mothers were dominant and masculine their boys preferred less masculine role and girl preferred greater masculine role.

According to Bronfenbrenner when the principal disciplinarian, boys tended to be more responsible when mother was the major authority figure girls were more dependable.

According to Hoffman the effect of maternal employment on children's social and personality adjustment are more consistently positive for girls than for boys. Daughters of employed mother are likely to have higher aspiration for achievement and education to want a career themselves and to choose a career that is not traditionally feminine.

Balay and Schaefer found that maternal expectations and demands for achievement were important for boys and not for girls. Mother's negative and rejecting attitudes had a severe effect on boys and little on girls. Intensive mothering benefited boys but girls responded negatively to it. These investigators also investigated that mother's affectionate, equalitarian behaviour inhibited children's personal, social manifestations. Similarly relationships were found between mother's behaviour and boy's cooperativeness and attentiveness, while girls were less affected by mother's behaviour. They seemed more self-sufficient.

In an examination of relationship between child rearing practices and attitudes of parents and identification among children Sears et al concluded (1) Children of both sexes initially adopted feminine maternal types of behaviour. (2) When opposite sex parent rewarded dependency the child tended to develop behaviour qualities characteristics of the sex.

In a study of children's behaviour involvement with parents, Livson found that significantly more sons than daughters showed high involvement with their fathers rather than with their mothers. Daughters significantly were strongly involved with their mothers than sons. Both boy's and girl's involvement with the mother was related to mother's maternal behaviour and affection.

(2) *Parental Acceptance.* Parental acceptance of children is believed to be one of the essential elements underlying the whole structure of parent-child relationship.

Burchinal found older mothers accepting their children more than younger mothers, as a result of experience of rearing older children.

According to Roy the educational level of parents is more important than their age. Parents of higher educational level gives more freedom to their children than parents with low educational level.

Parents with more education, to be more reasoning and use less scolding and physical punishment found by Gacas and Nye.

According to Nydeggar father who have their first child relatively lare are warmer and more involved with child rearing than are young father.

According to Crnic parents who have their first older are more attentive warm and parents than are people who begin child when they are satisfied with being their families early.

Findings of Medinnus and Curtis strongly supported the hypothesis that there is a significant positive relationship between maternal self-acceptance and self-acceptance of the child.

Hurley noted a positive relationship between parental acceptance and children's intelligence. Surprisingly maternal acceptance was not found to be more closely related to children's I.Q. than was paternal acceptance.

With respect to parental acceptance and rejection attitude Hatfield found that mothers reared aggressiveness in their sons but not in their daughters, while reverse is true of dependency.

Devdas et al observed the disciplinary techniques adopted by mothers differed according to their educational status. Praising and explaining the consequences and psychological techniques in disciplining children were adopted more by educated mothers. Beating was observed in uneducated mothers.

Sears observed that early parental warmth and acceptance were significant determinants of child's self-esteem. His findings indicated that rural mothers gave love and affection generously without bargaining.

Chandramani et. al. investigated that incidence of problem behaviour was the highest in low income group and in children from nuclear families. The higher the education of parents, the lesser the problems in children.

Mothers intimacy factor correlates positively with father's education was investigated by Lamb. More the education of the father more the mother was the engage in affectional support for the child.

Rohner et. al. perceived parental acceptance rejection and development of children's locus of control. A multiple regression correlation analysis revealed that internality increased significantly with subjects age and with their perceptions of increased parental acceptance.

Symonds sought to find out difference in behaviour between accepted and rejected children. He reported that the accepted children engaged themselves predominantly in socially acceptable behaviour while the rejected children manifested a numbed of unacceptable behaviour.

(3) *Parental Rejection.* Winstet found that totally rejected children exhibit more overt expression of anti-social and hostile behaviour than those living with their parents. He used controlled play situation in determining certain effect of maternal attitudes on children.

Kanner has pointed out that any child has a good chance for satisfactory mental health regardless of physical condition, intelligence quotient etc., if he is accepted by his parents.

Symonds pointed out that a child who was rejected developed feeling of insecurity and inferiority. He had a low conception of himself resulting from a low view of the child by his parents.

English found that parental attitudes of lack of affection for the child and disguised hostility to an unwanted child may presage the onset of neurosis and psychosis.

Maccord studied that parental conflict and rejection of the child were prominent in the family background of extremely dependent boys. These findings supported the view that dependent behaviour was a manifestation of feelings of insecurity in parent-child relationship. The high dependent children were the products of homes in which parents encouraged their children to rely on others for self care.

Digman and Hurley indicated negative relationship between the parental attitudes of harshness and rejection and the child's intellectual development.

Parental Rejection and Over Protection

Parent-child relations have been most widely studied and discussed in terms of rejection and over-protection (or over acceptance). There are, of course, all intermediate degrees between these extreme positions. The first extreme (rejection) may be characterized by parents' hypercritical attitudes, disregard, or neglect, numerous threats to the child's physical security and well being, actual desertion or failure to provide financial support. At the other extreme (over acceptance and over protection parental attitudes may be characterized by excessive contact of and association with the mother (sleeping together undue caressing, keeping the child always within sight). Prolongation of infant care (providing for his physical needs long after the child can take care of himself); prevention of the development of independent behaviour (defending and fighting for the child, too close and extensive supervision of activities); deficiency or excess of maternal control (on the one hand over-indulgence and revolving the household around the child; on the other hand, insistence upon complete obedience, resulting often in intensification of infantile traits).

It is clear that such disparate and extreme forms of treatment will have very appreciable effect upon the development of a child's personality and behaviour. It is not possible however, to predict exactly what consequences of extreme treatment will be; for a child's development and behaviour depend also upon other though often less powerful influence. Nor it is to be assumed that every child who has been the victim of parental rejection or over protection is doomed to a lifetime of maladjustment. Since a variety of forms of adjustment, as well as maladjustment, are possible.

Parental **neglect or rejection** at times may even be the primary cause of a child's delinquent behaviour, in the more extreme cases. In socially less severe instances parental rejection may create in the child anxieties, fears, hatreds, and unhappiness. Rejection may also produce on over aggressiveness which often persists for a large part or all of an individual's life time giving rise not infrequently to an over weening ambition. Such ambition, continued into adulthood, in the more extreme cases saddles an unfortunate industry community, or nation with 'leader' who are motivated by vindictiveness, which they attempt to rationalize in a variety of ways.

Parental over-protection, on the other hand, if it is primary and sucessfully dominating in character, often result in the child's being excessively submissive; that is, extremely obedient, dependent upon others and completely accepting authority.

This sort of child is regarded by too many adult as the 'good' child, for he does not disturb them; he does not interfere with their established ways of doing things; they can exercise their authority upon him without meting opposition. It sometime happens, however and paradoxically, that a child who has had too much care and protection from parents will later reject and rebel against authority. This paradoxical result is very probably due to the kinds of situations in which the child received the excessive care and protection and to the effect such treatment had upon that child's behaviour and status in his relationships with other members within his own family and with groups outside his family with which he has become identified. In other words, the individuals eventual reaction to childhood over protection and submissiveness will depend upon what kinds of situations he must live in and contend with at a later timer upon his later purposes and goals of activity, and upon the manner in which his earlier over protection and submissiveness influence the effectiveness of later adjustment.

Parental over-protection, however, may also takes the form of over-indulgence, when as already stated, the household revolves about the child and there is absence of authority. In such case, the child may develop into a commanding, bollying, lime-light seeking, authority-rejecting individual. Obviously traits such as these does not quality a person for well-adjusted association and living with his fellow men, even if it is true that such persons sometime become "leaders" in their communities or nations. But their so-called leadership is not motivated by an interest in social well-being; nor is it necessarily buttressed by superior abilities. It is a "leadership" motivated by a powerful desire for self-aggrandisement.

Cause of Rejection and Over Protection. Inasmuch as parental attitudes so profoundly affects a child's personality development, it is important to know, if possible, what the factors, are that cause these attitudes. Among the more immediate cause of over-protection, particularly in the case of mothers, are the following: earlier fustration in having children; hazard of childhood, especially if the child has any physical handicaps; sexual incompatibility with one's spouse, lack of social contacts and lack of other interests; thwarted ambitions and consequent "living out of parent's unhappy childhood and emotional impoverishment in early life; and second usually early assumption of a responsible role and continuance of this role into marriage. The presence of both these factors in a parent's early life, which occurs not infrequently, greatly enhances the possibilities of the appearance of an over protective attitude in parenthood.

Among the causes of rejection by parents again particularly by mothers, as revealed in several case studies, are the following emotional immaturity; dependence; insecurity; marital disharmony because of sexual maladjustment or for other reasons; unwelcome responsibilities and deprivations associated with raising children. When factors such as those are the causal ones in cases of rejection, the children become the objects of parental dissatisfaction and sometimes threats of displacing the parental dissatisfaction and sometime threats of displacing the parent in the family constellation.

Operative in parental over-protection or rejection are several other factors which are still more remote and less readily perceived than those mentioned above. One of these is *transference* to one's child of a feeling of hostility or protection, as the case may be, which the parent held and fostered toward another person, that other person might have been the parent's own parents, or the parent's brother or sister, or some other relative. The transference of feeling and attitude may be entirely unconscious. Yet the child, in such an instances may revive and perpetuate in the parents his (or her) former feelings, because the child recreates the formal situation in which those feelings were engendered.

A second factor among those less readily perceived is the projection by the parents upon the child of certain feeling and attitudes which the parent harbors toward himself, or herself. In severe instances of guilt feelings about one's self, created in a variety of ways (e.g., strong attachment of the parent to his own parent of opposite sex, sense of shame, exaggerated conscience, scruples and inhibitions) a parent might project this self-depreciation upon the child. Projection, however, may occur in many form, one of the most common of which and educationally very significant, is the projection of parental ambition and goal upon a child. In this case unfulfilled parental ambition and unattained parental goals are put upon the child; it is a form of vicarious self-fulfillment which is not in the parent's consciousness, or otherwise stated, the parental unconsciously lays upon the child an emotional "must". Parental ambitions for their children, however, are not always undesirable, nor unwholesome, if the ambitions and goals are within reach of the child's capabilities and if through wise guidance the child comes to accept them as this own. But when actual projection fosters in the parents attitudes of too great intensity, severity, and strictness, when it leads them to setup goals, that are too high, and to dictate the child's course of activity, the result can be extremely unwholesome. Another important form is the projection of a parent's own unresolved fears and insecurities upon the child, due to the parent's own unfortunate childhood experience. In short, it appears that many of these instances of projection derive from the parent's own trauma and unsatisfied needs of childhood and adolescence, the effects extending into parenthood.

An Alternative to Rejection and Over Protection

It might appear from the foregoing discussion of parental attitudes that there are no desirable and well adjusted parents. That is certainly not the case. There are many parents who have spent their childhood and adolescence under option or near optioned conditions, and who, therefore are able to provide their own children with initial environmental advantages. There are still other parents whose childhood and adolescence were less than optional, but who have sought and achieved insight into the nature and causes of their own feelings and attitudes, and who have there-by been enabled to provide more desirable interpersonal environmental condition to their children. It has been our primary purpose, in presenting these factors in parent-child relations, to indicate that parents' own histories and experiences profoundly affect their children's development. These children, in turn, become parents themselves; their feelings and attitudes too are rooted in their own histories and experiences; thus their own offsprings' development, in turn again, is influenced by the manner in which they, the newer generation of parents, were developed. And so the cycle of events goes on.

It is popularly assumed that children and marital happiness go together. Once the child series there are new stresses, and challenges and the role change is rather abrupt. Both parents experience new feelings of pride and excitement coupled with a greater sense of responsibility that sometime is overwhelming. Some men are envious of their partner's ability to reproduce and of the close emotional bond established between mother and infant.

Indeed there appears to be less communication and sharing of personal interests, more sexual problems, and near marital conflicts in many marriage following the birth of a child.

Influence of Parental Attitude on Children's Self-esteem and Self-concept. In a study mole examined relationship between the childs self-concept in school and parental attitudes and behaviour in child-rearing. It was found that parental satisfaction with child-rearing was significantly and positively related to child's self-concept. Also high ability achievement and creativity were associated with supportive family environment. Trusting that positive self concept represents socially accepted behaviour pattern. There is much scope to assert that parental attitude does influence the behavioural characteristics of children.

A study of children's self-esteem and child-rearing practices was done by Graybill. Results showed that children who viewed their mothers as using psychological pressure technique to discipline them, had low self-esteem and who viewed their mothers as being accepting had high self-esteem.

Parental behaviour and self-esteem in children was studied by Growe correlations between self-esteem and three dimensions of parental behaviour (rejection, indulgence and autonomy) indicated that parental behaviour was more highly related to boys than to girl's self-esteem.

Parental Encouragement, Freedom, Loving and Democratic Attitude. Lu showed that personality structure, the behaviour pattern and the roles the parents plays in the family have a tremendous effect upon the child's personality development and his relationship with other people. He further pointed out that the child in his struggle for independence and individuality need the strength of a parents to find fruitful ways of using his own strength. There is a conflict between child's wish to be independent and yet to be what his parents want him to be.

According to Fromm the ideal parental attitudes should grant the security of love as fundamental psychological requisite for normal growth towards later freedom and independence.

Many family pattern studies and the field research done by Sears, Maccoby and Levin have pointed out that warmth is the most crucial factor affecting the child.

Finney and Peterson showed that parental attitudes of lack of worth and rejection hamper the personality development of children.

Frank says that the family in the an essential agency of satisfaction. If the family lacks the necessary warmth of parental affection the young child becomes fearful and egocentric and uses defences in the form of distrustful and revengeful attitudes of mind.

Bronfenbrenner's research has speculated that 'love-oriented' socialization technique may have some negative as well as constructive aspect. It has now been more or less established that the effect of a satisfied need for action are deep and pervasive.

Jersild pointed out that love greatly affects the childs quality of the environment and conditions its relationship with the child. He remark "a basic and all pervasive feature of parental love for a child is that the child is liked for his own sake, he is viewed as something valuable per see, he is respected as a personality of his own right. The child who is loved himself is free to be himself. This suggest that such a child is free to mould his natural endowments and gifts.

Pikumas says that lack of mothering and affection may stunt his absorption of desirable emotions and attitudes. Antonovsky showed that a low level of affection prolongs the period of child dependency.

Stecker pointed out that children will be socially and emotionally immature if they are deprived of affection for a long time.

Backer found that if father's relationship with child was loving, democratic emotionally mature the child was rated by his mother as better adjusted, outgoing and less demanding. Becker emphasized that parental acceptance and support was a critical factor in child adjustment.

Chein studied the impact of parental attitudes on adjustment of elementary school children. Results yielded that 'Loving' dimension of child rearing behaviour had more influence than the 'demanding' dimension on the subjects' adjustment. Children of warm-restrictive and warm-permissive parents were better adjusted both personally and socially than children of hostile authoritarian and hostile-neglected parents. Girls were more readily influenced than boys by parental attitudes. These attitudes had greater effect on children's personal adjustment.

In an exploratory study Grant investigated various aspects of parent behaviour through interviews with parents. His results showed that children whose parents encouraged their development and expression of ideas were more resourceful, cooperative and self-reliant.

Read in a study that parents who approved freedom from adult control had children with more favourable behaviour. Results also showed that mother's attitudes had more impact on child's behaviour than the fathers'.

Mummary has shown that children who come from home where atmosphere is democratic and happy are assertive and socially accepted.

Becker concluded that restrictiveness may develop well controlled and socialized behaviour in children but it also tends to nurture fear submission, repressed, hostility, dependency and make intellectual striving dull.

Winder and Ross pointed out that overtly severe discipline accompanied by rigid moral standards results in a seriously repressed child who lacks spontaneity and warmth while overtly severe discipline accompanied by over strictness tends to produce children who are rebellious and socially deviant as they grow older.

Grant and Read showed that children are resourceful, cooperative, self reliant and well adjusted when they come from home where reasonable freedom is encourage.

Baldwin studied relations of parents' behaviour to child behaviour. The findings showed that children from democratic homes were characterized as active and free in school activities. The children were seen to be more creative and constructive in their behaviour and were asserting themselves more successfully than children from non-democratic homes.

Parental Punitiveness, Frustration Empathy and Authoritarian Attitudes. Shah studied parental authoritarianism in relation to the personality of children. He found the children with both the parents low in their authoritarian attitudes were good natured, ready to co-operate, attentive to people, soft hearted, kindly and adjusting in comparison with the children whose parents were quite high in authoritarian tendencies.

Hart found that mothers with authoritarian attitudes used fewer love-oriented controls over their children, than non-authoritarian mothers.

Baymrind showed distinction between 'authoritarian and 'authoritative' home. According to him both the homes are characterized by high level of control but in the former it is accompanied by lack of warmth and support while in the latter, severe demands are balanced by effective levels of supports observers rate children of authoritative parents as mature and stable while authoritarian parents have children with high displaced aggression and externalized conscience.

Relation of parental authority to child behaviour and attitudes studies by Radke demonstrated that children whose homes were characterised by a relatively autocratic discipline were more unpopular with other children inconsiderate or others, emotionally unstable, uninhibited and insensitive to praise, blame and did more fighting than did children from the democratic atmospheres.

Adorno, et. al. found that authoritarian parents demand unquestionable obedience and subordination in the child.

Hustan and Bandura in a study observed that identification of the child with the parent decreases as the parents increases the use of physical punishment.

Results of Baker and Krug indicated highest correlation between the father's use of physical punishment and girl's hostile defiant behaviour with him. Significant relations were found with submissiveness. Girls were submissive whose fathers were passive and when fathers were more strict than mothers, girls tended to be submissive, withdrawn, destructing and hostile defiant with father.

In an investigation Byrne and Sturr saw positive relationship between children's authoritarianism and strict parental discipline.

Sethi got supporting evidences to the hypothesis that children imitate parental responses to frustrations. In the event of consistency between parents and concerning response to frustration boys tend to imitate fathers and girls to mothers.

Barnett et. al. explored the relation between the young child's empathy and the parents' self-reported empathy, affection and emphasis on another individual's feelings in discipline and non-discipline situations. Heightened empathy in pre-school girls was associated with particular pattern of mother-father empathy. The facts believed to be more prevalent in the mother's interaction with the child than in the fathers'.

Kaliopuska administered an emotional empathy scale to 9-12 years old boys and girls and their parents. Children's empathy scores would be positively correlated to parents' higher scores. Mother's role would be more prominent than father's in socialization and empathy were expected. However, the results failed to support the assumptions. In addition it was found that mothers were more empathetic than fathers. Similarly girls were more empathetic than boys.

R. and D. Antrade obtained evidence to show that one of the way in which the child can develop low need for achievement is through having careless or indulgent parents who do not expect great things from him. Backer and Watson pointed out over indulged children have been found to be characteristically spoiled, selfish, inconsiderate and demanding.

Bossard and Boll, Henry and Sears et. al. pointed out that permissiveness, if not carried to the extreme of indulgence, will lead to healthy family life and better parents-child relationship.

Sears et. al. showed that high permissiveness and low punishment in the house were correlated positively with anti-social aggressive behaviour.

Father-Child Relationship. No doubt, mother's personality and adjustment are important to her ability to care for her children, but the father's personality and his adjustment are important to the mother's happiness and to all other family factors to which a child is exposed. Generally, it is the father's interests, educational background, occupation, socio-economic status, etc., that determine the way of life a child is going to live and kind of personality he would develop. A father influences his child development through many and diverse channels, through his genetic background, his manifest behaviour with his offsprings, the attitudes he holds himself and his children, the behaviour he models, his position in the family system, the material resources he is able to supply for his children and the vision he holds for his children. Though, father, directly and indirectly, plays an important role in the development of behaviour patterns and personality of the child, his role has been so generally overlooked in the past that it warrants special attention now. The contemporary research in developmental psychology is increasingly recognizing the importance of father's role. The concept 'fathering' is receiving an equal attention in comparison to emphasis on the concept 'mothering'. It is being realized that we need to know much more about the potentialities or the father-child relationship for child development. The traditional conceptions of the father as provider, disciplinarian, source of wisdom are giving way to conception of father as a sharer in the child's total development and in all aspects of family life. If the father-child relationship is good and there is affection and understanding between them the boy strongly identifies with his father. For a boy, his father is the primary source of learning and the supreme authority to whom he must conform. In a recent study by Radin and Epstein (1975), there appears to be a correlation between the warmth of the father-child relationship and the child's academic performance. This is consistent with modern learning theory prediction that the child who feels affection for the person modeling certain characteristics is more likely to identify and imitate these characteristics. An important point revealed by the study of Strodtbeck (1958) is that power assertion by the father over the son does not facilitate achievement or achievement-striving. Rosen and D'Andrade (1959) also support this view. They studied achievement motivation in boys studying in grades four through six and concluded that for high motivation to achieve to develop, the boy needs adequate autonomy from his father. The father who gives the boy a relatively high degree of autonomy provides him with the opportunity to compete on his own ground, to test his skill and to gain a sense of confidence in his own competence.

Hoffman (1960) found a probability that the mother's love and attention makes a boy feel warm and cozy, but father equips the boy to face the world. A healthy father-child relationship leads the boy to a feeling of being loved and accepted, a high degree of self-confidence, non-dependency and tendency to respond realistically and adaptively to frustrating situation.

Laudis (1962) found the role of father in family life an index of family interaction. Closeness of children to their parents is associated with positive values, desirable behaviour and self-evaluation in the children. Positive family values are more closely associated with father-close relationship than with mother-close relationship.

Majoribauks (1972) concluded from an extensive study of 11 years boys that father dominance correlates significantly, although at a low level, with boy's verbal ability. But there is also evidence that low father power fosters congitive competence in boys.

Strodtbeck (1958) has also found that low father power vis-a-vis his son was associated with high independence and mastery-value by boys 14 to 17 years of age, and these values are associated with high achievement. There is an evidence that paternal interference, or even an involvement in boy's mastery efforts may be detrimental to the youngster's congitive growth.

Lamb (1976) reviewing the available evidence suggested that father is most concerned with the adoption of traditionally defined sex roles in children. Father's masculinity and his status in the family are correlated with the masculinity of his sons and the feminity of his daughters. It is also assumed that father fosters sex roles particularly by his own behaviour. He, for example, mildly disapproves aggressive behaviour in girls while approves, even encourages, similar behaviour in boys.

Bertrand (1962), and Cerventes (1965) concluded from their studies that boys from father absent home are more likely than boys from father present homes to encounter difficulties in social, emotional and cognitive development. They are more likely to score lower on tests of academic aptitude and to perform below grades level on measures of academic achievement.

Gregory (1958) demostrated a significantly higher than average rate of delinquency among boys living with their mothers, following the loss of the father through death, parental separation or divorce. When the boy lived with his father following the loss of the mother, however, only an average rate of delinquency was found.

There are some evidence that father absence in the child is associated with overdependency of the child on the mother (Stolz, et. al., 1954) whereby the results of Pederson (1966) suggest that the mother-son relationship can have either a positive or negative effect on the father-absent boy's personality development.

In brief, it appears that having a father present in the home, serving as a competent, effective role model and expressing interest in his son and interacting with him, facilitates the development of attainment potential and influences its development in a masculine direction. It contrast, not having a father is likely to handicap the boy in his personality development.

Since 1961, several psychologists have commented on the oddity that the child's contribution to parent-child interaction is overlooked (Gewirtz, 1961; Kessen, 1963; Wenar, 1963; Korner, 1965; Bell, 1968, 1971; Scott, 1966; Rheingold, 1969 etc.). Although the systematic work in this respect began with David Levy work (1943) on 'maternal overprotection'. The situation of India is still remained worse. Parmeswaran (1972) surveyed 120 studies on Developmental Psychology in an ICSSR publication and found that only three of them related to parent-child relationship. He aptly remarked that, "Parent-child relation, which have been extensively investigated in the USA, has received little attention from Indian research workers." In Western countries, recently layman as well as academicans have shown an increase interest in the role of parent in child development (Biller, 1975; Shedd, 1975).

Recent cross-cultural studies in this area, clearly indicate that family happens to be the oldest and dearest cultural institution for nurturing and schooling of children. The nature of these basic functions very much depend upon the taste and temper of relationship on nuclear and parental dimensions. Interactions among parental roles, cultural expectations and need dispositions of the child in being, not only determine the 'growth space' of child's cognative-conative and affective patterns, but there 'apperceptive mass' clearly reflects the status and role of 'parenting' and 'culture' at work.

Studies in this context show the importance of parental roles in the development of specific personality traits (Kohlberg, 1969; Hoffman, 1970 ; Weisbroth 1970), verbal solutions (Jackson, 1956), academic performance (Jordan et al., 1975; Radin and Epstein, 1975), cognative development (Freeberg and Payne, 1967; Biller, 1974; Dreyer, 1975), adjustment as well as interpersonal interaction (Leiderman, 1959; Mitchell and Wilson, 1967; Sears, 1970; Fish and Biller, 1973; *Lozoff,* 1974) and sex-role adoption (Gray and Biller, 1973; Cazoff, 1974). One very alarming fact has been recognized by several researchers of this field that only the presence of mother and father is no gurantee of adequate 'fathering' and 'mothering', but stress must be given to the quality of fathers and mother's child relations (Lamb, 1976).

The above cited literature review shows that most of the studies have been done in the West and very few studies so far done in India

(Saxena and Saxena, 1975; Kiran and Singh, 1980; Chauhan and Tiwari, 1980; Tiwari and Tripathi, 1981 a, b).

The cross-cultural evidence also shows that father is the task or instrumental leader and the mother is the expressive leader or socio-emotional integrator of the family. Zelditch (1955), on the basis of ethnographers' reports, examined 75 cultures and characterized 'instrumental leader' (Father) as 'boss-manager', of the 'farm', 'leader of the hunt', the 'final court of appeals', 'final judge' and 'executor of punishment', 'discipline and control over the children'; whereas 'expressive leader' (Mother) is characterized by "such description as mediator or conciliator of the family—soothes over disputes, resolves hostility in the family—affectionate, solicitous, warmth emotional to the children of the family—the comforter, the consoler, relatively indulgent and relatively unpunishing."

Parental Competence and Styles. Competent human functioning patterns of psychological effectiveness and the genesis of competence in personality development have been relatively recent targets of psychological inquiry. Early considerations include Hartmann's (1958) definition of 'conflict free ego-sphere' and 'healthy adaptation,' Jahodes (1958) view of the healthy personality and Roger's (1961) 'fully functioning person' etc. Whereby child research focusing on competence began with Murphy et al. (1962) study of children coping effectively with stress. In 1973, Baumrind studied the 'instrumental competence' in preschool children and found that parental warmth and discipline play a leading role in its development. Bowlby (1973) found the growth of self-reliance as originating from infancy based secure parent-child attachment. Research with adolescents and young adults (Gatz, Tyler and Pargament (1998), Tyler (1978, 1979) have revealed the utility of the competence configuration. Mondell and Tyler (1981) study revealed that child of less competent parent interacted in an environment in which their actions and appeals were met with parental authoritarian control suggesting that a critical variable influencing which type of environment the child receives is the competence attributes of the child's parents.

Abraham and Prasanna (1983) on the other hand found from their study that there is close relationship between childs mental health, age and ordinal position in the family. Moreover, in problem-solving situation, children meet their inquiries with a parental style encouraging them to be in control of the situation and to experience their own success; they also receive much parental warmth and many problem-solving strategies. These behaviours have the potential to build the childs own sense of self-efficacy, trust and problem-solving/coping abilities.

Maternal Age and Parenting. Studies of subsequent child behavioural outcomes have emphasised that there is a positive relationship between maternal age and parenting. Rindfuss and Bumpass (1978) pointed out that child bearing should be accomplished between the ages of 22 and 31 suggesting an optimal period for maternal care of infants since at earlier and later ages, the biomedical risks increase, child behaviour outcomes are less optimal and/or maternal attitude and behaviour are less optimal. Actually the maternal age research is rooted in an applied social problem—i.e., teenage pregnancy. Stress associated with adolescent pregnancy (Baldwin and Cain, 1980) and emotional immaturity or ego-centrism of extremely young mothers (Epstein, 1980) have been considered as possible components of a behavioural construct of maternal age. As Field, et. al. (1980) found from their study that teenage mothers express less desirable child-rearing attitudes and have less realistic expectations for infants development then do older mothers. On the other hand adolescent mothers are apt to be less responsive to their new borns (Jones, Green and Krauss, 1980) and to engage in little verbal behaviour with infants (Osofsky and Osofsky, 1970; Sandler, et. al. 1976). The maternal age—child IQ relationship occurs when age effects have been isolated from confounding background variables and seems to reflect a small, positive, linear relationship across the entire child bearing age range (Boroman, 1981). Studies also show that there is significant maternal age effects on children's school readiness (Frustenberg, 1976) and achievement (Oppel and Royston, 1971; Maracek, 1979 and Boroman, 1981).

Parenting and Familial Retardation. There are no obvious bilogical abnormalities but there is a family history of one or both parents being retarded (Jenson, A.R., 1970; Zigler, E., 1968). It is not yet known whether familial retardation is due to primary or genetic factors or to the experience of being retarded parents. The familial retardates have no obvious biological defects. They have an IQ between 50 and 69 and a family history of retardation but the specific cause of their condition is not known. Most authorities regard familial retardation as a handicap that is passed through the genes from retarded parents to their children (Jenson, A.R., 1970 and Burt, C., 1975). This opinion is based on fairly substantial evidence that 50 to

70 per cent of the variability among people in IQ test scores can be accounted for by their genetic inheritance.

Nevertheless, some writers argue that intelligence is determined largely by a child's experiences and that retardation in the absence of any obvious biological disorder is due to psycho-social factors (Girardeau, F.L., 1971; Zajoric, R.B., 1975). While some hold that familial retardation is due to the limited intellectual stimulation provided by retarded parents as well as the deprived socio-cultural environment in which they live. Often, familial retardation occurs often among lower class than among middle class families especially when the family is living in a disadvantaged neighbourhood. On the other hand, being in a lower socio-economic class can be regarded as an effect rather than a cause of retarded in families. From this point of view—families whose retardation is inherited tend to drift toward socio-economic class, because of their limited social and vocational capacities. Hence their poverty can be seen as due to their limited genetic endowment, rather than as a reason for their own retardation or that of their children. Chauhan, N.S. (1963) found that the truents lacked love of the mother in early years of development whereas the non-truents got more mother affections in the earliest years.

An eminent Psychologist of India, Prof. M.C. Joshi (1977) rightly pointed out that, "there have been shifts in the attention that the various phases of child-rearing practice have attracted during the past 70 years (Cf. Walfenstein, 1967). However, the recent past decades have shown consistent efforts in the study of child's personality using child-rearing practices as a frame of reference. The studies of Sears et. al., (1957), Whiting (1963), Whiting and Child (1967) bring out the decisive importance of child rearing practices upon personality development of children cross-culturally. In a short study, conducted by Joshi and Dharwal (1971) which aims to investigate the main characteristics of child-rearing practices cross-culturally, revealed some subtle changes between the Satnaamee and Non-Satnaamee cultures.

Ames, E.W. and Randeri, R. (1965) made a study on the differences in the child-rearing practices of Indian and Canadian Mothers and found (i) although it is true that the Indian child spends more time in the presence of his mother than does the Canadian child, it does not seem to be true that the Canadian child receives any less warmth, sympathy, appreciation, attention, or expression of love from his mother during the time he is with her than does the Indian child, (ii) there seems to be a difference in the two groups' attitudes towards the child's accomplishment, with the Canadian mothers believing more in the practice of giving the child early training in how to do certain things and then refusing to help him with those things he is supposed to know-how to do. Ames and Randeri (1965) observed in this study that 'since Canadian mothers are not opposed to giving needed help, even in situation where, it inconveniences them, the difference does not imply that Canadian mothers are any less tolerant of their children's emotional dependency (need to be loved and protected) than are Indian mothers, but they do seem to want to accelerate the decline instrumental dependency (need to be helped in doing things). Canadian children appear to be pushed to instrumental self-reliance earlier than are Indian children.

One very alarming remark made by Canadian Psychologist, Elinor Wardwel Ames and American Psychologist Kalindi Randeri (1965) that, "One of the major problems confronting the student of Child Development in India today is the fact that almost all available sources of research findings on child-rearing norms and the relation of child-rearing practices to personality development are in non-Indian textbooks. Even books by Indian authors often have bibliographies containing no Indian references. With the increase in research training facilities, it is expected that the next few decades will see a drastic change in this situation, and that we may look forward to the day when the Indian student may get his training from theories and facts derived from research on Indian children. However, until that time, the student must be discriminating reader of British and American text books always evaluating their ideas in terms of the differences between Indian and British-American practices."

In numerous studies (Adorno, et. al., 1950; Haris, et. al., 1950, Allport 1954) comments, "it seems very likely that rejective, neglectful and inconsistent syles of training tend to lead to the development of prejudice." Other researches, revealing that prejudice in children is associated with harsh, strict and authoritarian parental discipline, are provided by Kates and Diab (1955) Lyle and Levitt (1955); Hart (1957); Siegman (1957); McClosky (1958); Smith and Rosen (1958); Dickens and Hobart (1959); Triandis (1962), and Epstein and Komorita (1966). Like prejudice self-image also has been found to be associated with parental discipline. Researches indicate that negative self-image in child is related to his/her strict parental discipline (Wylie, 1961; Rosenberg, 1965). Though there are numerous Indian studies on the relationship of self-image with factors like race (Anant, 1964), sex

(Deo, 1965; Sharma, 1969), caste (Sharma, 1969), scholastic achievement (Bhatnagar, 1969), achievement motivation (Mukherjee, 1965), personality traits (Sharma, 1956; Pathak, 1967; Deo and Hundal, 1969) and attitudes to others (Pareek and Khanna, 1960). In 1974, 1975, Hassan found from his study that authoritarianism and neuroticism in children are associated with harsh and punitive parental discipline.

Hassan (1976) studied the inter-relationships of child-rearing practices, self-image and three dimensions of social prejudice as well negative self-image of children was associated with their punitive parental discipline Singh and Singh (1986) studied the effect of family discipline on self-concept of graduate students and found that self-concept is more positively evident in normal discipline group than in harsh discipline group. Singh and Fatima (1980) study reveals that in case of males induction as disciplinary technique by mother had a positive relationship with social responsibility whereas in case of females, relationship between social responsibility and power-assertion by father and love-withdrawal by mother was observed.

Reddy (1973) found from his study that family plays a leading role in determining scientific ideas among elementary school children. Mehta (1969) study revealed that when the parents attitude was to harsh, dominant or indulgent, the bright children also became backward. Mehta (1977) studied the causes of jealousy in children and found the arrival of new baby in the family is the prominent variable in developing jealousy in the child. Garg Roop Rekha's (1983) Dotoral study revealed that parental disciplinary practices significantly and positively effects the development of personality needs, moral judgement and problem solving ability of the children.

Concluding Observation. The research results coverage in suggesting that parental acceptance, warmth and support are positively related to favourable emotional, social and intellectual development of children and that restrictiveness, authoritarianism punitiveness without acceptance, warmth and love tend to be negatively related to a child's positive self concept, emotional and social development. The various studies also indicate that parental attitudes and behaviour vary according to the sex of both parents and the child.

Research findings support the view that children's self-concept develops according to the pattern of parents' rewards and punishments. Many studies suggest that hostility on the part of the parents tends to produce counter hostility and aggression on the part of the children. When parents' attitudes place a positive model before children, such children tend to show self-confidence, friendliness and independence. Parental acceptance of children is believed to be one of the essential elements underlying the whole structure of parent child relationship.

Though there are several findings made earlier related to the present study in most cases there is cursory reference to the influence of marital happiness and marital adjustment on the behavioural characteristic of children, or the personality development of children. A few research findings which are related to the present study indicate that mothers who are happy and satisfied in their marital life are more lovable affectionate towards their children while the mothers who are unhappy and unsatisfied in their marital relationships use more authoritarian discipline, are more punitive and expect immediate obedience from the children. Children of these parents show characteristics such as emotional instability, low self-concept and anxiety. From the previous research findings it is observed that all these relationships are studied independently. An attempt has been made in the present study to investigate the total effect of all these relationships on the personality development of children. There is a great need of such investigations which can bring to light the sources and difficulties in these relationships.

Mother plays an important role in personality development of the child is a universal truth accepted by all the psychologists, parents, teachers, anthropologists. Thus in the present study mother child relationship is studied empirically, which is the backbone in the all round personality development of the child.

11

Plan and Procedure

Families continue to be one of the most important socializing influence for school-age children. Children acquire values, expectations, and pattern of behaviour from their families, and they do so in a number of ways.

Each family is unique in its composition, interrelationship and ways of bringing up children. Family structure is changing rapidly from joint family to nuclear family. In nuclear family roles are being redefined, the direction is towards greater participation of both husband and wife, sharing of responsibility and a joint decision making. The relationship of the marriage partners producės a climate conducive to the healthy emotional development of children.

The kind of child training used in the home has a pronounced influence on later social adjustment. Children are born normally gregarious persons. Child rearing is the process by which learning occurs, is the same for everyone. The specific environmental conditions that determine just what wants and actions will be learned are unique to each human being.

Sociologically speaking parent-child interactions are one separable class of events that prepare the child for continuing his life. Once he is beyond infancy youngster's personality is always a product of more social experiences than just those offered by his parents.

Parents and siblings serve as models for appropriate and inappropriate behaviour, and they reward and punish children's behaviour. Also, expanding cognitive abilities allow children to learn a range of social concept and rules, both those explicitly taught and those implied. And finally, social learning takes place in the context of relationship. Parental role sounds simple. It is to meet the needs of children, so they can grow. Within all children present, "The Seeds of growth", that is a natural inclination to develop to maturity.

The school-age of children's development is even more interesting than the early childhood. Boys and girls try out their own abilities and interests and gain more and more self-confidence and 'self-reliance'. They still need and count on the friendly care and backing of their parents and other in the family. They manage more and more their affairs. The feeling that the loyalty and service they render their family is appreciated, is highly enjoyable to them.

During this period child's personality becomes increasingly complex. It becomes more of a challenge to understand him. There is remarkable change in the development of independence and ability to think and reason for himself. New intellectual competencies give children tools for self-conceptualization. They understand the notion of family, kinship and association. Their relationship to others and to socially organized units is clarified.

During this age child begins to form a sex role preference. He is able to assess the advantages and disadvantages of his own sex role. A final contribution to the development of self-concept during school age is the development of sense of initiative.

There is no single method of child rearing that can be stated as the only way. Different methods are effective with different parents and of course with different children under different circumstances. No single method can be suggested that applies equally well to all cases. It is also true that no child is reared without any problem. The path of parent-child relationship is never perfectly smooth therefore, it is for the parents to prepare for every circumstances that arise.

The present study has been designed with a view to assess personality traits of primary school children in relation to their mothers' marital adjustment, happiness and child rearing practices employed by them.

On the basis of the objectives mentioned in earlier chapter the following hypotheses were formulated and the study was specially designed to test these hypotheses:

(1) Children reared by the mothers with better marital adjustment are significantly more outgoing, intelligent and emotionally stable as compared to the children reared by poorly adjusted mothers lives.

(2) Mothers who are better adjusted in their marital lives develop obedience and conscientiousness in their children while children of the mothers with poor marital adjustment express more assertiveness and are expendients.

(3) Harmonious marital adjustment helps in the development of sober and relaxed qualities of personality in children.

(4) Healthy child rearing practices are always employed by the mothers who are well adjusted in their marital lives. On the other hand the mothers with poor marital adjustment employ unhealthy child rearing practices.

(5) Mothers whose child rearing practices are unhealthy and whose marital adjustment is poor, produce children who are emotionally less stable, reserved and assertive. While children who are reared with better child rearing practices and whose mothers have better marital adjustment are emotionally stable, outgoing and obedient. The difference in the degree of personality characteristics is significantly large.

(6) Children reared up with healthy child rearing practices and of course by better adjusted mothers in their marital lives are significantly more bold socially, are self-reliant, and go readily with the group than those children who come from the families where inferior child rearing practices are adopted.

In the present study following technical terms are used:

1. Marriage

LOWIE defined marriage as "Relatively permanent bond between permissible mates". According to Lundberg, "Marriage consists of the rules and regulations which define the rights, duties and privileges of husband and wife with respect to each other."

2. Marital Role Relationship

RAINWATER defines role relationship between spouses as "Their typical ways of organizing the performance of tasks their reciprocal expectations, their characteristic ways of communicating and the kind of solidarity that exists between them.

3. Satisfaction

BURR Wesely defines satisfaction as a subjective to condition in which an individual experiences a certain degree of attainment of a good or desired results.

4. Marital Satisfaction

It is defined as the spouses subjective feelings of happiness and satisfaction when they consider all aspects of their marriage.

5. Marital Dissatisfaction

This suggests "a sick family" syndrome, in which the unsatisfactory marriage not only affects the child's behaviour but also it is made more unhappy by the apparent failure in child rearing.

6. Marital Adjustment

Marital adjustment is that state of relationship in which there is an overall feeling in husband and wife of happiness and satisfaction with their marriage and with each other.

RICE, defined marital adjustment as the dynamic nature of marriage the necessity to give and take in the continuing evaluation of the husband-wife relationship.

7. Parental Acceptance

The accepting parents recognize children's feelings and their rights to express their feelings. They value children's uniqueness within the limits of healthy adjustment and recognize their children's needs to become an autonomous individual. These parents love their children unconditionally.

Children of these parents are good matured, considerate, cheerful, cooperative and emotionally stable.

8. Indulgent Parents

These parents are unable to separate their own personalities from the personalities of their children and who tend to give them much care and protection.

9. Child Rearing Practices

LAFORE has classified child rearing practices into four groups:

(a) Dictators

These parents usually follow a dictatorial approach and emphasize authority and obedience.

(b) Co-operators

These parents are predominantly friendly who seem to deal with children on the basis of mutual respect and who appeared to feel that if things could be explained and if there could be joint action unquestioning obedience was necessary.

(c) Temporizers

These parents' approach to be preponderantly "Situational". These parents follow no consistent patterns of behaviour, but seem to fail into one situation after another.

(d) Appears

These parents' approach is predominantly conciliatory and who seem somewhat afraid of the child as though he is in control. These parents tend to avoid issues and try to circumvent problems that arise. Their apparent aim is to prevent trouble rather than to face an issue.

10. Parental Behaviour

Baumrind had delineated major patterns of parental behaviour as detailed overleaf.

(a) Authoritarian

These parents attempt to shape, control and evaluate the behaviour of the child according to a set of standard of conduct. Such parents value obedience, favour punitive, forceful measures to curb behaviour which they think is wrong. Verbal give and take is discouraged.

(b) Authoritative

These parents direct child's activities but in a rational issue oriented manner. Verbal give and take is encouraged and the child is given reasons for policy. Reason as well as power are used to achieve parental objective.

(c) Permissive

These parents attempt to behave non-punitively and an accepting and affirmative way toward the child. Child allowed to regulate his own activities by trial and error much as possible than by guidance and the parent avoids exercising control.

(d) Rejecting-Neglecting

The parents in this category fall into two groups---the non-authoritarian group who minimally independence and individuality, tend to fail encourage to enrich child's environment. The second group rejecting and neglecting in which parents are controlling and authoritarian.

Baumrind observed additional variety of parents. Known as harmonious parents. These parents are non-conforming, encourage independence and provide enrich environment.

(e) Democratic

These parents emphasize the need for discussions, explanations and reasoning to help the young understand why they are expected to behave in one way rather than another.

11. Child's Personality and Self Concept

(a) Self Concept

The 'Core' or centre of gravity of the personality pattern is the individual's concept of himself as a person as related to the world in which he lives. The quality of his behaviour expressed in the way he adjusts to people and things in his environment is related to and to a large extent is determined by his self-concept.

(b) Personality

As the term is, commonly used is, the cluster of potentialities for action characterize the individual. These can be of many kinds and relate to a great variety of actions.

HEISE states, "personality is formed in the first instance within the womb of family relationship".

Psychological Interpretation of Personality

According to the KOMF "Personality of those systems of habits that represent an individual's characteristic adjustment to his environment personality is essentially a product of a long process of many sided development such as physical, motor, mental, emotional, social and moral, personality is not just something but it is an organized whole. It has characteristics common with other individuals but their integration and organization is unique in the case of each individual.

Personality can be understood as the dynamically integrated psychological pattern that emerges from individual in relationship to the total environment, both biophysical and social. ALLPORT has given the following definition of personality. "Personality is dynamic organization within the individual of those psycho-physical systems that determines his unique adjustment to the environment."

Different Personality Traits

1. Reserved

The child who remains aloof, cool, detached from all the situations.

2. Outgoing

The child who is warmhearted, participating, responds favourably to teachers, peers, easy going and able to face the situation boldly.

3. Phlegmatic

Phlegmatic child is inactive, sluggish, calm, stodgy, is emotionally placid.

4. Excitable

This child always seems to be impatient, demanding, over active.

5. Assertive

Assertive child is independent aggressive stubborn and dominant.

6. Sober

The characteristics of sober child are, he is always calm and quiet sensible and serious.

7. Happy-go-lucky

This type of child is always gay and happy, enthusiastic lively and self-confident.

8. Expedient

This child always evades rules, feels few obligations and has weaker superego strength.

9. Conscientious

Conscientious child has stronger super ego, is rule bounded and persevering.

10. Shy

Shy child shows lack of confidence, is timid, restrained, more easily threatened and seeks to avoid social threat.

11. Venturesome

This child is socially bold, spontaneous, tough and daring. He interacts freely and boldly with people, shows positive emotional response to people.

12. Tough-minded

Tough minded child is self reliant, realistic, is more independent and "thick skinned".

13. Tender minded

This child is dependent, over protected sensitive, fearful.

14. Vigorous

Vigorous child goes readily with group, gestful, is more freely expressive, active and uncritical.

15. Forthright

This type of child is socially perspective, skillful, realistic, simple and freeminded.

16. Shrewd

Shrewd child is very calculating and penetrating. He is sharp keen and clever.

17. Placid

Placid child is untroubled child. He feels more secure, confident. He is peaceful, calm and quiet.

18. Apprehensive

This child is always worrying depressive, troubled, irritable and anxious.

Locale of the Study

The present study was conducted in Moradabad city of Uttar Pradesh within its Municipal limits to ensure optimum personal contact for data collection. Partly stratified random sampling technique was used to select the sample. A scroll of all Inter College and Higher Secondary Schools in Moradabad city was prepared. These are:

1. Hewett Muslim Intermediate College, Moradabad.
2. G.G. Hindu Inter-College, Moradabad.
3. Maharaja Agrasen Inter College, Moradabad.
4. K.G.K. Inter-College, Moradabad.

5. S.S. Inter-College, Moradabad.
6. S.R.A.N. Inter-College, Moradabad.
7. H.S.V. Inter-College, Moradabad.
8. R.N. Inter-College, Moradabad.
9. Moradabad Inter-College, Moradabad.
10. Ambika Prasad Inter-College, Moradabad.
11. Parker Inter-College, Moradabad.
12. P.L.J.L. Rastogi Inter-College, Moradabad.
13. Ansaar Inter-College, Moradabad.
14. Rajkiya Inter-College, Moradabad.
15. Methodist Girls Inter-College, Moradabad.
16. Kaushalya Girls' Inter-College, Moradabad.
17. Baldev Arya Kanya Inter-College, Moradabad.
18. Arya Kanya Inter-College, Moradabad.
19. J.R. Agarwal Kanya Inter-College, Moradabad.
20. Prabha Devi Kanya Inter-College, Moradabad.
21. Pratap Singh Kanya Inter-College, Moradabad.
22. L.N.J.S. Girls' Inter-College, Moradabad.
23. Rajkala P.D.A. Girls Inter-College, Moradabad.
24. Abdul Salaam Girls' Inter-College, Moradabad.
25. Ram Chandra Sharma Girls' Senior Secondary School, Moradabad.
26. Abbas Senior Secondary School, Moradabad.
27. Flahedran Senior Secondary School, Moradabad.
28. Shyam Lal Senior Secondary School, Moradabad.
29. Rishikul Senior Secondary School, Moradabad.
30. Phulvati Devi Girls' Inter-College, Moradabad.

Out of the list of 30 Intermediate Colleges and Higher Secondary Schools which existed on January 30, 1992, the following 8 Schools and Colleges. (4 boys and 4 girls) were randomly selected for the purpose of our study.

Boys Intermediate Colleges and Higher Secondary Schools

	Name of the Institution	*Strength*
1.	R.N. Inter-College	1371
2.	Moradabad Inter College	713
3.	Parker Inter-College	1145
4.	P.L.J.L. Rastogi Inter-College	400

Girls' Intermediate Colleges and Higher Secondary Schools

	Name of the Institution	*Strength*
5.	Methodist Girls Inter-College	2095
6.	Kaushalya Girls Inter-College	1615
7.	J.R. Agarwal Kanya Inter-College	1083
8.	Prabha Devi Kanya Inter-College	1143

Sample and its Selection

The present study "Personality traits of primary school children in relation to their mothers' marital adjustment and child rearing practices', is based on the notion that better understanding between husband and wife leads to positive effect on child's development and his personality.

The sample of the study consisted 400 subjects selected by stratified random sampling. The average age of children was 10 to 13 years, studying in V to VIII standard. Children of both the sexes were chosen for the study. Roll list of the student were first obtained from the school authorities. It was planned to include 250 girls and 250 boys in the sample, but the same number was not obtained as the number of girls and boys varied in each class. Therefore, emphasis was given to the total number of sample.

As one of the objectives of the study was to find out mothers' marital adjustment and child rearing practices used by them, mothers of these children were also included in the sample. The information regarding the mothers' educational background was collected through their children. Afterwards only those children were included in the final sample whose mothers' were at least matriculates. Following this criteria 400 children were selected for analysis. Of these 150 were girls and 250 were boys. However for the higher order of analysis, the final effective sample consisted of 320 children only. Of which 120 were girls and 200 were boys. Remaining subjects were deleted for various reasons such as incomplete answers, negligence on the part of the mothers in filling the inventory etc. Some of the mothers and their husband refused to disclose the required information regarding their marital life.

Psychometric Instruments and Techniques of the Study

Assessment Procedures

The information required for the present study was:

1. Mother's marital adjustment.
2. Mother's marital happiness.
3. Mother's child rearing practices.
4. Various personality traits of children.

To obtain above information following methods and tools were used.

1. Mother's Marital Adjustment and Happiness

To get information regarding mothers marital adjustment and happiness "Marital Adjustment Test" devised by Burgess and Cottrell was used. This test consists of 26 items based on five variables, namely—(1) Agreement and disagreement, (2) Common interests and abilities, (3) Demonstration of affection and mutual confiding, (4) Dissatisfaction with marriage, (5) Feelings of isolation and unhappiness.

Out of the 26 items the first 11 items refer to the extent of agreement or disagreement in various areas of marital adjustment such as finance, religion, caring for children, in-laws etc.

Items 12 to 15 of the schedule are concerned with the common interests and activities of the spouses. Items 16 to 19 are related to dissatisfaction regarding marriage and items 20 to 26 deal with feelings of personal isolation and unhappiness.

According to Burgess and Cottrell the reliability of the test is shown by rarely close correspondence between the adjustment scores computed from 66 pairs of schedules filled out independently by husbands and wives. The Pearsonian Coefficient of Correlation is 0.884 with a standard error of 0.027. While this coefficient of reliability is high enough to support a reasonable amount of confidence in the consistency with which the score discriminates among marriages.

It was to be expected that the adjustment scores would correlate fairly closely with happiness ratings. The tetrachoric coefficient of correlation between the ratings and the score is 0.92. Having decided the tool of research investigator distributed the Marital Adjustment Test through the children, who were included in the sample, for their mothers. The mothers who were not aware of the purpose of the study were invited to the school and investigator explained them the meaning of the test items in details and gave assurance that their information will not be disclosed to any person.

All the difficulties were solved to their satisfactions. For some mothers it was difficult to attend the school during that period, so the investigator collected addressed of these mothers and made personal contacts with them. Mothers who were included in the sample were asked to return the filled questionnaires within a weeks interval. After the collection of all forms, scoring was done on the basis of scoring key given in the test.

2. Mother's Child Rearing Practices

For the assessment of child rearing practices, Roma Pal and Shamim Karim's "Child Rearing Practices Scale" was used. This test has 30 statements and intends to measure both child rearing practices and child rearing attitudes of the mothers. Such as comfort, and encouragement, acceptance and harmony, authoritarian, punitive, controlling and intrusiveness to maintain boundaries between child and others etc.

This test was also distributed to the mothers along with the Marital Adjustment Test. Some mothers faced difficulty in understanding the meaning of certain statements in CRP Scale. To them Hindi version of the same questionnaire was provided by the investigator.

Scoring was done as per the instructions given in the manual. For the purpose of analysis the association between the child rearing practices and the personality factors was estimated with the help of coefficient of correlation.

3. Children's Personality Traits

For identification of childrens' personality characteristics, Early School Personality Questionnaire was used (ESPQ). This test is devised by Institute for Personality and Ability Testing.

ESPQ is divided into two Parts—Part Al and Part A2. Each part consists of 80 questions. These questions are concerned with the personality traits of children. The answer sheet of these questions is in the picture form. Each answer has different picture having two alternatives A or B. Each correct answer is given one mark. These 80 questions are based on thirteen personality factors. Approximately five questions are related to each of the factors.

These factors are denoted by different alphabets. These factors or personality traits are:

1. Factor A — Reserved vs. Outgoing.
2. Factor B — Less Intelligent vs. More Intelligent.
3. Factor C — Affected by Feeling vs. Emotionally Stable.
4. Factor D — Phlegmatic vs. Excitable.
5. Factor E — Obedient vs. Assertive.
6. Factor F — Sober vs. Happy Go Lucky.
7. Factor G — Expedient vs. Conscientious.
8. Factor H — Shy vs. Venturesome.
9. Tough minded vs. Tender minded.
10. Vigorous vs. Doubting.
11. Forthright vs. Shrewd.
12. Placid vs. Apprehensive.
13. Relaxed vs. Tense.

The ESPQ had been used widely and was found to be considerably reliable.

4. Administration of the Tests, Procedure for Collection of Data and Analysis

It is mentioned earlier that ESPQ has two parts, viz. Part A1 and Part A2. So the data were collected in two sessions keeping an interval of one week between them.

After completing the formalities of seeking permission etc. the Ss i.e., the selected children were asked to assemble in a room. They were seated at a considerable distance so that there should not be any scope for peeping through others' answer sheets. Cooperation of the class teachers of the respective classes was sought for supervising the children.

The Ss were explained the purpose and importance of the study. In the first session Part Al of ESPQ was administered. Copies of ESPQ answer sheets were distributed among the Ss. Once it was confirmed that every subject has received a copy of relevant answer sheet the investigator read the instructions. The Ss were also asked to read the instructions along with investigator then demonstrated the procedure on black board with illusive examples. Questions and difficulties were invited from the subjects and were replied to their satisfaction. Finally, the subjects were asked to write the answers after understanding the statements. In Hindi medium classes the test was explained in Hindi and then it was administered.

There was no time limit but the subjects were asked not to take much time on any particular statement. On an average 20 seconds were given to answer each question. The filled questionnaires, i.e., answer sheets were collected at the end. It was observed carefully that no subject has kept any question unanswered.

After completion of the first session the investigator distributed two questionnaires viz. Marital Adjustment Test and Child Rearing Practices Scale to subjects to fill in by their mothers and were asked to bring it back at the time of the second session.

Part A2 of ESPQ was administered on the same Ss after a week's interval. Same procedure was followed in conducting the test. After completion of both the tests the answer sheets of Al, A2 of each child were pinned together for the convenience of scoring.

Following similar procedures data were collected from different schools and also from the mothers of the respective children. Thus ESPQ Part I and Part II were administered on the children and CRP and marital adjustment (MA) were administered on the mothers.

In order to fulfill the requirements of the objectives of the study, the investigator intended to find out the effects of three independent measures viz. marital adjustment, happiness and child rearing practices employed by the mothers and the dependent thirteen above stated personality traits of children.

Since the bipolar adjectives were used to denote the personality traits it was obvious to relate marital happiness with the positive end of the continuum and unhappiness with the negative end of the continuum. Similarly, as the marital adjustment is strongly associated with the marital happiness invariably it is assumed that there is strong positive relationship between the marital adjustment and positive personality traits of children.

12

Result and Discussion

It is not a new fact that the childhood experience do influence the later personality characteristics. The experiences received in home, adopted child rearing practices and the relationship between parents have deep rooted effects on the personality of the individual. Number of boys and girls serving as effective sample varied, the proportion being approximately 2:1. Hence, the groups of boys and girls were treated separately.

At the first stage the major groups were classified on the basis of the degree of marital happiness and marital adjustment among the parents of Ss. The boys formed four group such as low marital adjustment among the parents of Ss. The boys formed 4 groups such as Low marital Happiness (LH), Poor Marital Adjustment (PA) as the first group (LHPA). The second group was of the Ss coming from Low Marital Happiness (LH), but better marital adjustment background (BA) represent by (LHBA). The Ss having high Marital Happiness (MH) but Poor Marital Adjustment (PA) formed the third group (HHPA). In the fourth group the Ss coming from High Marital Happiness (HH) and Better Marital Adjustment (BA) Background (HHBA) were included. The girls were also classified on the same basis and similar four groups of girls were formed. This for the final analysis four effective groups of boys and equal number of groups of girls were treated.

The first comparison of the groups were related to the first personality dimension measured in the study. The mean and standard deviation of the groups of boys and girls are given in Table 12.1.

Table 12.1 : Showing Means and Standard Deviations of the Four Groups of Boys and Girls

(*Reserved vs. Outgoing*)

Group	*Nos.*	*I*	*II*	*III*	*IV*
Boys	$\overline{X}$	7.70	7.72	8.34	7.90
	S	1.63	1.19	1.30	3.80
	$\overline{X}$	8.40	7.86	8.80	8.30
Girls	S	1.90	2.08	1.62	5.48

GR I-LHPA; GR II-LHBA
GR III-HHPA; GR IV-HHBA

It appears that the girls are relatively more reserved than the boys. The mean scores of the four classified groups are more than the mean score of the four groups of the boys. But examination of the SD values does not support the statement. In almost all the four cases the SD of groups of girls are larger than the SDs of the groups of boys.

Though the group of the girls and boys were classified following a predetermined criterion, the mean reserved vs. Outgoing (R-O) measures of the four group seem to be more or less similar. Hence the data were treated by the Analysis of Variance.

Table 12.2: Summary of 2 Way ANOVA of the Groups of Girls and Boys

Source of Variation	*df*	*MSS (Boys)*	*MSS (Girls)*	*F(B)*	*F(G)*
A: Marital Happiness	1	8.405	5.63	3.49	0.55
B: Marital Adjustment	1	2.205	7.50	0.92	0.73
A×B : MH×MA	1	2.650	0.033	1.10	0.003
Within	196	2.409	10.20		

The ANOVA results show that the groups of boys and girls classified on the basis of marital happiness and marital adjustment failed to show any significant difference. The main effect of A refers to Marital Happiness varied at two levels. Both for boys and for girls the MSS is non-significant ($P > .05$). But there is a basic difference, the F value associated with the main effect A is near to the minimum

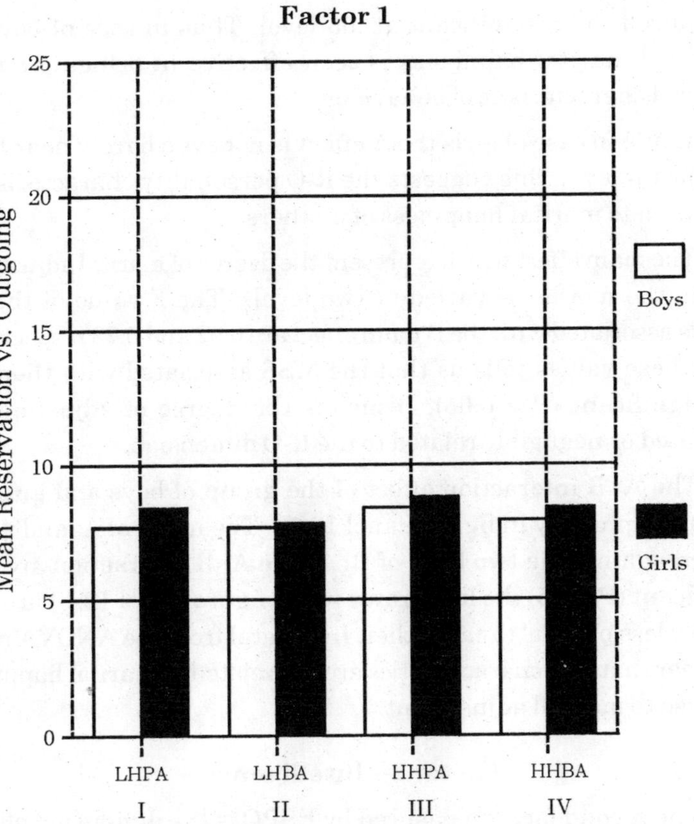

Fig. 1: Showing mean values of reserved versus outgoing dimension of personality

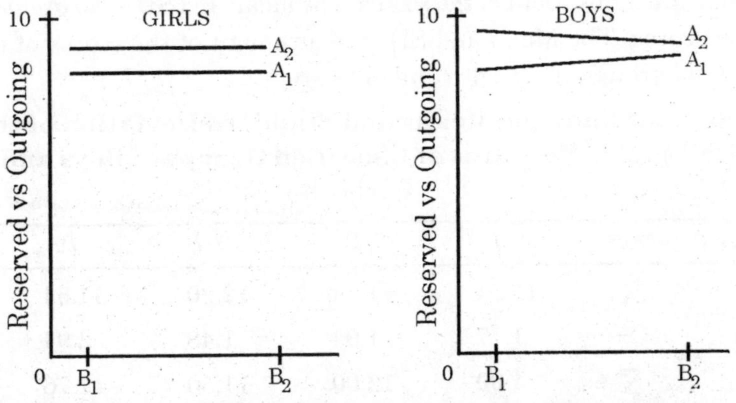

Fig. 2: Mean reserved versus outgoing values of A_1 and A_2 are plotted against two levels of B.

F required to be significant at .05 level. Thus in case of boys the degree of marital happiness is seen effective in bringing out the reserved characteristic of behaviour.

While in case of girls the A effect is not even barely near to the significant level, this suggests the R-O personality characteristic is unrelated to marital happiness of mothers.

The main effect which represent the degree of marital adjustment among the mother is varied at two levels. The F value of the two groups associated with the B main effect are 0.92 and 0.73 respectively. Both these values tells us that the MSS associated with them are non-significant ($P > 0.05$). It means the degree of adjustment is unrelated or negligibly related to the R-O dimension.

The A×B interaction effect of the group of boys and girls are shown graphically in figure Panel 12.14. The mean of A_1 and A_2 are plotted against the two level of B. As the A×B interaction are non-significant (P >. 05) the line drawn in the figure Panel 12.14 are seen more or less parallel to each other. In general from the ANOVA result it is clear that R-O characteristics are not related to marital happiness and also to marital adjustment.

Factor 2—Intelligence

The second factor measured by ESPQ is the dimension of Less Intelligence vs More Intelligence. It is one of the purposes of the study to see to what extent intelligence is influenced by the marital happiness and marital adjustment of the scores. The mean and SD measurement of the scores. The Mean and SD measurement of the scores of the classified groups of the boys and girls are :

Table 12.3 : Showing Means and Standard Deviation of the Intelligence Measures of Classified Groups of Boys and Girls

Groups	*Nos.*	*I*	*II*	*III*	*IV*
	$\overline{X}$	12.04	11.74	12.20	11.54
Boys	S	1.77	1.94	1.48	2.94
	$\overline{X}$	1.90	12.00	11.50	11.76
Girls	S	2.10	1.59	1.73	2.25

The intelligence scores seem to be unrelated marital happiness (MH) and Marital Adjustment (MA) Regarding sex differences with respect to intelligence measure.

In search of over all differences the classified groups of the boys and girls the data were treated by two ways ANOVA. The group of girls and the group of boys were treated by ANOVA separately. The findings obtained by 2 way ANOVA are given in Table 12.4.

Table 12.4 : Summary of 2 Way ANOVA of the Group of the Girls and Boys

(Less Intelligent vs. More Intelligent)

Source of Variation	*df*	*MSS (Boys)*	*MSS (Girls)*	*F(B)*	*F(G)*
A: Happiness	1	0.02	3.01	0.00	0.78
B: Adjustment	1	11.52	0.675	0.09	0.18
A×B : MH × MA	1	1.62	0.21	0.012	0.54
Within	196	134.07	3.84		

The main values displayed in Table 12.3 exhibited some differences in the four classified group. These differences can be seen in case of boys and girls also, but when the data, are treated by ANOVA the difference in the mean intelligence scores of the classified groups of both boys and girls are seen negligible. The F values associated with the A main effect are 0.00 and 0.78 for the groups of girls and boys respectively. All these values are non-significant ($P > .05$) suggesting that the difference in the mean intelligence occurred just by a chance only.

Similar results are obtained while asserting the influence of B main effect classified groups of boys as well as that of girls are seen having more or less similar mean intelligence scores.

To demonstrate A×B interaction effect on the intelligence scores, the value of A_1, A_2 were plotted against the two levels of B separately for boys and girls. These are seen in figure Panel 12.15.

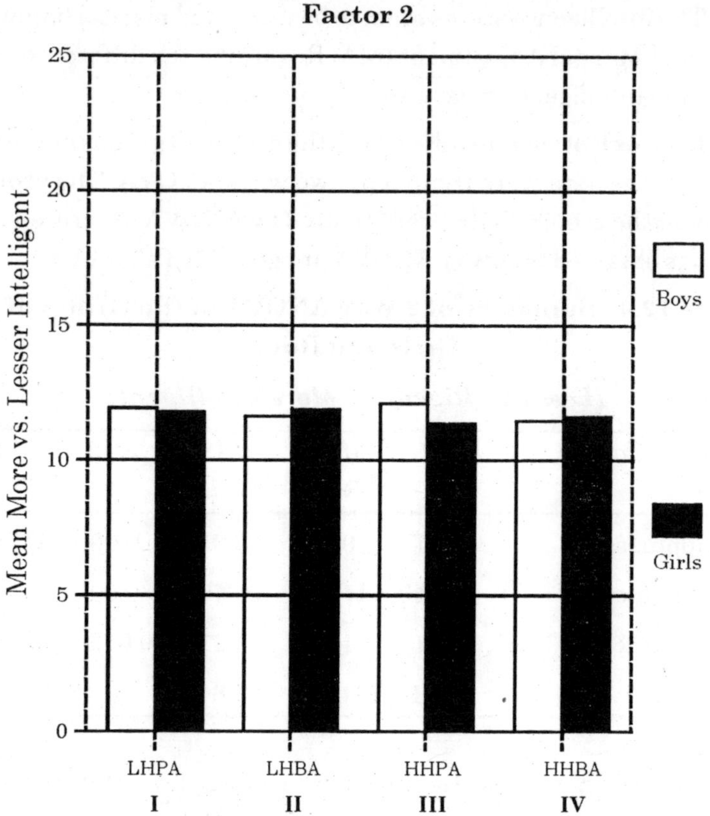

Fig. 3 : Showing mean values of less intelligent versus more intelligent dimension of personality

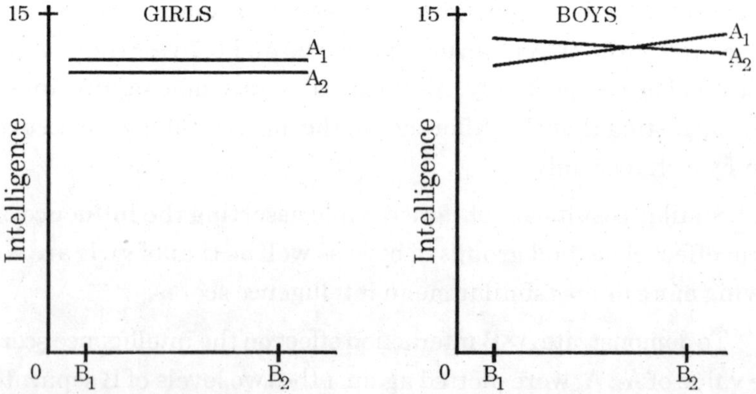

Fig. 4: Mean less intelligent versus more intelligent values of A_1 and A_2 are plotted against two levels of B.

As the A × B interactions are non-significant the Mean of A_1 and A_2 plotted against the two levels of B yielded parallel lines as can be seen in figure Panel 12.15. Thus the less intelligence vs. more intelligent dimension is seen uninfluenced by degree of marital happiness and marital adjustment of mothers.

Factor 3

Emotionally Stable vs. Emotionally Unstable

Emotional stability (ES) is believed to be mostly dependent on the early childhood experiences. To what extent the emotional stability vs. emotional unstability is influenced by the MH and MA of the mothers is tested in the study. At the initial stage the sex difference are examined on the basis of Mean and SD values and at higher order the results of ANOVA are examined.

Table 12.5: Showing Means and Standard Deviation of the Classified Groups of Boys and Girls

(Emotionally Stable vs. Emotionally Unstable)

Groups	*Nos.*	*I*	*II*	*III*	*IV*
Boys	$\overline{X}$	9.48	10.12	10.45	9.80
	S	1.96	1.43	1.45	2.10
Girls	$\overline{X}$	9.40	10.46	10.00	10.06
	S	1.94	1.55	1.45	1.68

The mean and standard deviation of ES Vs EUS measures are given in Table 12.5 separately for the classified groups of boys and girls. The LHBA and HHPA groups exhibited relatively more Es. The fourth group HHBA groups exhibited relatively more Es. The fourth group HHBA lies in between the 2 extremes. In case of girls on the other hand the LHBA group is highly Es while the LHPA group is at the lower end of this dimension. From the mean values it appears that the results failed to favour the assumption of the study. The girls are not emotionally stable than boys as was expected.

Like the findings of the other factors when the results of Es-Evs measured were subjected to 2 ways ANOVA. The result of ANOVA are presented in the following table 12.6.

Table 12.6: Summary of 2 Way ANOVA at the Group Girls and Boys. Emotionally Stable vs. Emotionally Unstable Characteristic

Source of Variation	*df*	*MSS (Boys)*	*MSS (Girls)*	*F(B)*	*F(G)*
A: Marital Happiness	1	1.28	1.87	0.41	0.58
B: Marital Adjustment	1	1.28	5.21	0.41	1.88
A × B : MH × MA	1	11.52	3.67	3.695*	1.33
Within	196	3.12	2.76		

*Significant at 0.5 level, the summary of 2 way ANOVA tells us that the A main effect which represent marital happiness failed to yield the significant MSS (F = 0.41:P > 0.5). It suggest that the ES-EUS dimension of personality remained unaffected by the degree of Marital Happiness of Mothers.

Similarly the B main effect which represents marital adjustment also yielded non-significant MSS (F = 0.41 : P > .05). It suggest that the degree of MA is not associated with the ES-EUS characteristics.

It is however, interesting to note that A × B interaction effect related to the groups of boys is presented graphically in the figure panal is based on boys data. Here the mean ES-EUS values of A_1 and A_2 are plotted against the two level of B. The significant interaction effect is demonstrated by the non-parallel lines.

In case of the groups of girls the picture is unfavourable to assumption. The two main effect are nonsignificant (P > .05). Examination of the last figures in figure Panel 12.16 tells that A × B interaction effect is also nonsignificant (P > .05).

Factor 4
Phlegmatic vs Excitable

Personality characteristic phlegmatic Vs excitable measured by ESPQ tells us to what extent the individual is peace loving or becomes excited early. The data relevant to this factor were first treated by Means and Standard Deviation technique. The result are given below.

Factor 3

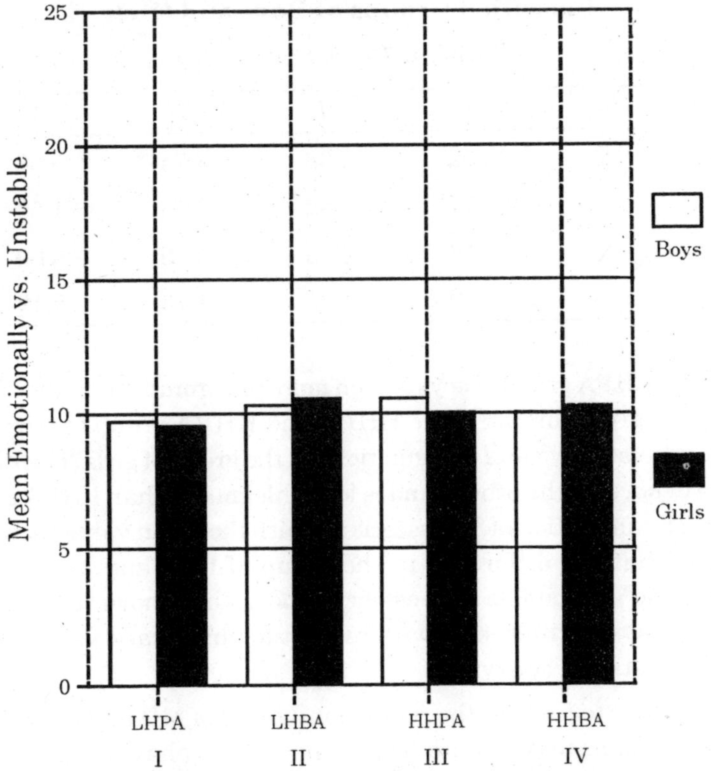

Fig. 5: Showing mean values of emotionally stable versus emotionally unstable dimension of personality

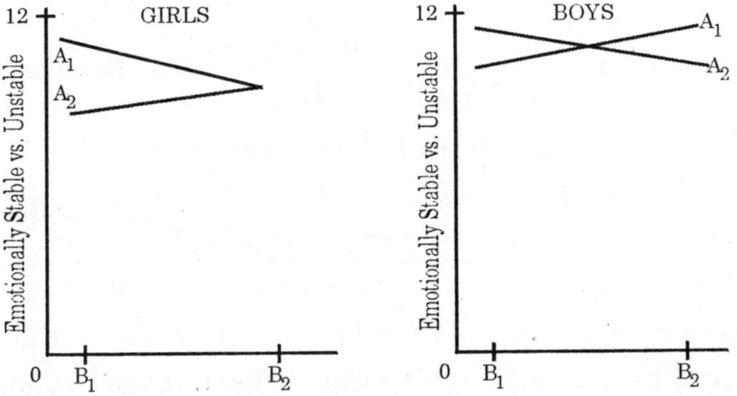

Fig. 6: Mean emotionally stable versus emotionally unstable values of A_1 and A_2 are plotted against two levels of B.

Table 12.7: Showing Means and Standard Deviations of the Classified Groups of Boys and Girls

(Phlegmatic vs Excitable)

Group	*Nos.*	*I*	*II*	*III*	*IV*
Boys	$\bar{X}$	3.92	3.38	3.74	3.58
	S	1.77	1.52	2.13	1.59
Girls	$\bar{X}$	3.56	3.50	3.50	3.00
	S	1.59	1.85	1.73	2.19

The LHPA group of boys is seen more phlegmatic than the LHPA groups of girls. Similarly the HHPA and HHBA group of boys also are seen relatively more phlegmatic than the group of girls. The LHBA group of boys on the other hand is less phlegmatic than LHBA group of girls. Examination of SDs associated with the mean values however tells us that the difference in the group of boys and girls on the phlegmatic Vs excitable dimensions are poor, thus showing that there do not exist sex differences with respect to phlegmatic vs. excitable characteristics of behaviour.

In order to find out the relative influence of MH and MA factors on the phlegmatic Vs excitable dimensions of behaviour data were tested by 2 way ANOVA.

Table 12.8: Summary of 2 way ANOVA of the group of girls and boys (Phlegmatic Vs Excitable) dimension of behaviour data were tested by 2 way ANOVA.

Table 12.8: Summary of 2 Way ANOVA of the Groups of Girls and Boys

(Phlegmatic vs. Excitable Dimension)

Source of Variation	*df*	*MSS (Boys)*	*MSS (Girls)*	*F(B)*	*F(G)*
A: Marital Happiness	1	.005	2.41	.002	0.21
B: Marital Adjustment	1	6.125	2.41	2.66	0.21
A × B: MH × MA	1	6.810	1.87	0.786	0.16
Within	196	2.30	11.89		

Factor 4

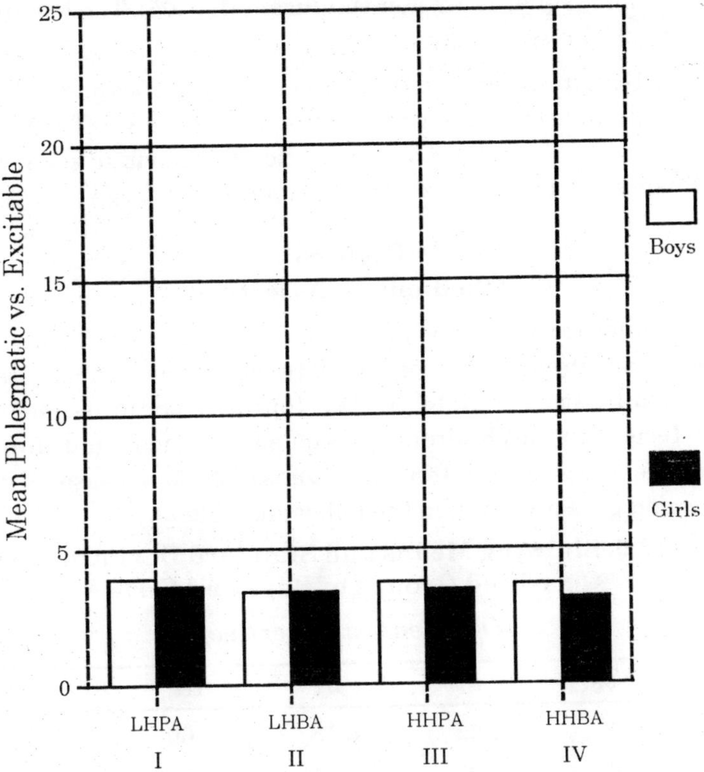

Fig. 7: Showing mean values of phlegmatic versus excitable dimension of personality

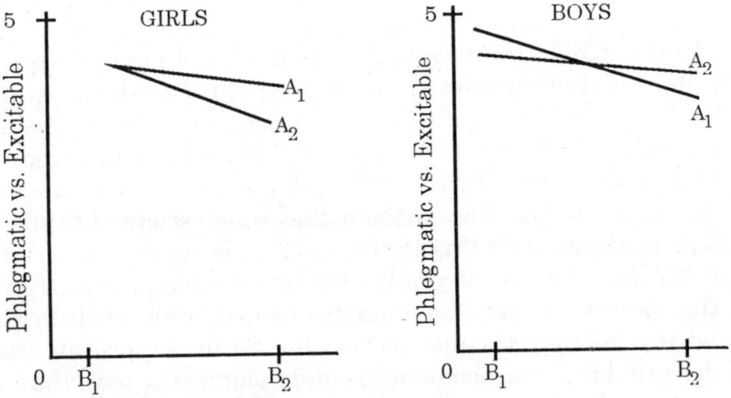

Fig. 8: Mean phlegmatic versus excitable values of A_1 and A_2 are plotted against level of B.

For both the groups that is for the groups of boys and of girls the A mean sum of squares are non-significant (P > .05). The F value are 0.002 and 0.21 respectively.

The B main effect seem to be though not significant, influential to a considerable extent in case of boys. The influence of MA on the phlegmatic vs. excitable characteristic of behaviour seem to be uninfluenced by the MA and MH of the Mothers.

Factor 5
Obedient vs. Assertive

The another dimension of personality is Obedient Vs assertive that was measured in the present study. The marital happiness and marital adjustment help in developing Obedient-Assertive characteristic in the children was studied. The mean and standard deviation of the Obedient Assertive Scores of the four classified group of boys and girls are given in the following table.

Table 12.9: Showing Means and Standard Deviation of the Classified Groups of Boys and Girls

(Obedient vs. Assertive)

Group	*Nos.*	*I*	*II*	*III*	*IV*
Boys	$\overline{X}$	6.22	6.18	5.60	6.28
	S	1.96	2.11	1.85	2.25
	$\overline{X}$	4.06	4.43	3.50	3.60
Girls	S	1.36	2.01	1.62	1.65

Contrary to the traditional old notion the findings of the present study showed that the boys are more obedient than the girls. In all the four classified groups the boys are seen exceeding the girls significantly. The mean obedience scores of boys is larger than the mean obedience scores of the girls. The fact however does not seem to be unusual. At the first place the Ss of the present study were primary school going children. At this age the girls are generally more mature physically than the boy. Secondly, there are more restrictions on the girls that causes frustration among them and they are likely to revolt against it. Probably because of this the Ss in the present study demonstrated that the obedience is more among the boys than it is among the girls.

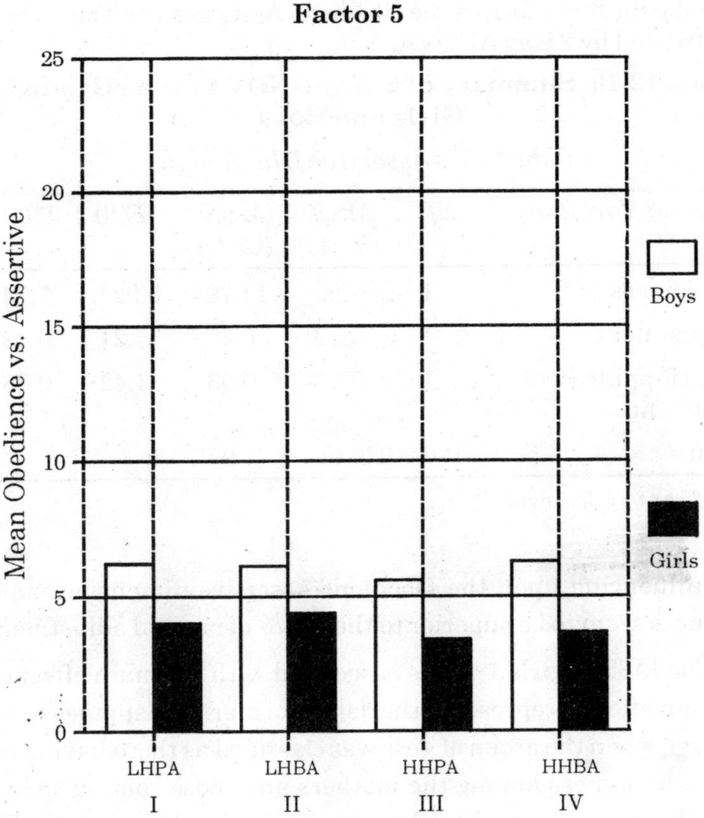

Fig. 9: Showing mean values of obedient versus assertive dimension of personality

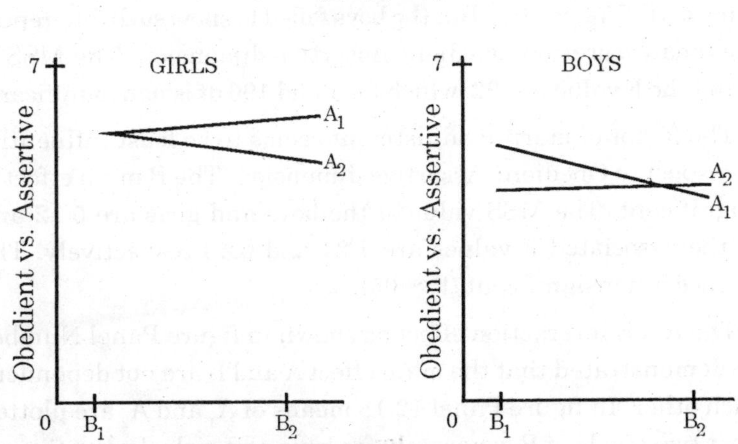

Fig. 10: Mean obedient versus assertive values of A_1 and A_2 are plotted against two levels of B.

Like the other factors the Obedient-Assertive Dimension Scores were treated by 2 way ANOVA.

Table 12.10: Summary of 2 Way ANOVA of the Groups of Girls and Boys

(Obedient-Assertive Dimension)

Sources of Variation	*df*	*MSS (Boys)*	*MSS (Girls)*	*F(B)*	*F(G)*
A: Happiness	1	3.89	14.70	0.92*	7.74
B: Adjustment	1	5.12	0.82	1.21	0.43
A × B: Happiness × Adjustment	1	5.97	0.53	1.42	0.28
Within	196	826.04	1.92		

*Significant at .01 level.

Influencing upon the Obedient-Assertive dimension marital happiness seem to be superior to the factor of marital adjustment.

The MSS of girls 14.70 is associated with the main effect of A. The main effect A represents the degree of marital happiness varied at 2 level, when the group of girls was classified as those having more marital happiness among the mothers and those coming from the family having poor marital happiness among the mothers. They showed significant differences with respect to Obedient-Assertive dimension (F-7.74, P < 01). But the boys failed to show such differences in the mean scores on Obedient-Assertive dimension. The MSS is 3.87 and the F value is 0.92, which for 1 and 196 df is non-significant.

The factor of marital adjustment seems to be least influential with respect to Obedient-Assertive dimension. The B main effect is nonsignificant. The MSS value of the boys and girls are 5.12 and 0.82, the associated F values are 1.21 and 0.43 respectively. The difference is nonsignificant (P > .05).

The A × B interaction effect as shown in figure Panel Number 12.18 demonstrated that the main effect A and B are not dependent on each other. In figure Panel 12.18 means of A_1 and A_2 are plotted against two levels of B separately for boys and girls. In the figures the lines are more or less parallel.

Factor 6
Sober vs. Happy Go Lucky

Home environment, parents' I marital happiness and marital adjustment might develop happy go lucky tendency among the children or they might become very sober in their behaviour. The sober vs. happy go lucky dimension is important personality characteristics that is measured by ESPQ. The following table presents a brief summary of means and standard deviations of sober vs. happy go lucky boys and girls separately.

Table 12.11: Showing the Means and SD of the Four Classified Groups of Boys and Girls

(Sober vs. Happy Go Lucky)

Group	*Nos.*	*I*	*II*	*III*	*IV*
Boys	$\overline{X}$	8.02	7.92	7.86	7.54
	S	2.21	2.16	2.10	2.60
Girls	$\overline{X}$	7.10	7.20	7.60	7.30
	S	2.59	2.61	1.56	1.90

Surprisingly the girls seem to be more happy go lucky than the boys who exhibited more sobriety. In all the four classified groups the boys surpass the girls in sober behaviour characteristics. Apparently it appears to be unusual but when the age level of the Ss is considered, one can observe more maturity among the girls than the boys at this age and hence their behaviour is "Happy Go Lucky" which is likely to be characteristic of boys after an year or two well in accord with the age.

The boys on the other hand also are seen behaving according to the age level, exhibiting the sober behaviour.

The marital happiness among the mothers and marital adjustment of the parents seem to be least effective in sober vs. happy go lucky behaviour dimension.

The data when put to 2 way ANOVA test brought out the following results.

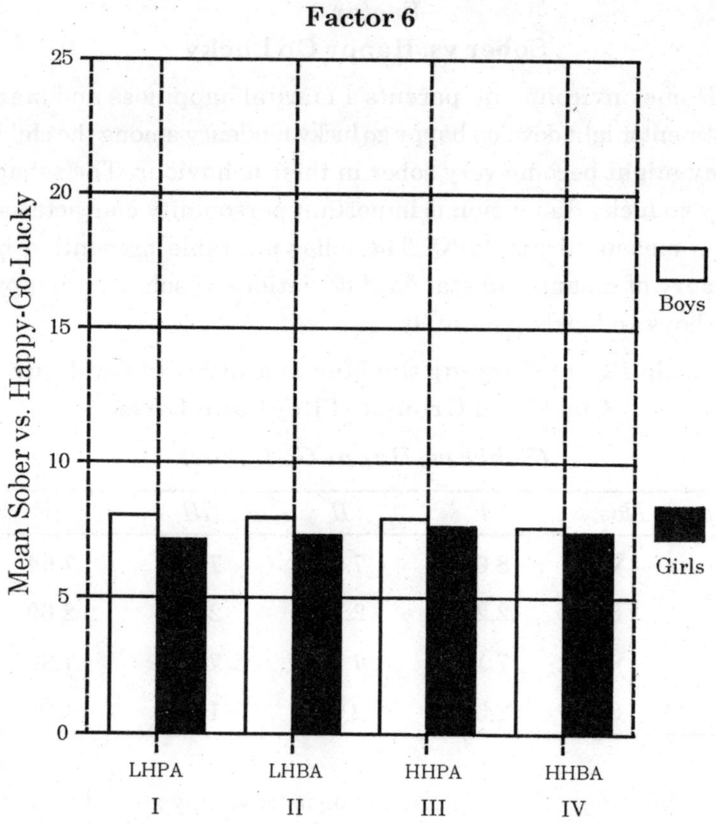

Fig. 11: Showing mean values of Sober versus Happy-go-Lucky dimension of personality.

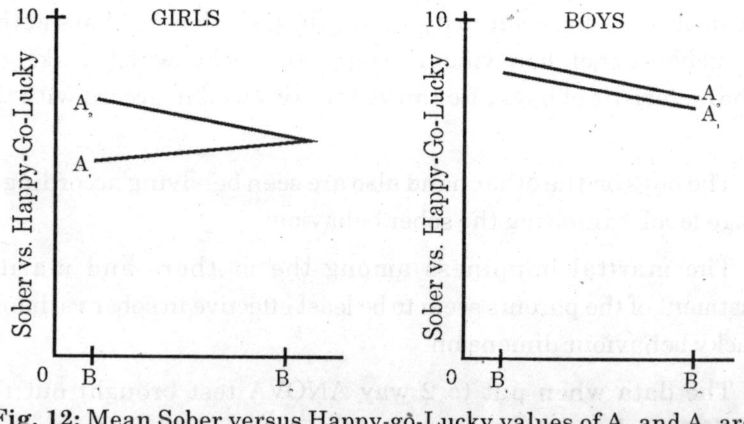

Fig. 12: Mean Sober versus Happy-gô-Lucky values of A_1 and A_2 are plotted against two levels of B.

Table 12.12: Summary of 2 Way ANOVA of the Groups of Girls and Boys

(Sober vs. Happy Go Lucky)

Source of Variation	*df*	*MSS (Boys)*	*MSS (Girls)*	*F(B)*	*F(G)*
A: Marital Happiness	1	3.645	3.67	0.98	0.75
B: Marital Adjustment	1	2.205	0.21	0.59	0.04
A × B : MH × MA	1	0.66	1.01	0.16	0.20
Within	196	3.71	4.91		

Both the A main effect as well as B main effect are nonsignificant. Neither the four classified groups of boys nor that of girls yielded significant differences. Like many other personality dimensions development of sober vs. happy go lucky behavioural characteristics depend upon several factors.

The A main effect represents marital happiness while the B main effect refers to marital adjustments. Though non-significant is compared to marital adjustment, marital happiness seems to be more influential in developing sober behavioural characteristics, among the children.

Obviously, the A × B interaction effect as shown in figure Panel 12.19 depicts two parallel lines when the mean sober vs. happy go lucky dimension score of A_1 and A_2 are plotted against B_1 and B_2 independently for boys and girls.

Factor 7
Expedient vs. Conscientious

Some individuals develop desirableness in their behaviour. Their behaviour includes conduciveness to the need of the moment. On the other hand there are individuals whose behaviour is regulated by conscientious. Does the development of expedient behaviour depend to some extent on marital happiness was one of the objectives of this study. The mean scores of expedient vs. conscientious behaviour dimensions show that there do not exist sex difference.

Table 12.13: Showing Means and SD of Expedient vs. Conscientious Dimension Scores for Boys and Girls Separately

Group	*Nos.*	*I*	*II*	*III*	*IV*
	$\overline{X}$	7.30	6.88	7.00	7.04
Boys	S	1.59	1.67	1.53	1.92
	$\overline{X}$	7.30	7.00	7.56	7.03
Girls	S	1.54	1.68	1.41	1.77

The LHPA groups of boys and girls had identical mean scores (X = 7.30) showing that sex difference is non-existent but the LHBA groups show considerable difference. The girls are found more expedient than boys. The mean score of the girls is 7.00 (SD = 1.68) and at the boys the mean score is 6.88 (SD = 1.67). Since the' SDs are more or less identical, the difference in the means can be attributed to sex difference.

The sex difference appears more sharply in HHPA groups. Here also the girls seem to be more expedient than the boys. The means are 7.00 (SD = 1.53) and 7.56 (SD = 1.41) for boys and girls respectively. The fourth classified group HHBA on the other hand shows that there do not exist sex difference.

After examining the sex difference broadly the inter-group differences were examined by putting the data to the ANOVA test.

Table 12.14: Summary of Two Way ANOVA of the Groups of Boys and Girls

(Expedient vs. Conscientious Dimension)

Source of Variation	*df*	*MSS (Boys)*	*MSS (Girls)*	*F(B)*	*F(G)*
A: Marital Happiness	1	0.25	0.41	0.09	0.16
B: Marital Adjustment	1	1.80	6.07	0.63	2.35
A × B: MH × MA	3	2.64	0.21	0.92	0.08
Within	196	2.86	2.58		

The A main effect is equality non-effective among the groups of boys as well as of girls. The MSS associated with the groups of boys

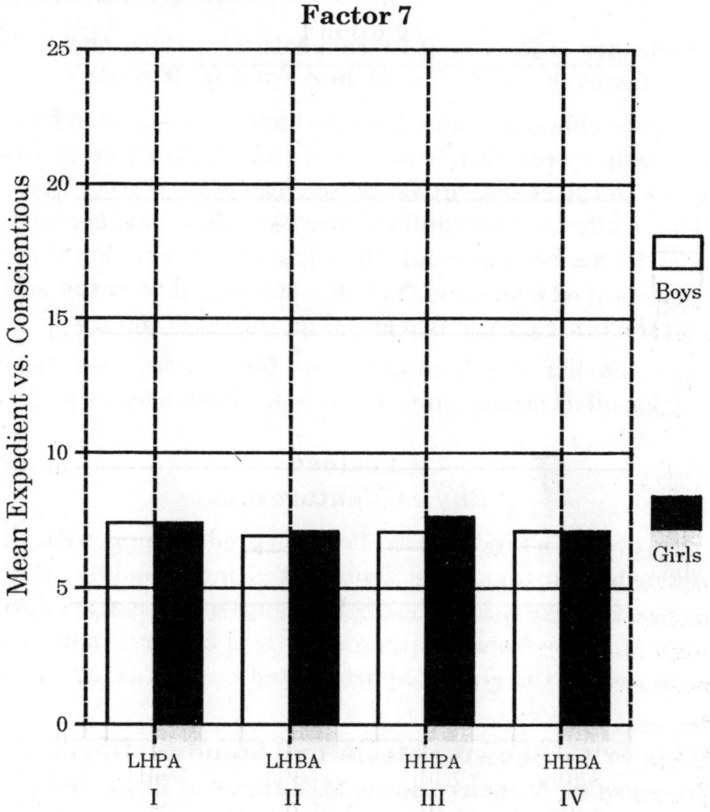

Fig. 13: Showing mean values of expedient versus conscientious dimension of personality.

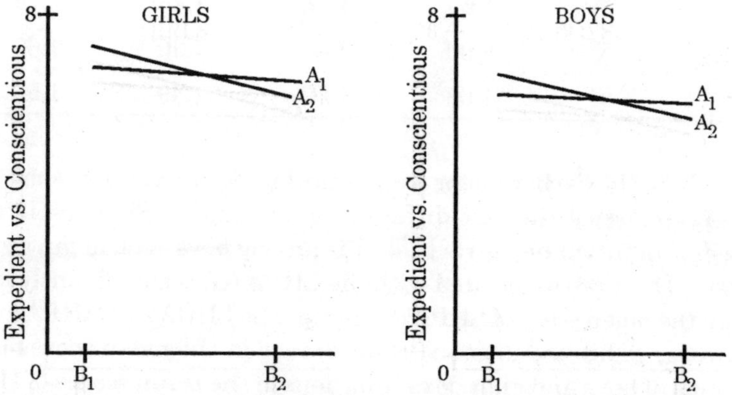

Fig. 14: Mean expedient versus conscientious values of A_1 and A_2 are plotted against two levels of B.

and girls are 0.25 and 0.41 respectively. Both the MSS are nonsignificant (F = 0.09; P > .05 and F = 0.16; P > .05).

Degree of marital adjustment which is represented by B main effect is seen more effective in case of girls than in case of boys with reference to the expedient vs. conscientious measures. Even when the B main effect is nonsignificant in case of the four classified groups of the girls, the F value is only little less than the table value of F to be significant at 0.05 level. The one associated with the groups of boys on the contrary is much less than the table value of V

Like earlier A × B interaction effects, here also the A × B interaction effect is nonsignificant. It is depicted in figure panel 12.20.

Factor 8
Shy vs. Venturesome

Shyness is a kind of fear. Persons predominant with shyness are not inclined to take risks. Venturesome individuals are those who are inclined to take risks. These behavioural tendencies are developed through training from family, society, and culture. In our country shyness among the girls is appropriated but discarded among the boys.

Table 12.15: Showing Means and Standard Deviation of Shyness vs. Venture some Measures of Boys and Girls

Group	*Nos.*	*I*	*II*	*III*	*IV*
Boys	$\overline{X}$	7.54	7.08	7.38	6.78
	S	1.64	1.48	1.48	1.74
Girls	$\overline{X}$	8.90	7.03	7.30	7.66
	S	1.68	1.00	1.49	1.56

Like the earlier factor with regard to shy vs. venturesome some characteristics the sex differences are sharp. Shyness is more predominant among girls than it is among boys. The mean score of 8.90 (SD = 1.68) associated with the LHPA (G) is significantly larger than the mean score of LHPA (B) group. The LHBA and HHPA groups however exhibited absence of difference in the mean scores of the groups of boys and girls. Examinations of the mean scores of HHBA (G) and HHBA (B) show a good amount of difference that can be attributed to sex difference.

The result thus shows that the social and cultural factors are distinctly important in the development of shyness or venturesome behaviour.

To search the relative importance or role of marital happiness and marital adjustment in developing these behavioural characteristics, the data were further subjected to ANOVA test.

Table 12.16 : Summary of 2 Way ANOVA for the Four Classified Groups of Boys and Girls Shown Separately For Shy vs. Venturesome Dimension of Personality

Source of Variation	*df*	*MSS (Boys)*	*MSS (Girls)*	*F(B)*	*F(G)*
A: Marital Happiness	1	0.25	0.41	0.09	0.16
B: Marital Adjustment	1	1.80	6.07	0.63	2.35
A × B : MH × MA	3	2.64	0.21	0.92	0.8
Within	196	2.85	2.58		

*Significant at .05.

In case of the groups of the boys the marital happiness of mother appears to be non-related to the development of shyness or venturesome behaviour in the children. Similar fact is true in case of the girls. The MSS values are 2.65 and 7.01 respectively for boys and girls. Though the difference in the means of four classified groups of boys are larger than that of the difference in the four classified groups of girls these are to be attributed to chance only.

The B main effect representing marital adjustment produced significant differences among the four classified groups of boys with respect to shy vs. venturesome dimensions of personality. The MSS is 14.05 ($F = 5.55$; $P < .05$).

Since the difference is significant the mean difference can not be attributed to chance only. Supporting evidence of this can be seen in the two factor interaction effect. As the A × B interaction effect in the groups of boys is non-significant (See figure Panel 12.21). The B effect is independent of A effect.

ANOVA findings of the groups of girls show non-relationship of marital happiness and marital adjustment with the development of

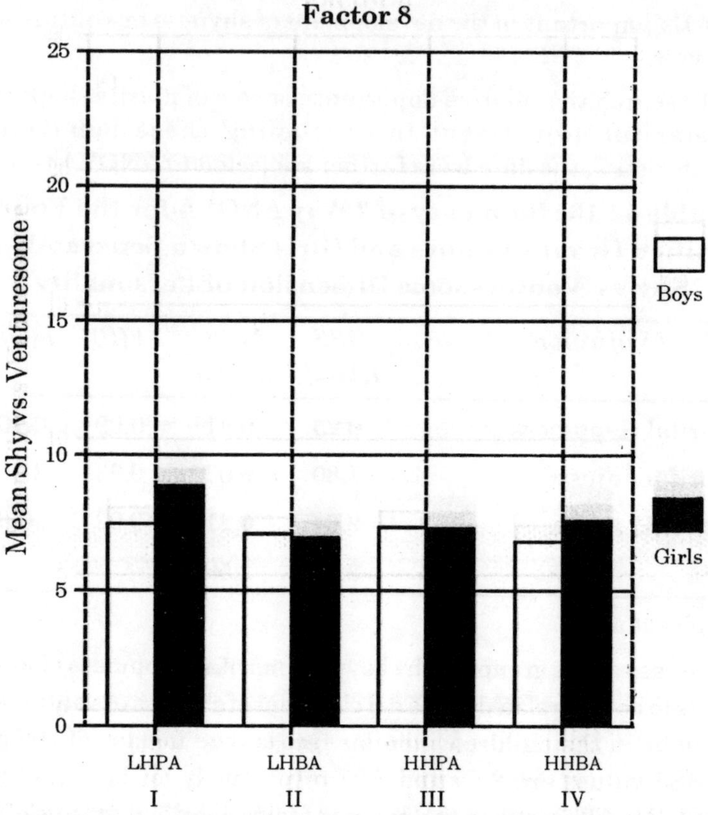

Fig. 15: Showing mean values of shy versus venturesome dimension of personality.

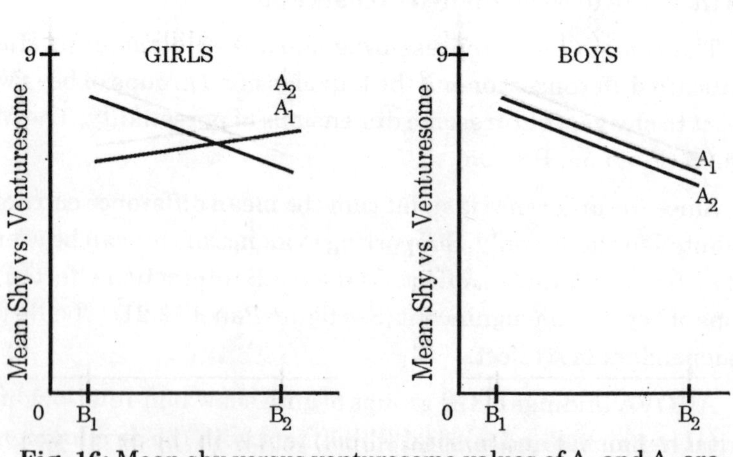

Fig. 16: Mean shy versus venturesome values of A_1 and A_2 are plotted against two levels of B.

shyness vs. venturesome characteristic of behaviour. The two main effects of A and B are non-significant (P > .05) also the A × B interaction effect is nonsignificant. But though the A and B main effects are nonsignificant whatsoever the little effect they might have is independent of each other though not significant.

Factor 9
Tough Minded vs. Tender Minded

Other important behavioural characteristics of the Ss that was studied here was tough minded vs. tender minded.

Table 12.17: Showing Means and Standard Deviation Scores on Tough Minded vs. Tender Minded Dimensions

Group	*Nos.*	*I*	*II*	*III*	*IV*
Boys	$\overline{X}$	6.74	6.36	6.54	6.24
	S	1.90	1.70	1.94	2.63
Girls	$\overline{X}$	8.03	8.23	8.30	8.10
	S	1.60	1.55	1.51	1.75

Well in accordance with the trend in all the four groups the girls are seen surpassing the boys in tendermindedness. The mean scores of LHPA Boys and Girls are 6.74 and 8.03 respectively. As the difference in the SD value is meagre the difference in the mean values can be attributed to sex factor.

The mean difference of 1.29 (8.03 – 6.74 = 1.297) is sufficiently large in the LHBA groups of boys and girls. So also in HHPA groups of subjects one can see that the boys exhibited more toughmindedness while the girls had inclination towards tendermindedness. Thus social acceptability in the behaviour is apparent in the groups of boys and girls.

The last classified group is HHBA. The mean scores of boys is 6.24 (SD = 2.63) and that of girls is 8.10 (SD = 1.75). The SD associated with the mean score of boys group is much larger than the SD associated with mean of girls. But apparently there is scope to state that the girls are more tenderminded than the boys.

Table 12.18: Summary of 2 Way ANOVA of Tenderminded vs. Toughminded, Scores Computed for the Four Classified Groups of Boys and Girls Separately

Source of Variation	*df*	*MSS (Boys)*	*MSS (Girls)*	*F(B)*	*F(G)*
A: Marital Happiness	1	1.28	0.13	0.29	0.05
B: Marital Adjustment	1	5.78	0.00	1.34	0.00
A × B : MH × MA	1	0.08	1.20	0.02	0.44
Within	196	4.30	2.73		

The ANOVA results show that tendermindedness or toughmindedness is mostly dependent on sex of the individual and not on the marital happiness or marital adjustment of the parents. It might be influenced by the family training or the social environment.

As the A and B main effects demonstrate the differences made on the basis of marital happiness among the subjects failed to bring in any significant change in tendermindedness among the children. Similar findings can be seen with B main effect representing marital adjustment. But the difference for the groups of boys is more sound than what it is in the groups of girls.

It is surprising that though marital happiness and marital adjustment are strongly associated like previous factors, in this case also A × B interaction effect is nonsignificant. The A × B interaction effect is graphically shown in figure Panel 12.22. Lines joining A_1 and A_2 values at B_1 and B_2 levels are parallel suggesting it to be absence of any kind of interaction.

Factor 10
Vigorous vs. Doubting

The means and standard deviations of vigorous vs. doubting characteristics are shown in the following table.

Table 12.19: Showing Means and Standard Deviation Score of Vigorous vs. Doubting Characteristics of Four Classified Groups of Boys and Girls

Group	*Nos.*	*I*	*II*	*III*	*IV*
Boys	$\overline{X}$	4.28	4.58	4.84	4.34
	S	1.52	1.80	1.81	2.00
Girls	$\overline{X}$	7.30	4.86	6.00	5.66
	S	1.91	1.91	1.61	1.77

Examination of the Means and SD values show that the results on vigorous vs. doubting dimension are complicated. Though in general the girls seem more vigorous than the boys, some groups displayed large size of disparity while in some groups the size of the disparity is meagre.

In the LHPA groups of boys and girls, the girls are significantly more vigorous. The means scores of the group of boys is 4.28 and of the group of girls it is 7.30. This difference is much larger as well as much difficult to interpret. The findings are contrary to the general expectations. Instead of girls having doubting nature, the boys showed more doubting behavioural characteristics.

The LHBA group failed to bring in any remarkable differences in the mean scores of boys and girls.

The last two groups HHPA and HHBA produced differences in mean scores of vigorous vs. doubting characteristics. But the difference are not so sharp as they were in case of LHPA group.

When the data were put to two way ANOVA test, the following results were obtained.

Table 12.20: Summary of the 2 Way ANOVA of Vigorous vs. Doubting Behavioural Characteristics of the Groups of Boys and Girls

Source of Variation	*df*	*MSS (Boys)*	*MSS (Girls)*	*F(B)*	*F(G)*
A: Marital Happiness	1	1.28	1.87	0.40	0.09
B: Marital Adjustment	1	0.50	57.41	0.15	2.69
A × B : MH × MA	1	7.80	33.07	2.42	1.55
Within	196	3.23	21.35		

In case of the groups of the boys neither the main effect A nor the main effect B produced significant differences. But the A × B interaction effect is seen producing MSS that is nearer to the one required to be significant. The values of A_1 and A_2 when plotted against the two levels of B, produced not the exactly parallel lines but at one point they are more closer to each other.

In case of the groups of girls on the other hand the main effect B has produced MSS that is nearer to the one required to be significant at .05 level. It suggests that the marital adjustment is more influential in case of girls in producing vigorous vs. doubting characteristics of behaviour.

The interaction effect is however nonsignificant ($P > .05$). it becomes clear from the figure Panel 12.23.

Factor 11
Forthright vs. Shrewd

At least apparently accepted behaviour in the society is to be straightforward or to be forthright. Those who are ill-natured mischievous or shrewd are not approved by the society.

Table 12.21: Showing Means and Standard Deviations of Forthright vs. Shrewd Characteristics of Behaviour of the Four Classified Groups of Girls and Boys

Groups	*Nos.*	*I*	*II*	*III*	*IV*
Boys	$\overline{X}$	3.90	3.64	3.80	4.20
	S	1.56	1.72	1.89	1.80
Girls	$\overline{X}$	5.06	3.43	3.30	4.06
	S	1.47	1.47	1.70	1.16

The mean values given in Table 12.21 suggest that the boys of HHBA groups are mostly forthright and next to them are boys from LHPA group. In hierarchy the HHPA group occupies the third position and the LHBA group enjoying as a tailender.

The group of girls on the other hand are displaying just the different picture. The LHPA, HHBA groups of girls are at the first and second position respectively. While LHBA, HHPA groups are at third and fourth positions.

Sex differences are more profound in case of LHPA groups of girls and boys, they are not so sharp in case of other three groups. The differences in LHPA groups are due to higher scores of the group of girls.

Table 12.22: Summary of 2 Way ANOVA of Forthright vs. Shrewd Characteristics of Personality Scores

Source of Variation	*df*	*MSS (Boys)*	*MSS (Girls)*	*F(B)*	*F(G)*
A: Marital Happiness	1	2.65	16.33	0.86	1.08
B: Marital Adjustment	1	0.25	10.80	0.08	0.71
A × B : MH × MA	1	5.44	32.03	1.77	2.11
Within	196	3.07	15.17		

The ANOVA results failed to support assumptions. It was expected that the marital happiness might be influential with regard to the development of forthright behaviour but none of the F values are significant either in the groups of boys or in the groups of girls.

Main effect independently appeared to be least influential but the interaction effect showed some inclination of affectivity. The picture becomes clear from the figure Panel 12.24 where the mean scores on forthright vs. shrewd category of the four classified groups are plotted separately for boys and girls. The mean A_1 and A_2 values plotted against the two levels of B produced straight lines which are closer to each other at one end, and wide apart at the other. The fact is true for both the groups.

Factor 12
Placid vs. Apprehensive

Behaviour pattern of some individuals is placid while the others develop apprehensive behaviour pattern. This dimension of personality when measured by ESPQ, the following results were obtained with the groups of boys and girls.

Table 12.23 : Showing Mean and Standard Deviation Values on Placid vs. Apprehensive Dimension of Personality

Group	*Nos.*	*I*	*II*	*III*	*IV*
Boys	$\overline{X}$	2.46	2.48	2.94	2.54
	S	1.94	1.98	1.82	1.98
Girls	$\overline{X}$	3.30	2.50	3.33	2.86
	S	1.51	1.45	1.78	1.67

On the whole placidity is dominant among the girls and not among the boys. Girls of LHPA groups have a mean scores of 3.30 while the boys of the same category scores 2.46. The difference in the means is large and might have occurred due to sex differences.

The second groups LHBA failed to bring out any such sex differences in the placid vs. apprehensive behavioural characteristics.

The last two classified groups HHPA and HHBA though exhibit differences in the means of groups of boys and groups of girls, the differences are not found enough to be seriously concerned with.

Another feature of the mean values can be noticed here. Arranging the four classified groups of girls hierarchically is easier but it is relatively difficult in case of the groups of boys. These findings suggest that the intergroup differences in the mean values of girls are larger than the intergroup differences among the boys.

Table 12.24: Summary of 2 Way ANOVA of Placid vs. Apprehensive Dimension Scores of Four Classified Groups of Girls and Boys

Source of Variation	*df*	*MSS (Boys)*	*MSS (Girls)*	*F(B)*	*F(G)*
A: Marital Happiness	1	3.65	1.20	1.03	0.46
B: Marital Adjustment	1	1.81	12.03	0.51	4.63
A × B: MH × MA	1	2.20	0.83	0.62	0.32
Within	196	3.55	2.60		

As was stated earlier the groups of boys scored more or less similar mean values on placid vs. apprehensive dimensions. The A and B main effect produced nonsignificant F values (1.03 and 0.51

respectively). Even the A × B interaction effect is nonsignificant (F = 0.62, P > .05). The A × B interaction effect when presented graphically demonstrated two parallel lines.

Marital happiness in case of girls also appears to be correlated with placid vs. apprehensive characteristic of behaviour. The MSS is equal to 1.20 and for 1 and 196 df the value is non-significant (F = 0.46, P > .05).

The B main effect which represent marital agreement varied at two levels had produced highly significant differences. The mean sum of squares is 12.03. The F is 4.63 for which for 1 and 196 df is significant beyond 0.05 level. Thus the differences in the means of two groups varied at two levels on marital adjustment has not occurred by chance.

The A × B interaction depicted in figure Panel 4.25 tells us that the main effect B is independent of the main effect A. Thus marital adjustment seems to be much influential with respect to placid vs. apprehensive characteristics.

Factor 13
Relaxed vs. Tense

The means and standard deviations of the relaxed vs. tense characteristics of personality are given in Table 12.25.

Table 12.25: Showing Means and Standard Deviation of Relaxed vs. Tense Dimension Scores

Group Nos.		*I*	*II*	*III*	*IV*
Boys	$\overline{X}$	2.92	3.23	3.16	3.10
	S	1.90	1.79	2.06	1.91
Girls	$\overline{X}$	3.03	2.60	2.83	3.06
	S	1.86	2.17	2.07	2.14

Classified groups of boys seem to have more relaxed than the classified groups of girls the only exception being LHPA group. However, the differences in the means of four groups are poor and might have occurred due to chance only.

Likewise the intergroup differences appear to non-significant. The fact becomes clear from the ANOVA results. The summary of the two way ANOVA result is presented in the following tables. All the F values shown in the summary table are much less than what is required to be significant.

Table 12.26: Summary of 2 Way ANOVA of Relaxed vs. Tense Personality Characteristics of Behaviour of Four Classified Groups

Source of Variation	*df*	*MSS (Boys)*	*MSS (Girls)*	*F(B)*	*F(G)*
A: Marital Happiness	1	0.13	0.53	—	0.12
B: Marital Adjustment	1	0.85	0.30	—	0.017
A × B MH × MA	1	724. 02	0.83	—	0.77
Within	196	3.69	4.28		

Examination of the MSS and related F values tells us that all the four classified groups of boys have almost similar mean scores, even the interaction effect is nonsignificant as seen in Table 12.26.

More or less similar case can be observed in case of girls also.

In sum, it can be said that both the marital happiness and marital adjustment failed to bring out any change in the relaxed vs. tense behaviour characteristics.

Correlation coefficient computed between child rearing practices of mother and different personality characteristics in children.

The two groups of subjects are treated separately even after investigating the strength of association between the child rearing practices and thirteen personality factors measured by ESPQ. It is expected that the families adopting approved child rearing practices are likely to develop approved personality characteristics among the children. However it seems that the personality factors are not functions of only the child rearing practices. There might be many other factors that directly influence the development of personality factors. The picture becomes clear when one examines the coefficient of correlations computed between CRP and 13 personality factors.

Among the groups of girls in all, not all the cases the coefficient of correlations for 190 df are seen non-significant. The first factor dealt in the present study is reserved vs. outgoing characteristics of behaviour. The correlation between Child Rearing Practices measures and this dimension of personality was 0.008. It means that the distribution of scores in the scattergram failed to show any directionality in scores. There is much scope to assert that development of reserved vs. outgoing characteristics of behaviour might be mostly dependent upon the other factors than the Child Rearing Practices.

It is obvious that intelligence is a multifactor phenomenon and hence searching relationship between intelligence and Child Rearing Practices is spurious. Well in congruence with this statement the correlation between intelligence and Child Rearing Practice is seen nonsignificant ($P > .05$).

Emotional stability more or less rely upon the early family experiences. Some children are being hampered by the parents while to the others much freedom is given. This ultimately results in development of emotional stability or imbalance hence it is natural to search the strength of association between the emotional stability measures and Child Rearing Practices measure. The r – 0.05 which again was seen non-significant. It seems that the childhood experiences seem to be unrelated to the later development of emotional stability.

Since the period of Kretchmer (1926), the personality types were systematically examined. Kretchmer and Sheldon found that some of the personalities are phlegmatic while there are a few others which can be categorized as excitable. Their emphasis was mostly on the body built or the body structure, and hence the characteristics of phlegmatic or excitability is not related to the others. Which can be categorized as excitable. Their emphasis was mostly on the body built or the body structure and hence the characteristics of phlegmatic or excitability is not related to the other factors except the genetic factors. In the present investigation the relationship between phlegmatic vs. excitable and the Child Rearing Practices are seen negligible $r = 0.05$ indicating that the genetic factors are more dominant than the Child Rearing Practices.

To be obedient or assertive depends mostly upon the home condition and there are no two opinions that the type of Child Rearing Practices adopted does play a significant role in developing obedience or assertiveness among the children. However, the findings of the present study fall to support this generalization. One probable reason might be that the age group of the present study is homogenous, had it be heterogenous the different might have been more sharp.

Family background especially the socio-economic status of the individual in one or the other way develop either happy go lucky tendency among the children, or soberness. Apparently it appears that the training exerted by the parents is responsible for development of these personality characteristics. But the findings of these correlations in no way support this assumption correlation is poor between Child Rearing Practices and soberness vs. happy go lucky dimension.

Conscientious is an important factor in the development of personality. The other dimension is expedient vs. conscientious treated in the present study. As the correlation coefficient is just negligible. It is apparent that the Child Rearing Practices and the development of expedient vs. conscientious dimensions are unrelated.

Shyness among the girls is an accepted behavioural characteristics in Indian culture. The other end of the dimension is venturesomeness. However even in case of girls it seems that shyness is more social than a family affair. In other words apart from the Child Rearing Practices the other factors are more influential in the development of shyness and venturesome behaviour.

Thoughmindedness and tendermindedness to a great extent depends upon the childhood experiences. It is not out of place to expect that adopted Child Rearing Practices in one of the other way helps in the development of toughmindedness vs. tendermindedness, but like earlier factors this factor also seems to be a result of multivariate phenomenon.

The findings of coefficient correlations relevant to the other dimensions of personality namely vigorous vs. doubting, forthright vs. shrewd and placid vs. apprehensive are more or less depicting the same poor relationship. The only dimension that deviates from the trend observed is placid vs. apprehensive dimension. In this case the correlation-coefficient is relatively high though not significant. The value is just on the threshold of significance. Similar findings could be seen in case of tense vs. relaxed characteristics of behaviour.

Both the groups of girls and boys are similar depicting absence of relationship between the child rearing practices and the development of different personality characteristics. Though it is accepted that behavioural characteristics or personality characteristics are the result of several antecedent variables, assuming that along with other factors the child rearing practices do help in developing particular type of behaviour. The strength of association is measured between the child rearing practices and behaviour characteristics measures.

Out of the 13 correlation coefficient computed between the 13 personality characteristics and child rearing practices, only in one case the relationship is found to be significant. The remaining 12 correlation coefficient on the other hand show no relationship of any kind.

Correlation between reserved vs. outgoing characteristics and child rearing practices is found to be 0.14 only, but in the measure of intelligence and child rearing practices it was 0.50, which is significant beyond 0.01 level. It can be stated about this relationship that better the Child Rearing Practices more the intelligence and vice versa. Correlation between emotional stability vs. instability and Child Rearing Practices and phlegmatic vs. excitable and Child Rearing Practices are 0.034 and 0.085 respectively. Though the df. for examining the significance of correlation is larger the correlation values are less. The findings fail to show, any kind of relationship between Child Rearing Practices and behavioural characteristics.

The next two measures are obedient vs. assertive and sober vs. happy go lucky. None of these two are seen related to Child Rearing Practices. The correlation coefficients are 0.088 and 0.03 respectively which obviously are nonsignificant.

Expedient vs. Conscientious and shy vs. venturesome behaviour would have been to a considerable extent associated with the early treatment received in the family. But here also the values of correlation coefficients are much below the expectation, i.e., 0.06 and 0.04 respectively. Thus the findings failed to support the assumptions.

There is much possibility of coupling toughmindedness with vigorous behaviour. Assuming that the Child Rearing Practices plays significant role in developing these characteristics the correlation coefficients are computed. The values are 0.05 and 0.02 respectively. These values also are more or less negligible.

The last three factors of personality characteristics are forthright vs. shrewd, placid vs. apprehensive and relaxed vs. tense. Their correlation coefficients are 0.02, 0.02 and 0.003 respectively. These results are also not found in accordance with the earlier expectations.

On the whole correlation coefficients failed to show strength of association between the Child Rearing Practices and behaviour characteristics. It can be stated that development of behavioural characteristics in no way is unidimensional phenomenon. There are many factors which influence the development of different behavioural or personality characteristics. The fact becomes clear from the poor relationships observed between Child Rearing Practices and different dimensions of personality.

Discussion

There is a dearth of studies, estimating the effect of marital happiness among the parents on the development of varied behavioural characteristic in the children. Such studies as estimating the influence of parental separation are many but the present investigation deals mainly with the marital adjustment and marital happiness, one has to rely mainly on the secondary sources.

Likewise, the theories of child development had touched the aspect of family atmosphere, though there is no direct relationship depicted with marital adjustment and marital happiness in any of the theories of development.

Here it will not be out of place to assume that congenial home atmosphere depends to a great extent on the marital adjustment and marital happiness among the parents. Disagreement poor adjustment and unhappiness among the parents affect adversely the Psychosomatic development of the children. However, the findings of the present study failed to confirm the above assumption. Mostly marital adjustment and happiness found to be unrelated to the development of socially approved characteristics, hence, the relevant theories of child development are discussed here in brief.

Freudian theory has emphasized that the relationship of the child to his parents of the opposite sex is critical in the development of his personality. All parents have an implicit or explicit ideal of what their children should be like what knowledge, moral value and behavioural standard they should acquire as they grow. Parents try many strategies designed to move the child toward that goal.

There are at least two ways of looking at styles of parenting. The first way is to observe the particular behaviour and attitudes of the parents and the resulting behaviour of the children.

Parental behaviour toward a child can strongly determine how well the child achieves social intimacy, personal autonomy and an understanding of his place in the social environment. The parents behaviour affects the child's behaviour approximately in three ways. Firstly, the parents serve as models for the child to identify with them and imitate. Secondly, most parents have specific expectation about the way they want their children to respond and behave. Finally parents control the reward and discipline child receives.

Many studies have dealt with such specific parental behaviours and their effects on children's behaviour and personality. Becker (1964) sees parents behaviour as having three key dimensions. In his view each and every parents' attitudes and actions fall somewhere along each of three continuums.

(1) Restrictiveness vs. Permissiveness,

(2) Warmth vs. Hostility,·

(3) Anxious emotional involvement vs. calm detachment.

Several research studies have given an important insights into the different influences of restrictiveness and permissiveness behaviour of parents. The Principal findings indicate that restrictive parents usually tend to have dependent submissive and complaining children. Research finding have also discovered. Some interesting traits about sex differences in children's reactions to restrictiveness. It is found that the long term affects of childhood restrictiveness were much more stable in girls than boys.

Some research studies also suggest that boys are more sensitive and susceptible than girls to the influence of parents. It is partially because boys experience less positive supportive behaviour from their parents. They also experience more satiation effects of this behaviour and as a consequence become less susceptible than boys to parental influence. Some findings were obtained in the present study, indicating that girls are more emotionally stable than boys. Also it is interesting to note that boys tend to be more obedient than girls which may be the effect of changing social pattern.

Although permissiveness is the opposite polar of restrictiveness, it does not necessarily produce independent children. The results of few studies indicate that permissiveness is related to active outgoing creative and aggressive behaviour in children (Baldwin, 1949; Watson 1957) when permissiveness is used in a Climate of detached warmth seems very likely to produce fairly positive characteristics and when it is accompanied with high hostility it is more likely to result in non-compliance and aggressiveness.

Thus, overprotection, restrictiveness and more permissiveness in one or the other way deviate the normal development of children, but the inferential statistical measures, as stated elsewhere could not, satiate the assumption of the present study, though the hypotheses were based on sound footing.

Pearson, studied marital adjustment of the mothers and personality adjustment of the child. Surprisingly, his findings are well in accordance with the present investigation, which suggested that relationship between the mother's marital adjustment and the personality adjustment of the children are not significantly related.

Many research studies concerning marital relationship of the parents emphasize the importance of the parents marriage as a model for their children because children tend to imitate parents both consciously and unconsciously. The way parents relate to each other influences the child's attitude towards marriage in future.

If a child grows up seeing parents give each other positive psychological strokes, he or she learns to view marriage as a pleasant relationship. Another factor found to be strongly related to marriage success in an individuals personal happiness in childhood. An individuals who was happy in childhood is more likely to have a happy successful marriage. This findings reflects the importance of a positive parent child relationship and the importance of parents relating to the child is warm, accepting and supporting manner to prepare him for successful and fulfilling relationship with other.

None of the studies can provide a full proof recipe for raising children to personal specifications. But they all indicate the importance of the parents' role in child's development which is characterized as a period of developing skill and of increasing motivation to meet goal of peers in the social environment. In piagetion theory these early School year mark the transition from concrete to formal operational thought.

The result of various studies gives us a general idea of different ways in which parental styles as well as specific acts and expectations can influence the children's later standards, anxieties, his green of self-reliance and self-esteem and the quality of his peer relationship in the social environment.

The Child Rearing Practices measures and the development of particular personality traits were believed to have strong association. But it is surprising to observe that even the Child Rearing Practices seemed to be unrelated to the development of behavioural characteristics.

13

Recommendations and Suggestions

Marital Relationship

Marriage of the relationship that most adults find conducive to attaining satisfaction from life but marriage in itself does not create happiness. Marriage can add to one's feeling of self worth if one enters it. Happiness does not lie in the institution of marriage. It lies within people and depends upon the way they relate to each other.

Marital Happiness and Child Rearing

Studies on marital satisfaction report that marital satisfaction results in development of socially approved characteristics among the children. It is popularly assumed that children and marital happiness go together and are causally related. Child rearing generally refers to all interactions between parents and their children. Mother's role is very important in upbringing her child.

In the present study alongwith the marital happiness and marital adjustment of mothers, their influence on child rearing practices used by them, on their children have been assessed. Much of child's early development reflects the mother's personality. Thus, focal emphasis is placed on mother and her personality, in the personality development of her child, child is the visible product of parental child rearing effort.

The effective sample in the present study consisted 320 subjects of which 120 were girls and 200 were boys, in the age group of 10 to 13 years. For assessing mother's marital adjustment and child rearing practices, Marital Adjustment Test and Child Rearing Practices Scale were administered on mothers, respectively. To assess children's personality traits ESPQ was administered on children. Thus, the effective variables in the present study were marital happiness and adjustment and dependent variables were thirteen personality factors of children. In order to evaluate the effect of marital adjustment and happiness on different personality traits of children 2 × 2 factorial design was used. To find out the strength of association between the child rearing practices and the development of different personality characteristics the data were subjected to correlation coefficients.

In the light of the findings of the present study the conclusions drawn were as follows:—

1. Marital adjustment and child rearing practices seemed to be poorly influential in developing outgoing and emotionally stable characteristics in children.
2. Better adjusted mothers were found helpful in developing obedient and conscientiousness in their children.
3. Harmonious marital adjustment was seen remotely associated with the development of placid and relaxed qualities of personalities.
4. The well adjusted mothers were found using healthy child rearing practices, but the correlation coefficients failed to bring out any significant association or relationship.
5. Emotional instability was more among the children coming from the family where marital adjustment was poor. However, the difference was not significant.

In sum, it was observed that behavioural characteristics or personality characteristics are the results of multiple factors and cannot be attributed to one single variable.

Recommendations for Further Research

1. In the light of the present nuclear family situations it is very essential to conduct more intensive and longitudinal studies of family relationships. Such as father-child, mother-child, husband-wife relationships. This may help to investigate the problems and solutions can be resolved. This will definitely impart guidance to all members of the society and then there will be an emergence of healthy society.
2. Interesting results can be obtained in the same type of studies, if different age groups, can be studied separately.

3. Both teachers and parents should be considered while studying children's personality characteristics. Rapport between them may given good results.
4. Variables such as different socio-economic conditions, educational status of parents, working and non-working mothers, mothers, from different religions, comparison between mothers from joint families and nuclear families can be studied. The results of these studies will also be interesting.
5. Intensive study of children's personality characteristics can be of great help to improve the parents-child relationships. Each personality factor such as emotionally stable and unstable, reserved vs. outgoing, phlegmatic vs. excitable, obedient-assertive etc. can be studied separately of boys and girls from different age groups.

Suggestions

1. Each family is an important constituent of a social group. It has its functions toward the society. These functions can be fulfilled when all the members in the family are well-adjusted, satisfied and happy, their interpersonal relationships are harmonious. To develop such type of relationships, it is essential that parents should have knowledge of different developments of children.
2. Many child psychologists have emphasised the importance of parent-child relationship in child's personality development. Parents can rear their children in a better way when they are happy, satisfied in their marital life. Therefore, it is of utmost importance that each spouse must have a knowledge as how to build up a good marital relationship. Such type of knowledge can be imparted through different medias—films, social welfare centres, marriage counselling centres etc.
3. Results from various studies have shown that where father and mother have conflicts between them, the atmosphere in the home is full of stress and strain, children may develop negative personality characteristics. Thus, vicious circle starts in the home. The sufferers ultimately are the children. This can be avoided when much attention can be given during the formative years of childhood. Parents, specially

mothers must have knowledge as how to develop healthy personality of the child.

4. Apart from society and family the other important institution which can take part in the healthy personality development programme of the child is School Teachers must be aware of the different developmental stages in child's life. Teachers can observe children in different situations, this observation may help them to detect the children who are not normal socially, physically or emotionally. They can discuss the problems of these children with their parents. Such type of discussions may be helpful in improving the child's condition.

5. For the child's healthy personality development parent education programmes are very helpful. These programmes can be conducted teacher-parent meetings, films, lectures, posters, seminars etc. It is better to start this education during early adulthood years because then would be parents can prepare themselves to face the problems with confidence which may arise during the parent-child interactions.

Some General Advice to Parents

Optimal child-rearing practices should help the child to develop social needs which are in harmony with the major social values of his culture. They should further help him to acquire the necessary perceptual-response skills for satisfying his social needs in a culturally acceptable manner.

Other things being equal the following conditions appear conducive to wholesome personality growth in our culture:

1. Environmental factors that promote optimal physical growth and health: adequate nutrition, opportunities for rest and relaxation, protection from debilitating diseases and physical injuries.

2. Environmental factors that promote optimal perceptual-motor, intellectual, and social skills: abundant learning opportunities when the child is maturationally and experientially ready for them, social stimulation to realize his potentialities for further growth, appropriate guidance for his learning efforts, opportunities to make mistakes and profit from them.

3. Environmental factors that promote optimal emotional stability: a secure home in which affectional bonds can be permanently established, consistent methods of discipline and socialization, opportunities for the release of emotional tensions through "man-to-man" talks and the like, parental acceptance of the child as a personality in his own right.
4. Environmental factors that promote socially acceptable values: parents provide reasonably acceptable models by their own behaviour, approval and disapproval used in an intelligent and consistent manner to reflect the personal-social values of the homes and the larger community, opportunities for the child to participate in the activities of various agencies and institutions designed to transmit social values (school, church, youth groups, and the like).
5. Environmental factors that promote initiative, planfulness, flexibility, self-responsibility, and self-understanding: freedom to explore, permissive attitudes in the home, democratic structure in sub-groups to which the child belongs, encouragement to examine his needs, purposes, and potentialities for further growth.

This is not an exhaustive list by any means, but it is sufficiently inclusive to demonstrate that not all of our children enjoy even these advantages. Almost any parent or teacher would fail to "measure up" to some of these conditions. In other words, there is undoubtedly more knowledge in child psychology than parents, teachers, and other youth counsellors customarily apply.

The wise parent, teacher, or youth counsellor will do well to take the long view of child guidance by being relatively consistent in his interactions with children, but sufficiently flexible to allow for minor changes when indicated; by adopting a critical attitude toward "new discoveries" that run counter to his programme of child guidance; by accepting some behaviour deviations in children as a natural consequence of growth that is sometimes "painful"; by being calm when personality aberrations threaten, and by systematically varying the environmental condition in an effort to correct them; by accepting each child as a unique personality who may never be like the child next door; by seeking help from a reputable psychologist or psychiatrist when an environmental approach to child guidance is not sufficiently effective.

The positive and negative reinforcements that the growing child receives in the home determine, in large measure, his behaviour tendencies, his personality characteristics, and his general orientation toward life. Mother, father and brothers and sisters (if any) all have the opportunity to reward, ignore, and punish the child's responses. The child also has the power to delight and demoralize other family members by his actions. These interactions within the family are complex and little understood. However, child psychologists have made numerous efforts to identify and measure the molar variables of child-rearing and to relate these variables to the behaviour tendencies of the developing child. The child-rearing practices of the mother have been most extensively studied because of her relatively greater accessibility for questioning and experimentation. Fathers and siblings have been too long neglected as important influences on the child and the "group atmosphere" of the family unit. There are promising signs that this neglect may be corrected in psychological research within the near future.

The research findings reviewed in this book shed a modest amount of light on the manner in which children's personalities are influenced by parental actions and attitudes. Some general and broadly defined variables appear as significant antecedents in many different studies; e.g., acceptance-rejection, permissiveness-restrictiveness, and so on. There is reason to believe that these may be first approximations to fruitful description and prediction of parental influence on child growth and behaviour.

Let us round out some general comments about discipline and child management. These are not oracular preachments to govern one's handling of children, but broad considerations that might profit a parent or a teacher to ponder.

Behaviour is Motivate. There is a reason, a cause for every behaviour. Usually these causes are nct apparent at the conscious level: the child does not know why he does the things he does. To pinch his arm and ask, "Why did you do it?" is preposterous. If he knew why, he probably would not have had to act as he did in the first place. Yet the adult must try to ascertain and understand the cause. What is the child trying to achieve? Is he trying to gain acceptance? Attention ? Recognition? Affection? Meanness is not a cause but an interpretation.

Discipline is concerned too frequently with actions. Feelings are disregarded. The action or behaviour may be stopped, but what happend to the feelings? These must be dealt with, too. The child needs the opportunity to express them. He will fell better if he can air his feelings and adults may learn something in the process. Since restrictions are frustrating, the child needs to give vent to his feelings. The young child usually does so; the older child learns not to, but this does him no good.

Because restrictions are frustrating, they should be kept to a minimum. The fewer there are the better. The simpler they are the better. And they should always be geared to the child's level of understanding.

Then, too, the adult might examine his own thoughts. What are his motives? Are his demands reasonable? Was the child's behaviour truly not permissible, or was the adult's level of tolerance unusually low? Too great a price may be charged for conformity.

Finally, the parent-child relationship is unique; all authority, all the power, all the weight is invested in only one individual, the parent. The child must obey. For a parent to take advantage of such a relationship reflects little basic human understanding. Physical punishment is violence. It breeds a response detrimental to the individual and the society of which he is a part. Kindness, respect, and sensitivity, on the other hand, are qualities worth cultivating in a growing human being and these may well develop out of the intimate relationship between parent and child. They flourish in a climate of mutual trust, and for mutual trust to be truly mutual, it takes the full cooperation of both parties.

Limitations

1. Probing into an individual's marital life is by no means an easy task. Usually the spouses especially the women do not like to talk about their marital life to an outsider and are specially reluctant to divulge any unpleasantness they might be experiencing. Under these circumstances obtaining truthful answers becomes a challenge.
2. Previously it was planned to study 500 children during the research work and accordingly more than 500 children were included as subjects. But at the time of final analysis certain cases were deleted for various reasons such as (a) Children did not responded to the test properly. (b) Some mothers did not fill the forms accurately. (c) Some mothers having no knowledge of its importance lost the forms. (d) Husband

of some spouses refused to fill the questionnaire, since the information sought for was of very personal and private nature. (e) Some mothers were deleted from the sample as they were not matriculate, which was the minimum educational qualification for mothers.

Due to all these difficulties the final sample consisted only 320 subjects and their mothers. Of these 200 were boys and 120 were girls. The investigator had to satisfy herself with the remaining sample.

3. For the studies like this, it is essential to establish rapport with the individual subjects before interviewing them. Unfortunately the investigator could not establish rapport with the subjects due to limitation of time.

4. The tests used in the present study Marital Adjustment Test and Early School Personality Questionnaire were devised in foreign countries. Therefore, it may have affected the results of the present investigation.

5. In the study where children are the subjects, cooperation from teacher is very important. In some schools, due to non-cooperation from the teachers, the investigator could not collect larger sample.

The conclusions drawn and suggestions offered on the basis of the findings of this study may have therefore, to be considered in the light of limitations of this study.

Bibliography

Abraham, K.G., Christopherson V.A., Kuchl R.D., "Navj and Anglo Child Rearing Behaviours—A Cross Cultural Comparison", *Journal of Comparative Family Studies*, Vol. 15(3), 1984, 373-338.

Adorno, T.W. et. al., *Authoritarian Personality*, Harper and Row, New York, 1950.

Agarwal, R., "A Study of Feeling of Security in Morally Developed and Underdeveloped Adolescents as related to their Self-Concept and Personality Pattern', Ph.D., Agra University, 1985.

Agrawal, G. and Saxena N.K., "Emotional Development of the Child and the Role of the Parents", *An Interview, Child Psychiatry Quarterly*, (Oct.) Vol. 10(4) 1977, 1-7.

Alexander, E.. *The Dynamics of Personality Development*, Soc., Sasewk, Vol. 32, 1951, 139-43.

Allinson, J. and Endsley R.C., "Influences of Sex of Child and Parent on Parental Reactions to Hypothetical Parent-Child Situations", *Child Development*, 1970, 41.

Allport, G.W. and Kahn, J.H., "Human Growth and the Development of Personality", *Ind-edi.*, Oxford, Perganon, 1971, 10.

Allport, G.W., *Pattern and Growth in Personality*, New York, Holt, 1960.

Bacon, M.K., Child I.L., Berry H., "A Cross Cultural Study of Correlation of Crime", *Journal of Abnormal Social Psychology*, Vol. 66, 1963, 291-300.

Baldwin, A.L., "The Effect of Home Environment on Nursery School Behaviour", *Child Development*, Vol. 20, 1949, 49-61.

Baldwin, A.L., Kalharn J., Brese F.H., "Pattern of Parents Behaviour", *Psychological Monographs*, 58, 1945.

Bandura, A., Huston A., "Parent Child Relationship", A Decade Review of Research, *Journal of Marriage and Family*, Vol. 33, 1971, 70-77.

Bandura, A., Ross, D., Ross, S.A., "Transmission of Agression Through Imitation of Aggressive Models", *Journal of Abnormal and Social Psychology*, Vol. 63, 1961, 575-582.

Bandura, A., Walter H., "Social Learning and Personality Development", New York, Holt, Wrinehart and Winston, 1963.

Banner, C.N., "Child Rearing Attitudes of Mothers Under College and over achieving Children", *British Journal of Educational Psychology* (Jan.), Vol. 49(22), 1979, 150-155.

Barker, G.H., Adams W.R., "Comparison of the Delinquencies of Boys and Girls". *Journal of Criminal Law*, Vol. 53, 1962, 470-75.

Barnett, M.A., King, E.M., Howard, J.A. and Dino, G.A., "Empathy in Young Children, Relation to Parent's Empathy Affection and Emphasis on the Feelings of others". *Developmental Psychology*, (May), Vol. 16(3) 1980, 243-244.

Bates, J.E., Pettit, G.S., "Adult Individual Differences as Moderators of Child Effects", *Journal of Abnormal Child Psychology*, Vol. 9, 1981, 329-340.

Baumrind, D., "Effects of Authoritarian Parental Control on Child Behaviour", *Child Development*, Vol. 37, 1966, 887-907.

Baumrind, D., "The Development of Instrumental Competence, Through Socialization", *Symposia on Child Psychology*, Vol. (7), Uni. of Minnesota Press, 1973.

Baylay and Schaefer, Psychology of the Child, Parental Influence-Chapter 12, 1964.

Becker, W.C. and Krug, S.R., "A Circumplex Model for Social Behaviour in Children", *Child Development*, Vol. 35, 1964, 384-392.

Becker, W.C., "Consequences of Different Kinds of Parental Discipline", *Review of Child Development Research*, Vol. (1), 1964, New York.

Becker, W.C., "Parent-Child Relationships", A Decade Review of Research, *A Journal of Marriage and Family*, Vol. 33, 1971, 70-79, 95-99.

Behrens, M.L., "Child Rearing and the Characteristics Structure of the Mother", *Child Development*, Vol. 25, 1954, 225-228.

Bell, R.Q. and Harper, L.V., *The Effects of Children on Parents*, Hill Sdale, N.J. Eribaum, 1977.

Bell, R.Q., "Parent Child Reciprocal Influences", *American Psychologist*, Vol. 34, 1979, 821-26.

Bell, R.R., "The Related Importance of Mother and Wife Roles, Among Black, Lower class women in the Black Family", Belmen, California, Wordsworth, 1971.

Berman, S., *Adjustment of Parents to Children in the Home*, J. Pediat, Vol. 32, 1948, 66-77.

Bernreuter, R.G., Ayer, M.E., "Study of Relationship Between Discipline and Personality Traits in Little Children", *Journal of Genetic Psychology*, Vol. 50, 1973, 165-170.

Bhogles, S., "Child Rearing Practices Among Different Culture", A Project Report of ICSSR, 63-70.

Bhoota, Dr. Kamla, *Your Child from 6 to 12*, Vora and Co. Publishers Pvt. Ltd., Bombay-1966.

Biller, H.B., *Father-Child and Sex Role*, Lexington, Mass, Health-1971.

Bishop, N.M., "Mother-Child Interaction and the Social Behaviour of Children", *Psychology Monograph*, Vol. 65, No. 11, 1951.

Blood, R.O. and Urdy, "Marital Satisfaction as Perceived by Wives", by Naheel Jeris, *Home Economics Research Journal*, (Mar.) Vol. 74, 1979.

Blood, R.O. and Wolfe, D.M., *Husband and Wives, The Dynamics of Married Living*, Free Press, New York, 1960.

Bollmen, "Parent Child Relationships", A Decade Review of Research *Journal of Marriage and Family*, Vol. 33, 1971, 70-79, 95-99.

Bowman, H.A., Marriage for Moderns, London, 3rd edition, MacGrew Hill Book Co., New York-1, 1959.

Brotenbrenner, "Parent Child Relationships", A Decade Review of Research, *Journal of Marriage and Family*, Vol. 33, 1971, 70-79.

Buirt C., *The Causes and Treatment of Backwardness*, London Press, London, 1950, 77.

Burchinal, L.G., "Parents Attitudes and Adjustment of Children", *Journal of Genetic Psychology*, 92, 1958, 69-79.

Burge, P.L., "Parental Child Rearing Sex Roles Attitudes Relation to Social Issue, Sex Role Attitudes and Selected Demographic Variables", *Home Economics Research Journal*, Vol. 9(3), (Mar.), 1981, 193.

Burgess, E., Cortrell, L., *Predicting Success of Failure in Marriage*, Inc., New York, Prentice Hall, 1934.

Burr, W.R., Wesley, "Satisfaction with Various Aspects of Marriage Over the Life Cycle", *Journal of Marriage and Family*, Vol. 32 (1-2), 1970, 32-36.

Buss, D.M., "Predicting Parent-Child Interactions from Children's Activity Level", *Developmental Psychology*, Vol. 17(1), 1981 (Jan.), 59-65.

Byrne and Sturr, "Parent Child Relationship", A Decade Review of Research, *Journal of Marriage and Family*, Vol. 33, 1971, 70,79-95, 99.

Carlow W.R Reynolds R. Green W.L., Khand N.I., "Underlying Sources of Agreement and Communication Between Husband and Wives", *Journal of Marriage and Family*, Vol. 33, 1971, 576-581.

Carlsmith L., "Effect of Early Father Absence on Scholastic Aptitude", Horward Educational Review, Vol. 34, 1964, 3-21.

Cattell, R.B., *Personality a Systematic Theoretical and Factual Study*, New York, McGraw Hill, 1950.

Centres et. al., "Conjugal Power Structure", A Re-examination American Sociological Review, Vol. 36 (April), 1971, 264-278.

Chandramani M., Salmomy, K.C., Indulekha, K.V., "Family Background Versus Problem Behaviour of Children of Pre-School Age, *Indian Journal of Home Science*, Vol. 9 (Dec.) No. 4, 1975.

Chein, M., "Impact of Parental Attitudes on Adjustment of Elementary Children", *Bulletin of Educational Psychology*, 1978, (Jun.), Vol. 11, 1978, 63.86.

Christenson, H.T., Johnson K.P., *Marriage and the Family Living*, 3rd Ed. New York, Ronald, 1971.

Cioate, E. "The Influence of Stressful Events in Early Childhood on Personality in Preadolescence, *Psychological Abstracts (1980)*, Vol. 63(4), 1980, 837.

Clapp, "Parent-Child Relationships", A Decade Review of Research *Journal of Marriage and Family*, Vol. 33, 1971, 70-79, 90-97.

Clayton R.R., *The Family, Marriage and Social Change*, Lexinton, Massachusets, Heath, 1975.

Clifford, E., "Discipline in the Home", A Controlled Observational Study of Parental Practices, *Journal of Genetic Psychology*, Vol. 95, 1959, 45-82.

Craig, G.T., *Child Development*, Prentice Hall Inc., Englewood, Cliffs, New York, 1979.

Cutler, B.R., Dyer, W.G., "Initial Adjustment Process in Young Married Couples", *Social Forces*, Vol. 44(2), 1965.

Davis, A. and Havinghurt, R.J., Social Class and Colour Differences in Child Rearing", in Amer. Social Rev., Vol. 11, 680-710.

Dean, D.G., Karlson, Robert, S., "Definitions of Life Situations and Marital Adjustment", *Journal of Comparative Family Studies*, Vol. 15(3), 1984, 441-448.

Delaney, "Parent Child Relationships—A Decade Review of Research", *A Journal of Marriage and Family*, Vol. 33, 1971, 70-79, 90-99.

Desai, A.N., "A Study of Relationship Between Maternal Attitudes and Mother Child Interaction, With Special Reference to Child Rearing in Urban Community," ICSSR Annual Report, 1970-71.

Devdas R.P. et al., Sheela K., Nalini Devi R. "Child Rearing Practices of Employed and Non-Employed Mothers", *Indian Journal of Home Science*, (Oct.), Vol. 2, 1970.

Devdas R.P., Jaya N., *A Text Book of Child Development*, Mc Millan India Ltd., 1984.

Devidson, Bernard, 1984, "A Test of Equity Theory for Marital Adjustment", *Social Psychology Quarterly*, (Mar.), Vol. 47(l), 1984, 36-42.

Digman and Hurley, "Parental Child Relationship", A Decade Review of Research, *Journal of Marriage and Family*, Vol. 33, 1971, 70-79, 90-95.

Dollard, J., *Frustration and Aggression*, Yale Uni. Press, 1939.

Dunbor, F., *Symbiosis of Parents and Child*, Amer. J. Orthopsychiat, 1952, Vol. 22, 809-824.

Edmonds, V.H., Withers, G., Diabaltista, B., "Adjustment Conversation and Conventionalism". *Journal of Marriage and Family*, (Feb.), Vol. 34, 1972, 96-103.

Elder, G.H., "Structural Variations in the Child Rearing Relationship", *Sociometry*, Vol. 25, (Sept.) 1962, 24-25.

ElGuebalay, N. and Offord, D.R., "The Competent offspring of psychiatrically ill parents", A search for behaviourial variable. Canadian, *Journal of Psychiatry*, (Oct.), Vol. 25(6), 1980, 464-467.

Erickson, E.H., *Childhood and Society*, New York, Norton, 1950.

Escalona, S., "Pattern of Infantile Experience", *The Development Process in Psychoanalytical Study of the Child*, Ed. R.S., Vol. 18, International Uni. Press, New York, 1963.

Eschleman, J.H., "Mental Health and Marital Integration in Young Marriages", *Journal of Marriage and Family*, 27 May 1965.

Eysenk, H.J., *The Structure of Human Personality*, New York, Wiley, 1953.

Fe A Domingo, M. "Child Rearing Practices in Barrio", *Journal of Psychology*, (Jul.-Dec.), Vol. 10(2) 1977, 3-6.

Feldman H., Rilling Boyd., "Marital Satisfaction over the Family Life", *Journal of Marriage and Family*, Vol. 32(1-2), 1970, 24-26.

Filsinger Erik, "Social Competence and Marital Adjustment", *Home Economics Journal*, (Dec.), Vol. 9(2), 1980, 159.

Friedman, "Parent Child Relationships", A Decade Review of Research, *Journal of Marriage and Family*, Vol. 33, 1971, 70-79, 90-99.

Frued, S., *An Outline of Psycho-Analysis*, New York, Norton, 1949.

Gardner, L.P., "An Analysis of Children's Attitudes Towards Fathers", *Journal of Genetic Psychology*, Vol. 70, 3-28.

Garrison, K.C., *Growth and Development*, 2nd Edition, New York, Longmans, 1959.

Geismar, "A Decade Review of Research", *Journal of Marriage and Family*, Vol. 33, 1971, 70-79, 95-99.

Ghosh and Sinha, "Parent Child Relationships", A Decade Review of Research, *Journal of Marriage and Family*, Vol. 33, 1971, 70-80, 90-99.

Glen, M.L., "Intimacy and Oppression", *Marriage and Family in a Decade of Change*, Edited by G.B. Carr, Readings, Massuchusett Wesley, 1972, 109-111.

Govalas R. and Briggs, P., "Concurrent Scheduled of Reinforcement", *A New Concept of Dependency, Merril Palmer*, Quarterly, Vol. 12, 1966.

Grace, J. Gaig, *Human Development*, 4th Edition, Prentice-Hall, New Jersey, 1986.

Grant, "Effect of Certain Factors in the Home Environment Upon Child Behaviour", M.A. Thesis State Uni. of Iowa, 1937.

Grosby, J.E. "Illusion and Disillusion", *The Self in Love and Marriage*, Belment, California, Wordsworth, 1973.

Grossman, "Parent Child Relationships", A Decade Review of Research, *Journal of Marriage and Family*, Vol. 33, 1971, 70-79, 95-99.

Growe, G.A., "Parental Behaviour and Self Esteem in Children", Psychological Reports, (Oct.), Vol. 47(2), 1980, 499-500.

Groybill, D., "Relationship of Maternal Child Rearing Behaviours to Children's Self Esteem", *Journal of Psychology*, (Sept.), Vol. 100(l) 1978, 45-45.

Gupta, R. and Agnihotri, R., "Self Confidence as a Function of Perceived Maternal child rearing behaviour., Deptt. of psychology, R.G. Post-Graduate College, Meerut, Psychology and Educational Sciences, Indian Science Congress, 1987, 21.

Gurin et al., "A Feminist Review of Marital Adjustment Literature". The rape of the Locke-by Laws J.L., *Journal of Marriage and Family*, Vol. 35, 1971, 495-505.

Harper, L.V., *The Effect of Children on Parents*, Hills Dale, N.J. Eribaum, 1977.

Harris and Tseng, "Children's Attitude towards Peers and Parents as revealed by sentence completion", *Child Development*, Vol. 28, 1957, 401-411.

Hatfield J. Ferguson L., Allport R., "Mother Child Interaction and the Socialization Process", *Child Development*, Vol. 38(1-2), 1967, 365-411.

Hawkes, G.R., Burchinal, L.G., Gardner, B.M., Forter, M.B., "Parents Acceptance of their Children", *Journal of Home Economics*, (March), Vol. 48(3), 1956, 195-199.

Hawkes, G.R., Pease, D., "Behaviour and Development from 5 to 12", Deptt. of Child Development, Iowa, State Univ. Harper and Bow, New York, 1966, 40-42.

Heathers, G., "Emotional Dependence and Independence in Physical Threat Situation", *Child Development*, Vol. 24, 1953.

Heise, D.R., *Personality and Socialization*, Chicago, R and McNally, 1972.

Hicks, M., Platt, M., "Marital Happiness and Stability", *Journal of Marriage and Family*, Vol. 32(3-4), 1970, 558-563.

Hicks, Mand, Platt, M., "Marital Quality—A Review of the Seventies", *Journal of Marriage and Family*, Vol. 42(1-4), 1982, 94-96.

Hill, D.L., "Interaction of Sex of Subject and Depending Training Procedures in a Social Reinforcement Study", *Merrill Plamer*, Quarterly, Vol. 15, 1969, 185-198.

Hodges, W.F. Buchsbaun, H.K. and Tierney, C.W., "Parent Child Relationships and Adjustment in Pre-school Children in Divorced and Intact Families", *Journal of Divorce*, Vol. 7(2), 1983, 43-58.

Hoffman, L.W., "Effect of Maternal Employment on the Child", *Child Development*, Vol. 32, 1961, 187-197.

Hoffman, M.L., "Power Assertion by the Parent and Its Impact on the Child", *Child Development*, 31, 1960, 129-143.

Hurley and Palonen, "Marital Satisfaction—As Perceived by Wives", *Home Economics Research Journal*, (March), Vol. 7(4), 1979.

Hurlock, E.B., "Developmental Psychology", *A Life Span Approach*, 5th edition, MacGrew Hill Publishing Co. Ltd., Delhi, 1983.

Hurlock, E.B., *Child Development*, 6th Edition, Tata McGraw Hill, Publishing Co., 1978.

Hurlock, E.B., *Personality Development*, Tata McGraw Hill, Publishing Co., Ltd., New Delhi, 1983.

Ismail, M.I. and Hana, A.M., *The Problem Child*, Egypt, J. Psychol., 1950-51, 6, 20, 9, 218.

Jacobson, D.S., "The Impact of Marital Separation, Divorce on Children, Parent, Child Communication and Child Adjustment and Regression Analysis of Findings from overall study, *Journal of Divorce*, Vol. 2(2), 1978, 175-194.

Jersild, A. T., Sawrey, J.M., Telford, C.W., *Child Psychology*, 7th Edition, Englewood Cliffs N.J. Prentice Hall of India Pvt. Ltd., New Delhi, 1978.

Jones, D.C., Ricklel, A.V. and Smith, R.L., "Maternal Child Rearing Practices and Social Problem Solving Strategies Among

Preschoolers, *Developmental Psychology*, Vol. 16(3), 1980, 241-242.

Kafiluddins, S., "*A Study of Parental Discipline Family Structure and Ordinal Position* as Antecendent Factors in the Genesis of Aggression", Ph.D, Psy. Bhagalour U., 1980.

Kagan and Lenkin, "Parent Child Relationships—A decade review of Research", *Journal of Marriage and Family*, Vol. 33, 1971, 70-79, 95-99.

Kagan, Freeman, *Psychology of the Child*, Parental Influences (Ch. 12), 1963.

Kagan, Spencer, Knight, George, P. 'Maternal Reinforcement Style and Cooperation, Competition among Anglo-American and Mexican-American Children, *Journal of Genetic Psychology*, (Sept.), Vol. 145(1) 1984, 37-47.

Kale S.V., "Child Psychology and Child Guidance", *Self and Personality*, Ch. 6, Orient Longmans, Bombay, 1978.

Kalliopuska, M., "Relation Between Children and Parents Empathy", Psychological Reports, (Feb.), Vol. 54(1) 1984, 295-299.

Kamath, R. and Udipi, Shobha, "Guide to Thesis Writing", S.N.D.T. Women's University, Bombay, 1989.

Kapadia, K.M., *Marriage and Family in India*, 3rd Edition, Oxford Uni. Press, Bombay, 1970.

Kappuswami, B., "Advanced Educational Psychology", New Delhi, Sterling Publishing Pvt. Ltd., 1976, 17, 43.

Kappuswami, B., *A Text Book of Child Behaviour and Development*, Vikas Publications House Pvt. Ltd., Delhi, 1976.

Kapur, Promilla, *Marriage and Working Women in India*, Vikas Publications, Delhi, Bangalore, Bombay, 1970.

Kardiner, A., *The Psychological Frontiers of Society*, Columbia, University Press, 1945.

Karian G., "Structural Changes in the Family in Kerala", India in R.R., Williams Socialization and Communication in Primary Groups, *The Hague*, Morton Publishers, 1975, 59-79.

Kephart, W.M., *The Family Society and the Individual*, 3rd Edition, Buston, Honghton, Millan, 1972.

King, C.E., "The Burgess Cottrell Method of Measuring Marital Adjustment Applied to Non-White Southern Urban Population", *Journal of Marriage and Family*, Vol. 14(4), 1952.

Klemer, R.M., *Marriage and Family Relationships*, Harper and Row Publications, New Delhi, 1970.

Kotler, T., "Marital Happiness and Stability" by Hicks Hanel Platt, *Journal of Marriage and Family*, Vol. 32(4), 1970.

Krause, Rainer, "Relationship Between Mental Health Socialization and Creativity", *Psychological Abstracts*, Vol. 65(3073), 1981, 330.

Kretschmer, E., *Physique and Character*, New York, Harper Brace, 1926.

Lafore, G.G., "Practices of Parents in Dealing with Pre-School Children", *Child Development Mono*, Colombia University.

Lamb, "Assessment of Child Rearing Behaviour of Mid-Western Rural Parents", *Home Economics Research*, Journal (Dec.), Vol. 9(2) 1980, 163.

Landis, J.T. and Landis, M.G., *Building a Successful Marriage*, 6th Edition, Englewood Cliff, New Jersy Prentice Hall, 1973.

Landis, P.H., *Making the most Marriage*, Appleton Century Crefts Inc., New York, 1960.

Laws, J.L., "A Feminist Review of Marital Adjustment Literature, The Rape of the Locke", *Journal of Marriage and Family*, Vol. 33, 1971, 483-516.

Lerkowtiz, M.M., "Parent Child Relationships", A Decade Review of Research by Walters James Stinett Nick, *Journal of Marriage and Family*, Vol. 33, 1971, 70-79, 90-95.

Levin, M.J., "Psychology, A Biographical Approach", New York McGraw Hill Book Co., 1978.

Levinger and Senn, "Marital Happiness and Stability", *Journal of Marriage and Family*, Vol. 32(3-4), 1970, 558-563.

Lewis, R.A., "The Marital Disenchantment—Disagreement Paper Presented at the Meeting of the International Gerontological Society. June, 24, Jerusalem, Israel, 1975.

Livson, "Parent Child Relationships", A Decade Review of Research, *Journal of Marriage and Family*, Vol. 33, 1971, 70-79, 90-95.

Locke, J.J. and Karlson, G., "Marital Adjustment and Prediction in Sweden and United States, *American Sociological Review*, Vol. 16, 1952.

Maccoley, E.E. and Gribbs, P.K., "Methods of Child Rearing in Two Social Classes", in W.E. Martin and Alia B. Stendler, Eds. *Reading in Child Development*, New York, Harcourt Brace, 1954, 380-396.

Maccord, W., "Familial and Behavioural Correlates of Dependency", Child Development, Vol. 37, 1962.

Mace, D., "We can have better Marriages if Really want them", Nashville, Tencsee, Abingdon, 1974.

Maier, Henry, W., *Three Theories of Child Development*, New York, Harper and Row, 1965.

Martin, B., "Parent Child Relations", *Review of Child Development Research*, Vol. 4, Chicago, Uni. of Chicago, 1975.

Martin, E.K., "Relation of Parental Strictness to Competitive and Comparative Attitudes of Primary School Children", Psychological Reports, (Jan.) Vol. 54(3), 1984, 864-866.

Maw, W.H. and Maw, E.W., "Children Curiosity and Parental Attitudes", *Journal of Marriage and Family*, (Aug.), Vol. 28(3) 1966, 343.

Medinus and Curtis, "Parent-Child Relationships", A Decade Review of Research, *Journal of Marriage and Family*, Vol. 33, 1971, 70-79, 95-99.

Medling, J.M., Mercury H., "Marital Adjustment over Segments of Family Life Cycle, The Issue of Spouses Value Similarity", *Journal of Marriage and Family*, Vol. 43, 1981, 198-201.

Merill, B., "Relationship between Mother-Child Interactions and the Social Behaviour of Children", Ph.D. Dissertation, State Uni. of Lowu, 1974.

Meyer, C., "Assertive Behaviour of Children as Related to Parent Behaviour", *Journal of Home Economics*, Vol. 39, 1947, 77-80.

Miller and Swanson, "Parent Child Relationships"—A Decade Review of Research, *Journal of Marriage and Family*, Vol. 33, 1971, 90-99.

Miller, B.C., "A Multivariate Developmental Model of Marital Satisfaction", *Journal of Marriage and Family*, (Nov.) Vol. 30, 1968, 643-57.

Miller, B.C., "Marital Quality—A Review of Seventies", *Journal of Marriage and Family*, Vol. 42(1-4) 1980, 94-96.

Mohr, G.J., "Influence of Mothers Attitudes on Mental Health", J. Pediat-1940, Vol. 16, 641-646.

Mole, "Parent Child Relationships", A Decade Review of Research, *Journal of Marriage and Family*, Vol. 33, 1971, 70-79, 95-99.

Moore, "Parent Child Relationships", A Decade Review of Research, *Journal of Marriage and Family*, Vol. 33, 1971, 70-79, 90-99.

Morris, H.H., Escoal P.J., Wexler R., "Aggressive Behaviour Disorders of Childhood A Follow Up Study", *American Journal of Psychiatry*, Vol. 112, 1956, 991-997.

Mukerjee, Nanuta, "Changing Pattern of Child Rearing Practices in Three Religious groups and its Relation to Behaviour Adjustment in Children" in ICSSR, Annual Report, 1973.

Murphy, D.C., "Mendelson, L.A., "Use of Observational Method in the Study of Love Marital Communication", *Journal of Marriage and Family*, Vol. 35(5), 1973, 256-263.

Murstein, Gladin, "Marital Happiness and Stability", by Hicks M. Platt, M., *Journal of Marriage and Family*, Vol. 32(3-4), 1970, 558-563.

Mussen, P.H., Conger, J.J. Kagan, J. Juston, A.C., *Child Development and Personality*, 6th Edition, Harper International Edition, 1984.

Naheel, Jeris, "Marital Satisfaction—A Perceived by Wives," *Home Economics Research* Journal (March), Vol. 7(4), 1979.

Nalini, Devi and Anandam, K., "Child Rearing Practices of Rural Families at the two Income Levels", Abstract of Home-Science Research, 1967, 6, 27.

Nancy, D., Colletta, International Journal of *Sociology of the Family*, Vol. 9, (Jan.-June), 1974, 27-33.

Navranl, "Communication and Adjustment in Marriage", *Family Process*, 6 (Sept.), 1967, 173-184.

Newtan, B.M. and Newman, P.R., *Infancy and Childhood, Development* and its Contents, John Wiley and Sons., 1977.

Nye and Gecas, "Assessment of Child Rearing Behaviour of Midwestern Rural Parents", *Home Economics Research*, Journal, (Dec.) Vol. 9(2), 1980, 163.

Olim, E.G., "The Self Actualizing in the fully Functioning Family"—A Humanistic View Point", In American Marriage a Changing Scene", Edited by P.D. Cese Dubuque, Lowa Univ., Brown, 1972, 182-193.

Orden, S.R., Bradburn, N.M., "Dimension of Marriage Happiness", *The American Journal of Sociology*, (May) Vol. 73(6), 1968.

Papalia, D.E., and Old, S.W., "Psychology", McGraw-Hill Book Company.

Patterson, G.R., "Mothers, the Unacknowledged victims Monographs of the Society for Research" in Child Development, *Child Development*, Vol. 45(5), 1980, 64.

Pavenstedt, E., "A Comparison of Child Rearing Environment of Upper-Lower and Very Low-Lower Class Families", *American Journal of Orthopsychiatry*, Vol. 35, 89-89, 1965.

Peterson, D.R., "Child Behaviour Problems and Parental Attitudes", *Child Development*, Vol. 32, 1961.

Philliber, S.G., Graham, Elizabeth, "The Impact of Age of Mother on Mother-Child Interaction Patterns", Journal of *Marriage and Family*, Vol. 43, 1981, 112.

Plash, E.J. and Johnston, C.A., "A Comparison of the Mother Child Interactions of Younger and Older Hyperactive, and Normal Children", *Child Development*,Vol. 53, 1982, 1371-1381.

Powers, W.G., Hutchinson, "The Measurement of Communication", Apprehension in the Marriage Relationship Journal of *Marriage and Family* (Feb.), Vol. 41, 1979, 89-95.

Radin, N., "Maternal Warmth Achievement Motivation and Cognitive Functioning in Lower-Class Pre-School Children", Sociometry-13, 1971, 154-71.

Radke, M., "Relation of Parental Authority to Children's behaviour and Attitudes", Minneapolia Min Uni. of Minoesota Press, 1946.

Raj, H., *Society in India*, Jagrati Printers, 1988, 77-123.

Rapp, D.W., "Child Rearing Attitudes of Methods in Germany and U.S.A.", *Child Development*, Vol. 32, 1961, 669-78.

Read K.H. "Parents' Expressed Attitudes and Children's Behaviour", Journal *Consultant Psychology*, 1945, 95-100.

Renne, K.S., "Correlates of Dissatisfaction in Marriage", *Journal of Marriage and Family*, (1-2), Vol. 32, 1970, 60-62.

Rhyne, D., "Bases of Marital Satisfaction among Men and Women", *Journal of Marriage and Family*, Vol. 43, 1981, 944-53.

Rice, P.F., "Marriage and Parenthood", Allyn and Bacon Inc., 1979.

Ricep, F., "Contemporary Marriage" Part 1, by Allyn and Bacon Inc. 7, Well Avenue Newton, Manssachuaetts, 1983.

Robert, H. and Deluty, "Consistency of Assertive, Aggressive and Submissive Behaviour for Children", Uni. of Marryland, Battimore Conty, *Journal of Personality and Social Psychology*, Vol. 49(4), 1985, 1054-1065.

Rohner, B.C., Chaille, C. Rohner, R.P., "Perceived Parental Acceptance, Rejection and the Development of Children's Locus of Control", *Journal of Psychology* (Jan.) Vol. 104(1), 1980, 83-86.

Rollerova, B. and Cap. J., "Influence of Child Rearing Practices on the formation of a well-rounded personality", *Psychological Abstracts*, Vol. 62(2), 1981, 342.

Roth, J. and Peck, R., *Readings in Marriage and Family*, by Landis J.T. and Landis M.G. Prentice Hall Inc. New York, 1952.

Sachdeva, V.B., *An Introduction to Sociology*, Kitab Mahal, 1984.

Santrock, J. N. Warshak R.A., "Father Custody and Sociological Development in Boys and Girls", *Journal of Social Issues*, Vol. 35(4), 1979, 112-125.

Saraswati, T.S., Sunderson J., "Perceived Maternal Disciplinary Practices and their relation to development of moral judgement", *International Journal of Behaviour Development*, Vol. 3 (Apr.) 1, 1980, 91-109.

Sarkar, U., "Contribution of some Home-Factors on Children's Scholastic Achievement", Ph.D. Psy. Calcutta U., 1983.

Saxton, L., *The Individual Marriage and the Family*, 3rd Edition, Belment, California, 1977.

Schafer, R.B., Kath, M.P., "Equity in Marital Roles across the Life Cycle", *Journal of Marriage and Family*, Vol. 43, 1981, 362.

Schneider, L.J., Dewinne, R.F., Overton, T.D., "Influence of Congruity between Parental personality types of offsprings personality Development", *Journal of Counselling Psychology*, Vol. 27(1), 1980, 40-43.

Schrem, R. N., "Marital Satisfaction over the Family Life Cycle", A critique and proposal, *Journal of Marriage and Family*, (Feb.) Vol. 41, 1979.

Schrfman, M. and Clerk, R.W., "Delingment Adolescent Girls, Residential Treatment in a Municipal Hospital Setting", *Arch, Genetic Psychiatry*, Vol. 17(4), 196-197, 441-447.

Sears, R., Whitting, J., Nowlis, V., Sears, P., "Some Child Rearing Antecedents of Aggression and Dependency in young Children", *Gentic Psychology Monograph*, Vol. 47, 1953, 135.

Sears, R.R., "Relation of early Socialization experience to self concepts and gender role in middle childhood", *Child Development*, Vol. 41, 1970, 267.

Sears, R.R., Maccoby, E.E., Levin, H., *Patterns of Child Rearing*, New York, Harper, 1957.

Sears, R.R., Rav, L. and Alpert, R., *Identification and Child Rearing*, Standford, California Stanford University Press, 1965.

Serot, N.M. and Teevan C.R., "Perception of the Parent Child Relationship and its relation to Child Adjustment", *Child Development*, Vol. 32, 1961, 373-378.

Sethi, "Parent-Child Relationships", A Decade Review of Research, *Journal of Marriage and Family*, Vol, 33, 1971, 70-79, 95-99.

Shainberg, D., "Motivation of Adolescent Military Offenders", *Adolescents*, Vol. 26, 1967, 246, 254.

Sharma, Pratima, "Parents Role in the Development of Creative Behaviour", Proceedings of 74th Session of the Indian Science Congress, Bangalore, 1987.

Sheldon, W.H., *The Varieties of Temperament*, New York, Harper, 1942.

Shoben, E.J., "The Assessment of Parental attitudes in relation to child adjustment", *Genct. Psychol. Nonogr*, 1949, Vol. 39, 101-148.

Shoemaker, D., Paeterson, D., Quey, H., Baker, W., Heller, L., "Parental Attitudes and Child Adjustment", *Child Development*, Vol. 30, 1959, 119-130.

Shrivastava, S.S., "Anxiety among Primary School Children in relation to employment of their Mothers", Proceedings to 74th Indian Science Congress 1987, Part III, 22.

Sidana, Usha and Sinha, D., "Child Rearing Practices and the Development of Fear in Children", *Indian Journal of Psychology*, Vol. 18(2), 34-48.

Siggelman, A.E., Hass, B.M., "The Working Mother—A Review of Research", *Child Development* (Mar. to Dec.) Vol. 34, 1963, 513-542.

Singh, M.B., Miss Kiran, "Parental Acceptance of preschool Children of Rural and Urban Mothers", *The Indian Journal of Home Science* (March), Vol. 14, 1981, 23.

Singh, P.N., Huang, S.C., Thampson G.G., "A Comparative Study of selected attitudes values and personality characteristics of American Chinese, Indian Student", *Journal of Social Psychology*, 57, 1962, 123-132.

Sinha, L.K.W. and Krishna, K.P., "Child Rearing practices in young and old Adults", *Indian Journal of Gerontology*, Vol. 3(324), 74-75.

Smith, "Social Competence and Marital Adjustment", by Filsinger, E., *Home Economics Journal* (Dec.) Vol. 9(2), 1980, 159.

Spainer, G.B., Lewis, R.A., "Marital Quality—A Review of Seventies", *Journal of Marriage and Family*, Vol. 42(1-4), 1980, 94-96.

Stendler, C.B., "The learning of Certain Secondary Drives by Parison and American Children", *Journal of Marriage and Family*, Vol. 16, 1954, 198-200.

Stinnett, N., Walters, J., *Relationships in Marriage and Family*, Macmillan Publishing Co. Inc., New York, 1977.

Strecker, E.A., *Their Mother's Sons*, Philadelphia, Lippincott, 1946.

Stroup, A.L., "Marital Adjustment of the Mother and the Personality of the Child", *Journal of Marriage and Family*, May 1956, 109.

Stukert, "A Feminist Review of Marital Adjustment Literatures, The Rape of the Locke", by laws J.L., *Journal of Marriage and Family*, Vol. 33, 1971, 495-505.

Symonds, P.M., *Psychology of Parent Child Relationships*, New York, Appleton century Crafts, 1936.

Tandon, R., "Study Habits as Related to Personality Adjustment, Intelligence, and Scholastic Achievement". Project Report, Rohilkhand University 1980-81, 21-22.

Tasch, R.J., "Interpersonal Perceptions of Fathers and Mothers", *Journal of Genetic Psychology*, (Sept.), Vol. 87(1), 1955, 59-65.

Tayler, "Marital Happiness and Stability", by Hicks M. and Platt, M., *Journal of Marriage and Family*, (Nov.) Vol. 32, 1970.

Thomas Banta, Leonard Eran, "Comparison of data obtained from Mothers and Fathers on Child Rearing Practices and their relation to Child Aggression", *Child Development*, Vol. 32, 1961, 457-72.

Thompson, K.S., "A Comparison of Black and White Adolescents Belief s about having Children", *Journal of Marriage and Family*, Vol. 42 (Feb.), 1980, 133-139.

Uday, Shankar, *Personality Development*, Atma Ram and Sons, Delhi, 1981.

Uday, Shankar, *Problem Children*, Chap. III, Atmaram and Sons, Delhi, 1978.

Udry, J.A., *The Social Extent of Marriage*, 3rd Edition, New York, J.B. Lippincott, 1974.

Waiters, J., Stinnett, N., "Parent Child Relationships", *Journal of Marriage and Family*, Vol. 33, 1971, 70-79, 95-99.

Watson, G.B., "Some Personality Differences in Children Related to Strict or Permissive Parental Discipline", *Journal of Psychology*, 1957, 227-244.

Westbrook, M.T., "The Reactions of Child Bearing and early Maternal Experiences of Women with differing Marital Relationships", *British Journal of Medical Psychology*, Vol. 51, 1978, 191-199.

White, M., "Social Class, Child Rearing practices and Child Behaviour" *Amer. Social Rev.*, Vol. 22, 704-712.

Whitehurst, "Marital Happiness and Stability", by Hicks M, Platt, M., *Journal of Marriage and Family*, Vol. 32(3-4), 1970, 558-563.

Whiting, Beatrice, B., *Six Cultures Studied of Child Rearing*, New York, John Wilcy and Sons.

Winder C.L. Rau. L., "Parental Attitudes associated with Social Deviance in Preadolescent Boys", *Journal of Abnormal and Social Psychology*, Vol. 64, 1962.

Index

H

I

J

K

L

M

N

O

P

R

S

T

U

V

W

Y